Programs for Older Americans

Evaluations by Academic Gerontologists

Volume 1

Research Series, Center for Gerontological Studies

Communications relating to gerontology at the University of Florida should be addressed to the Center for Gerontological Studies, 3357 GPA, University of Florida, Gainesville, Florida 32611. This publication and all other publications of the Center for Gerontological Studies may be obtained from University Presses of Florida, Gainesville, Florida.

Programs for Older Americans

Evaluations by Academic Gerontologists

Edited by

Gordon F. Streib

Published for the
Center for Gerontological Studies
by
University Presses of Florida
Gainesville

Research reported in this volume was supported in part by a grant from the Administration on Aging, Office of Human Development, U.S. Department of Health, Education, and Welfare, to the Gerontological Society, Washington, D.C.

University Presses of Florida is the central agency for scholarly publishing of the State of Florida's university system. Its offices are located at 15 NW 15th Street, Gainesville, FL 32603. Works published by University Presses of Florida are evaluated and selected for publication by a faculty editorial committee of any one of Florida's nine public universities: Florida A&M (Tallahassee), Florida Atlantic University (Boca Raton), Florida International University (Miami), Florida State University (Tallahassee), University of Central Florida (Orlando), University of Florida (Gainesville), University of North Florida (Jacksonville), University of South Florida (Tampa), University of West Florida (Pensacola).

Library of Congress Cataloging in Publication Data

Main entry under title:

Programs for older Americans.

  (Research series; v. 1)
  Bibliography: p.
  1. Gerontology—Research—United States—Case studies. 2. Aged—Services for—United States—Evaluation. I. Streib, Gordon Franklin, 1918– II. University of Florida. Center for Gerontological Studies and Programs. III. Series: Research series (University of Florida. Center Gerontological Studies and Programs) [DNLM: 1 Geriatrics—United States. 2. Fellowships and scholarships. WT 100 P963]
HQ1064.U5P73   305.2'6'0973   81–11645
ISBN 0–8130–0705–4   AACR2

Typography by Williams Typography
Chattanooga, Tennessee

Printed in U.S.A. on acid-free paper

Acknowledgments

THE success of the gerontological fellowship program has been due to the widespread support of members of the Gerontological Society who contributed leadership and ideas to the program. The first Steering Committee, under the direction of Gordon F. Streib in 1974–77, gave generously of time and expertise: Marjorie Cantor, Margaret Clark, Donald Cowgill, Antonia Dolar, Carroll Estes, Bennett Gurian, Marion Hughes, Eleanor Slater, and Charles Taylor. This book is the result of the first three years' activities. In subsequent years the Steering Committee was under the direction of Margaret Clark, 1977–78; Tom Hickey, 1978–79; Mary Wylie, 1979–80; and Robert Hudson, 1980–81. Edwin Kaskowitz, executive director of the Gerontological Society during six years of the program, offered administrative support and assistance.

Special thanks are due to Jane White, program director from 1974 to 1978, and to her able assistants Gail Alter, Barbara Hanlon, Linda Lillienfeld, and Gail Pearl. Suzanne Wood and Linda Krogh have been program directors since 1978.

Members of the review committee were Tom Hickey, Jim Florini, Lissy Jarvick, Harold Orbach, and Kermit Schooler.

The Research Fellowship Program was supported by a grant from the Administration on Aging, Department of Health and Human Services (formerly Department of Health, Education, and Welfare). Al Duncker of the Administration on Aging was involved in the early days of the program, and Sean Sweeny, Marvin Taves, and Lorraine Thompson offered administrative guidance.

Throughout the program a number of regional and state administrators have supplied valuable counsel and support: Gerald Bloedow, Minnesota; Eleanor Cain, Delaware; Chaz Kawabori, Region X; Marion Miller, Region V; Clinton Hess, Region VIII; Claire Monier, New Hampshire; James Pennestri, New Jersey; and Janet Levy, California.

Persons affiliated with national organizations who were helpful during the planning stages include Carella Laycayo, Association National Pro Personas Mayores; Delores Davis, National Caucus on the Black Aged; and Dan Quirk, National Association of State Units on Aging.

Contents

Contents

Contributors

Coordinating Committee

Gordon F. Streib, Ph.D., Graduate Research Professor, University of Florida, Gainesville; Chairman, Gerontological Society Summer Research Fellowship Program, 1974–77

M. Margaret Clark, Ph.D., Professor of Medical Anthropology, University of California, San Francisco; Member of Steering Committee and Chairman, 1977–78, Gerontological Society Summer Research Fellowship Program

Julio L. Ruffini, Ph.D., Staff Anthropologist, Medical Anthropology Program, University of California, San Francisco

Charles Taylor, Ph.D., Professor of Psychology and Human Development, Pennsylvania State University, University Park; Member of Steering Committee, 1974–77, Gerontological Society Summer Research Fellowship Program

Authors of Cases

Michael A. Allen, M.A., Assistant Professor of Sociology, George Fox College, Newberg, Oregon

James O. Carpenter, Ph.D., Associate Professor, Health Specialization, School of Social Work, University of Pennsylvania, Philadelphia

David P. Fauri, Ph.D., Division of Social Work and Community Services, College of Human Resources, Southern Illinois University, Carbondale

Charles E. McConnel, Ph.D., Assistant Professor, Health Care Sciences, School of Allied Health Care Sciences, University of Texas, Dallas

Elizabeth W. Moen, Ph.D., Assistant Professor of Sociology, University of Colorado, Boulder

George R. Peters, Ph.D., Associate Professor of Sociology, Director, Center for Aging Studies, Kansas State University, Manhattan

Robert A. Solem, Ph.D., Research Director, Office of Research, Department of Social and Health Services, Olympia, Washington

Jack E. Sigler, M.A., Institute for Community Studies, Long-Term Care Education Center, University of Missouri, Kansas City

Charles B. White, Ph.D., Assistant Professor, Department of Psychology, Trinity University, San Antonio, Texas

Preface

THIS book will be of interest to a broad range of readers: gerontology students, both graduate and undergraduate, professors who teach gerontology, sociology, social work, and public administration, and administrators and practitioners in some fields, particularly in aging. The book can be read in its entirety or just in part. It can be used as a casebook (a text) for courses in gerontology, sociology, and social work.

Its descriptions of the Gerontology Research Fellowship Program, now in its sixth year, will interest those in other human service fields, for they may see merit in adapting such a program to other situations.

The cases, taken as a unit or read separately, are diverse and rich in content and cover a wide range of concerns: needs assessment, problems of aging among American Indians, tapping and pooling of resources, and training of agency staff, among others.

Graduate students in gerontology and in other fields will find the case studies instructive of the kind of research that is needed and can be conducted in public agencies.

Finally, the book is of value to persons considering careers in human service fields such as aging because it offers a realistic and honest account of how a complex bureaucracy operates. Nine different observers present their perspectives of the operation of the organizational structure.

The theme of "academics in the real world" is a metaphorical concept—not a precise analytical one—and it describes the general ambience in which the fellows operated. The book has some similarities to *Sociologists at Work* (edited by P. E. Hammond), published some years ago, in which distinguished social scientists gave personal histories of some well-known studies and showed, among other things, how theories had to be adapted to reality which is sometimes intractable. In a similar vein, we hope that this book will offer a candid, insightful account of some phases of aging programs.

1. The Research Fellowship Program of the Gerontological Society

Gordon F. Streib

THE elderly gentleman attended session after session of the Gerontological Society's annual meeting. He sat in the front row and listened attentively to speakers talking about cohort analysis, locus of control, empirical assessment, and causal models. Finally his frustration could no longer be contained, and he burst forth: "All you professors do is talk—talk—talk! When are you going to *do* something for us old folks? Why don't you get out of your ivory towers and into the *real world*?"

This incident, a true one, inspired the theme of this book. The comparison of the "real world" to the "ivory tower" is a metaphoric concept held by many people outside of academic life. For the gerontologist, it involves the misunderstanding that the only valuable arena is in the organization and delivery of services to the elderly and that "doing" is more legitimate than understanding.

Also implicit in the expression "ivory tower" is an aloofness, a social distance from the real world, and a belief that the activities themselves are remote from reality—they have an abstract, theoretical quality. The ivory tower is seen as set off from the real world because academics employ technical language, or jargon, in an attempt to be more precise. Further, it is thought that in the ivory tower there is a relaxed time schedule, that activities are carried out without consideration for their costs, utility, or practical value. Since the phrase ivory tower is used to describe schools and colleges whose residents tend to be young, the cliché takes on added meaning, for youth is a time of idealism and inexperience, and universities may be places where young people "mark time" until real life begins.

Obviously this notion of academia as the ivory tower is a caricature, for the ivory tower is the "real world" in many respects: there are schedules and deadlines, there are budgets and cost cuts, certain services are delivered, and there are politics and power struggles and manipulative Machiavellians. So when we speak of the "real world" in this book, we are writing metaphorically. We use the term not in a precise definitional or conceptual manner but to create a sense of contrast. It conveys an ambience which is understood by almost everyone. The chapters that

1

follow and the case studies will illustrate the theme. In fact, it becomes clear that academics can function in the "real world" and make definite contributions.

HISTORY OF THE PROJECT

Some well-established professions, such as medicine, nursing, and social work, have institutionalized the notion of an internship or residency in which the aspiring professional has the opportunity to observe and participate in the professional work for which he is training. In the social sciences, especially in a new field such as social gerontology, this kind of exposure and apprenticeship has been rare. Far too often, the student and professor read about the problems of service delivery to the elderly, read about the bureaucratic organization involved, read about the problems of funding and execution of programs, but rarely experience or observe them firsthand.

With some of these thoughts in mind, a committee of the Gerontological Society met in 1973 to try to develop some plans on how to bridge this gap. The Summer Internship Project was initiated in 1974 by the Committee on Research and Development (CORAD) of the Gerontological Society under a grant from the Administration on Aging (AOA). This program was intended to provide a unique and mutually beneficial eight-week experience for ten gerontologists and ten State Offices on Aging (SOA). Its dual purpose was generally to offer resource and learning opportunities in program evaluation to the state directors on aging, and at the same time to provide gerontologists with field experiences in which to conduct research that realistically reflected the planning, design, and impact of social services for the elderly. It was anticipated that exposure of researchers to the needs of the field and to AOA priorities would encourage them to bridge the gap between theory and practice.

The program was designed to allow for both immediate and long-term benefits to all parties involved. Specifically, in this first cycle, gerontologists would bring their expertise in evaluative research to the state units, thereby assisting the staff in the evaluation of ongoing programs in the state and providing them with the skills necessary to plan, design, and implement future programs which incorporated evaluative components. It was assumed that the program would include some in-service staff training, which would occur as an informal extension of the process, rather than as a formal program. It was hoped that communication between agency directors and gerontologists would continue beyond the eight-week internship. To facilitate this last objective, it was planned that all interns would be placed in their states of residence.

One of the principal values of the program to the gerontologist was the opportunity to become familiar with the operations of the state unit on aging and thus to gain a better appreciation of services offered and some insight into those still needed.

The Steering Committee saw the advisability of obtaining the closest match possible between the needs and desires of the interns and the state offices. To facilitate optimal placement of interns, state directors were encouraged to make recommendations and requests for gerontologists with whom they were acquainted. After selection and assignment of academicians to offices, all participating in the program met for a two-day workshop, so the researchers and directors could jointly delineate basic criteria, expectations, functions, and goals for the project. If the relationship between intern and state director was positive, it would promote a continuing liaison.

Consultants were to spend at least two days per week in the agency office and approximately three days in the field. This plan assumed that consultants would have regular weekly contact with agency directors. The consultant was also required to prepare a final report on the summer's activities, which would be submitted to the agency director and also presented in a symposium at the annual Gerontological Society meetings. Not only would the interns and state offices benefit but the project would be of some value to the field of gerontology, the AOA, and the aged themselves.

Because of the overwhelmingly favorable reactions of both interns and agencies, application was made to AOA to double the number of placements the second year, to twenty gerontologists matched with twenty agency offices. Although the project operated with the same goals in the second summer, some additions and changes were made. The project's name was changed to "Consultantship in Administrative Agencies on Aging." Activities were expanded to include HEW regional offices and city offices on aging, in addition to state units. The training workshop for participants was extended to three days.

In 1974 all gerontologists were placed in offices of their home state to increase the probability of continued liaison and further cooperation. But some states with a great need for the contribution of gerontologists' expertise had very few, if any, such resources available within their boundaries. Therefore, in 1975 additional funds were allocated to some consultants to live away from home to help meet the needs of some states.

In the third year, the project was still receiving highly positive support from both administrative units and the gerontological research community. Over 150 gerontologists applied for the 20 fellowships available, and 28 state units requested participation in the program, in addition to ten city and six federal regional Offices on Aging. In 1976 the gerontologists were designated "research fellows" rather than consultant-researchers. The program was offered also to persons with training in biomedical fields, and one fellow was placed in the same agency for a second summer.

In all three summers the steering committee appointed by the Gerontological Society continued to provide coordination and leadership. Each fellow and the agency in which he worked were visited by a member of the steering committee, who monitored the experience, offered suggestions, and acted as a liaison, counselor, and ombudsman where required.

The program continued for three more years, with support from the AOA. By 1980 almost 100 gerontologists had participated in the research fellowship program.

The research fellows represent a wide range of professional backgrounds, skills, experience, and academic affiliations. They have applied for the summer fellowships for a variety of reasons; some wished to explore the benefits of practitioner-research interaction; others wanted to gain a more realistic understanding of the administrative process; others wanted to have first hand experience in agencies serving the elderly so as to better advise and place their students; and all wanted to broaden their perspectives by experience in applied gerontology.

Basic or Applied Research

A perennial controversy in academic research is whether the focus of a particular investigation is basic or applied. Applied research has three general characteristics that differentiate it from basic research: the aims or intentions of the participants (the gerontologists) are oriented to the goals and programs of the agencies; the expected results from the project are of an applied nature; the role definitions that prevail suggest a strong applied orientation. In a basic research situation, the gerontologist would have had more autonomy in selecting his research problem, some latitude in altering his methods and time schedule to meet the constraints set forth by the research itself, and the work would be judged primarily by his peers in his specialty. In all three respects, the gerontology program tended to be of an applied nature. The choice of problem resulted from negotiation between the gerontologists and the persons in the agencies where they would work. Second, although the researcher had some latitude in how a problem would be studied, the work had time constraints which were more demanding than might be found in a typical academic research situation. Finally, the work was judged by a mixture of gerontologists who were peers and agency persons who came from a variety of backgrounds, including business, management, public administration, social services, and public relations.

Very early in the project there was the problem of what to call the participants, since many agency personnel considered themselves gerontologists. For the purposes of clarity, we shall consider gerontologists to be those persons, selected by the society to hold the fellowship, who had academic training in gerontology; and we will refer to persons working in administrative positions as "agency personnel."

GOVERNMENT STRUCTURE AND THE OLDER AMERICANS ACT

The Older Americans Act (OAA), passed in 1965 and amended seven times, provides the framework for programs and services related to older Americans. The act is divided into nine "titles," which are parts of the law specifying areas of purpose, operation, and funding:

Title I Objectives
Title II Establishment of the Administration on Aging
Title III Grants for state and community programs on aging
Title IV Training and research
Title V Multipurpose senior centers
Title VI Grants for Indian tribes
Title VII Nutrition programs for the elderly
Title VIII Repealed
Title IX Community service employment for older Americans

The intern project was originally funded under Title IV but was supported later as a model project under Title III. The activities were centered principally in the state and area agencies (organized under Title II). The gerontology fellows were concerned with many of the areas specified in the titles, as employment (Title IX), Indian tribes (Title VI), or needs assessment (specified under Title III). A list of the projects of the fellows during the first three years appears in the appendix. Nine of the fellows have described their research in chapters 4 to 12 of this book.

Title II established the AOA in the Department of Health, Education, and Welfare. The administration is headed by a commissioner on aging, appointed by the President by and with the advice of the Senate. Under the OAA, each state must designate a "sole state agency" if it wishes to receive the grants and funds allocated by Congress. The law further provides that the state agency shall designate subunits of government for planning and service, called Area Agencies of Aging (AAAS). The area agencies vary greatly in size and population—some comprise one city, some many counties. The AAA must develop a plan to establish a comprehensive and coordinated system for delivering social services in its area.

There are also ten federal regional offices on aging, which coordinate the programs in their regions. The fellows in the summer gerontology program were assigned to these three levels of bureaucracy, federal, state, and area.

The Consulting Process and Its Continuity

"Consultation" is a label which covers a multiplicity of generalities and relationships. The kind of consulting reported here is not the conventional relationship between consultant and client, such as that extensively reported in the literature on psychological counseling and psychotherapy. Lippitt (1959, p. 5) has offered a general definition of consultation which describes broadly the relationships of this program: "The consultation relationship is a voluntary relationship between a professional helper (consultant) and help-needing system (client) in which the consultant is attempting to give help to the client in the solving of some current or potential problem, and the relationship is perceived as temporary by both parties. Also, the consultant is an 'outsider,' i.e., not a part of any hierarchical power system in which the client is located."

One of the goals of the gerontology consultantships was to help establish relationships that would continue beyond the summer experience. Continuity in the consulting process seems very appropriate for the aging field, since much of the focus concerns those problems of life which are difficult or impossible to solve, and the source of people with such problems is constantly replenished. Thus, in many cases, effective consulting involves continuous contact and counseling. We assumed that if agency and consultant established a useful relationship, they might want to continue it beyond the summer, either formally or informally. This approach of promoting continuity in a consulting process is contrary to the operations of traditional consulting, where there is a definite point at which the relationship is ended and the consulting role is terminated. The traditional consultant may have been more of a trouble-shooter, dealing with a single critical situation, but very few of the summer consultants were so viewed.

The exploratory nature of the program resulted in changing the terminology from "consultant" the first summer to "intern" the second summer and finally to "research fellow," but the nature of the relationship and the activities pursued were essentially the same throughout the program.

Figure 1.1 shows the relationships between the academic gerontologist and the administrative gerontologist. In the upper left we see that the academic gerontologist brings resources in the form of knowledge and technical skills. In the upper right, we see the policy concerns of the administrative gerontologist—the agenda to be decided upon, tasks to be accomplished, and problems to be solved. In the lower left are listed the diverse roles that the gerontologist might assume in the administrative setting: regional, state, or area offices on aging.

PLAN OF THE BOOK

A general overview of the research fellowship program is given in chapters 2 and 3. The politics of interaction are presented, and the research fellow's role as an "outsider" in the agency is described. The role of the outsider as consultant, researcher, observer, or intern would have some of the same characteristics in a variety of public or private complex organizations.

In chapter 2, Charles Taylor points out the politics of interaction, highlighting the context in which the relationship takes place. In chapter 3, Margaret Clark and Julio Ruffini explore how the politics of interaction are involved in the negotiating of the contract between the two parties— how the outsider, as researcher, intern, or consultant, needs to specify his goals and roles and how problems of loyalty and accountability will be defined.

In the second part of the book, a series of case studies are presented describing in detail the roles and activities of nine academic gerontologists in their research fellowship roles. The underlying theme of all of the case studies is the complexity of understanding and improving government organizations in dealing more effectively with the needs and problems of America's older population. All of the cases illustrate that knowledge of government bureaucracies is essential to developing more responsive programs and policies. Although each research fellow had a different task during the fellowship period, the underlying goal was understanding the

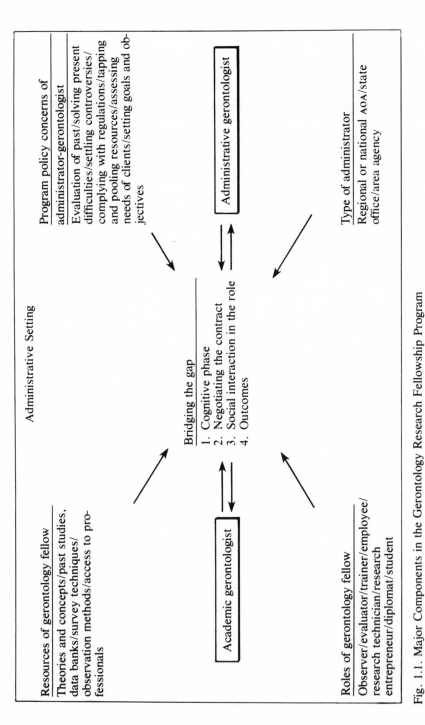

Fig. 1.1. Major Components in the Gerontology Research Fellowship Program

bureaucracies and implementing their goals through input of academic knowledge and research skills.

David Fauri developed a detailed plan for a sample survey to determine the needs of older persons in Tennessee. He shows the importance of interorganizational relations between federal and state units in the aging network. Federal law mandates that a needs assessment be made. State agencies attempt to comply with federal regulations with inadequate financial resources and a staff untrained in survey research.

Elizabeth Moen's assignment was similar to Fauri's. She employed a method more suitable to her interests and those of her husband, a professional photographer, who worked with her in rural Oregon. Her method was essentially a qualitative study of a small number of older rural Oregonians. She became well acquainted with them, and entered into their homes and lives. Moen's case is of interest because she concentrated on direct interaction with older persons, while most of the researchers dealt with agency personnel and less directly with the ultimate consumers—older people.

The work of George Peters focused on interorganizational relations. His role of field worker involved a combination of theorist, researcher, interviewer and diplomat. He discovered that due to contradictory purposes and failure to communicate clearly, problems emerge when two levels of government try to coordinate their activities. Problems of complex organizations arose in Kansas because the Area Agencies on Aging were new organizations trying to determine program goals and train new staff while facing a unique situation. Time smooths out some of these hazards in organizing problems and services for older clients. Peters emphasizes the structural organizational issues rather than the personal and psychological factors. Based upon his experiences and observations, he sees the importance of structural change in building a more effective service network.

Michael Allen had an even more complicated organizational structure to describe and analyze: a group of sovereign nations—Arizona Indian tribes. His task was more difficult due to suspicions of some Indian informants regarding white social scientists and administrators. Thus, Allen had to convince his respondents of his qualifications and neutrality. When the data were gathered, he faced the challenge of assimilating and interpreting diverse viewpoints. As an analyst he felt it was important to present the diversity of opinions, while maintaining his own integrity as researcher and analyst.

Charles White's experience as a research fellow was an explicit attempt to assist the New York State Office on Aging to anticipate a problem—the possibility that older New Yorkers might be caught in a fuel shortage crisis. Many persons assume that government bureaucracies are sluggish organizations, bogged down in procedures, tied up in their own red tape, and unable to respond quickly to a new situation. White's research was aimed at overcoming this difficulty by setting up a detailed procedure for carrying out a sample telephone survey of older residents. His plan could be put into operation quickly.

Robert Solem faced still another set of issues and problems while working with the Regional Office of the Administration on Aging. He attempted to establish a region-wide information system which could gather and assimilate statistical facts for planning thus avoiding the time and expense of carrying out household surveys. Solem's work shows the difficulty in implementing a sound and useful idea if the requesting agency does not have the power or the sanctions to require compliance. The coordinating agency must convince the constituent units that it would be in their long-term interest to assist in gathering the information. Solem shows how the gathering of solid information in the health and social service fields is often uncoordinated and incomplete. His fellowship activities illustrate how needs assessment information could be gathered in another way than by expensive surveys of individual elderly people. Solem's research was an attempt to "tap and pool resources" as part of the broad mandated plan for the establishment of area Agencies on Aging.

James Carpenter's research was an attempt to create a clearer understanding of the interorganizational dynamics of a social delivery system. His work involved constructing criteria for use in evaluating existing service contracts and which could also be used to determine which applications for support should be funded. In a government agency the administrators must make decisions based upon universalistic criteria to insure that funds will be used effectively and allow competing agencies to be judged equitably.

The day-to-day activities of the agency staff must be translated into more generic questions which can then be restated as problems for which solutions can be offered. Carpenter approached his fellowship as a theorist and researcher of complex organizations and he shows how the conceptualization of the problem is the first step in determining organizational effectiveness.

Charles McConnel honed his economic tools of analysis upon a specific problem area: how public employment programs provide services for older workers. McConnel shows that the rational utilization of funds in a public agency is not always possible due to constraints of daily opera-

tions. These concerns take priority over the systematic utilization of information which might insure that more older persons receive job placement. McConnel's analysis, like a number of others in this casebook, show very clearly that political issues—power and decision-making— may dominate service programs and determine how resources are allocated.

The last case deals with gerontologic training as seen from a regional office of the Administration on Aging. Jack Sigler offers a realistic description of how the training process operates. Target groups, involved in training, must be clearly identified if training is to be efficacious. Sigler found that training is like many other aspects of government service delivery in that more urgent day-to-day demands may take priority over training. However, a better trained staff may result in a clearer understanding of agency objectives and produce a higher degree of effective communication and delivery of needed services to older persons.

The nine cases reported here were selected by the project's steering committee, representing the Gerontological Society. It was a difficult task to choose these nine cases from the 50 excellent reports submitted. The cases included were chosen to satisfy several criteria: to provide illustrations of the range of projects; to represent the geographic locations; to show the varied approaches in meeting the assignments which resulted from the negotiations between the research fellow and the agency staff; to show how the three major levels of government were involved (local AAA's, state offices on aging, and the regional offices of the AOA); and, to present variations in outcomes from the summer fellowship—for both the agency and the individual research fellow. Further, we chose authors who could bring the perspective of different disciplines to their reports: sociology (Peters, Carpenter, and Sigler); psychology (White and Solem); demography (Moen); social work (Fauri); economics (McConnel); and anthropology (Allen).

There was a deliberate decision not to restrict cases to "success stories." The editorial selection committee felt that a frank presentation of problems encountered would be particularly valuable to students of gerontology and other disciplines who hope to enter government agencies or direct service delivery in organizations that serve the elderly.

Beyond the sheer description and analysis of the experiences and outcomes, these cases should provide persons planning to enter areas of applied gerontology with some realization of the complexities of government operation. Also, an understanding of what is involved in the administration of laws specifying services to America's older population should evolve. One value of the book lies in the disparate nature of the contributions. The editorial committee felt it was important to bring together, in one volume, some of these varied experiences, and to leave a record of a most successful program sponsored by the Gerontological Society.

The continued interest and support for the program is shown in Appendix listing the 1974–1980 research fellows, their report topics, and present affiliation.

REFERENCE

Lippitt, R. 1959. Dimensions of the consultant's job. *Journal of Social Issues* 15:5–12.

2. Insiders and Outsiders: The Politics of Interaction

Charles Taylor

IN the context of today's scholarly vocabulary, it would be stylish to describe the experiences reported in this volume as an interface between two systems of thought and action: the "insider"—the social agency and its administration, and the "outsider"—a person from outside the agency who has been designated to perform a limited task for the agency. An interface serves as a conceptual model only when the characteristics of its two systems are clearly defined.

In this case, agencies related to aging are vaguely defined. Rather, they are in a period of rapid adjustment and change, with short and poorly documented histories and extremely fluid characteristics; "loose amalgamations of segments which are in movement" (Bucher and Strauss, 1961). Furthermore, the outside persons who provided service to the agencies were heterogeneous in training and experience. They came from established disciplines, but the range of their values, skills, and techniques was so great that they too may be considered fluid systems. Instead of two abutting walls, or even two busy computers in communication, a better simile is that of a hasty mating of two active organisms who have no reliable mating instincts.

The agencies involved were of several sorts, both organizationally and geographically. Their similarities are largely the result of the fact that they all were created and/or monitored and funded by the federal government. The outsiders came from many disciplines and orientations largely from the wish to involve many disparate lines of expertise in the cooperating venture. Indeed, so great was the desire to extend the opportunity that some pressure was brought to bear to include cell biologists as consultants to a public service agency project related to aging!

The changing terms used to describe the outsiders from year to year shows the lack of a clear definition of their roles; they were in succeeding years called gerontologists, interns, consultants, and research fellows. "Gerontologist" had to be abandoned because many *agency* people were members, for example, of the Gerontological Society, and by any measure of public life equally as much gerontologists as the outsiders. Consultancy is well-known in business and professional life; most would accept the

13

idea that the consultant is a temporary staff member operating at the will of the agency (Golton, 1968; Beisser and Green, 1972). In this relationship the outsider responds to the wishes of the agency, even though he may have considerable freedom to act within his own specialty. The person placed in the agency reserved a larger amount of autonomy than could be considered typical in the consulting experience, because his position was funded by the grant mechanism, not the agency. The term "intern" signifies someone engaged in a late-stage of professional training, who will later enter full professional life. In this program, almost all were full professionals and some were persons of national note. A fellowship implies that a period of time has been granted to explore the potential of a situation or setting in order to advance personal understanding and growth. In many ways, the role of the outsider was an amalgam of consultant and fellow, with gains for both agency and individual. In no case could the service provided by this project have been funded by and legitimized by the normal funding patterns of the agency. Outsider and agency were expected to benefit mutually from the experience.

There were attempts to formalize or dichotomize both sides of the cooperative venture. At times the terms "research" versus "action" seemed to be properly descriptive. There were difficulties in the use of these terms, however. Often the outsider's research and evaluation skills were already minimally represented within the agency. The term research has many meanings, and, in retrospect, the work done by the outsiders was more often part of the "action" and would probably not meet even the most lenient canons of formal research. Some of the research was designed to meet the parochial needs of one agency, even though the methodology could be duplicated with routine resources elsewhere. Some was of very little help to the agency for its current or future operations but rather asked broad questions about the nature of the older persons. Some did new things and broke new ground, and some was of high quality but routine in design and treatment. A great deal of task specification came from the agency; indeed the application forms required it. Some products were almost surely in process before this funding was available, and in those cases the tasks were clear, suitability of the outsider to fulfill them was obvious, and progress was rapid. In other cases, even the delineation of what was needed and could be researched was an important exercise in formative evaluation.

The problems inherent in building the kind of relationships envisioned by the project lie in differences between systems of thought which can be differentiated by the terms "academic" and "bureaucratic"; the latter term is not meant to have any perjorative undertones. The term "academic" is similar to but less provocative than the one used in an analysis of the "intellectual" (Merton, 1957). All of the outsiders were affiliated, at least in their major professional roles, with colleges and universities. Some had had agency experience and were knowledgeable about the bureaucratic way of life. Likewise, several of the agency staff had held academic teaching or staff positions. Discrepancies between these two systems of thought and action, rather than between individuals, provide the basis for the following discussion.

DIFFERING ROLES OF INSIDERS AND OUTSIDERS

No matter what the assigned task, the interplay between the two professional modes is one which contrasts values, personal and professional styles of conduct, and bases of power and authority (Ganesh, 1978). When a consultant, the academic's particular knowledge and skill are means for acquiring status in the agency. Almost surely there will be a tendency for some to play the role of the elitist in order to gain status (Benveniste, 1972).

An agency can provide several scenarios for the visiting expert. Often he or she is called on to fulfill a specific task, the scope of which is well understood and the technical demands of which are clear-cut. The expert acts like a practitioner, an engineer, or a technician, in order to plan, to sort, to evaluate, or to gather and analyze data. The level of expertise can be very high or only moderate; but since it is relatively easy to develop low-level continuing staff, the probability is that a big project or a thrust in a new direction will suggest a consultant of some standing.

A second role is that of the co-worker, a helping hand in a continuing or emerging activity. Here it is expected that a fresh evaluation, coming either from prior experience with the same type of problem or a different disciplinary outlook, can give sharper dimensions to the ongoing problem-solving efforts.

A third role is like that of an "artist-in-residence" who becomes an honorary staff member, reacting to the atmosphere and the conceptual and theoretical world of the agency ventures and uncovering unrealized difficulties and resources. Only very self-confident agencies will tolerate this free-wheeling outsider.

The last type of consultantship is that which seeks neither special expertise nor presents any special task but asks only that the expert be an attractive façade or even a camouflage. The presence of an expert of note may disarm critics by giving a look of contemporaneity and depth; if the agency should fall in acceptance and stature thereafter, a convenient scapegoat is available. The more eminent the outsider, the less specific the assignment and the more limited the contact is likely to be.

Each type of relationship brings into focus some of the discrepancies between the academic and the agency. The entry point is particularly critical (Rhodes, 1974; Lippitt and Lippitt, 1978). If the system is under siege and the consultant is known to possess the skill and experience to solve a problem which must be solved quickly, entry is simple and arrangements fall readily into place, with accommodation not too necessary on either side. If the need is not great, or the consultant is only icing on a rich cake, or the expertise is equally useful on a number of fronts, entry is conditional, and considerable time is required to make functional arrangements. When a consultant with special expertise is offered to an organization at little or no cost, some projects which otherwise would have been indefensible luxuries become enterprises of high priority and good sense.

A major part of the consultant's problems derive from the fact that he *is* an outsider. New entrants into any social system, large or small, cannot expect to be openly welcomed by all of the staff. Even if the person is of considerable note, an academic newcomer is likely to meet indifference and an ill-veiled hostility from those who are anti-intellectual or who downgrade any notion of expertise. On the other hand, the line staff know that the actions of anyone who has so temporary a place in the agency will be unlikely to affect them directly or make much of a permanent change in the bureaucracy. Politeness aside, newcomers are either replacements for functionaries whose place and abilities are well understood or they are almost surplus. No matter if the consultant is believed in and welcomed effusively, his reasons for being there are vague and suspect. The social worker who consults in a social work agency faces the same kinds of problems as the academic who enters the agency (Golton, 1968). Problems intensify, however, when there are different educational and cognitive elements to separate the principals. "Psyching out" (Oleson and Whittaker, 1968) is particularly important, since line staff are quite expert in using regulations and situational elements to put the entrant in situations quite at variance with those wished by the managerial staff.

EDUCATIONAL AND COGNITIVE FACTORS

The role of the academic consultant is amorphous and does not provide a clearly defined, well-bounded, and carefully protected niche. For this reason, more than any other, the different value systems and professional orientations assume a high degree of importance in the relationship. The typical agency, like all bureaucracies, is likely to employ many workers of modest education and minimal responsibility in a vertical structure (Harries-Jenkins, 1970). On the other hand, academics are arrayed in a horizontal structure; indeed, though ranks and privileges do exist, "collegiality" means that all participate somewhat as equals in the ventures of the institution of higher learning. In the classroom an instructor, no matter what the rank, stands virtually unchallenged as the final authority. Administrators, though they often rise from the academic ranks, are seen by many of the teaching staff as adversaries, and it is not uncommon for academics to be very contentious with all persons of administrative authority. The academic is socialized to expect deference to his training and knowledge and does not function skillfully in situations which prompt him or her to parade expertise and openly strive for position. On the other hand, the agency directorship, familiar with the ascriptive pattern of authority, is likely to view the role of the consultant as "his" or "her" "man" or "woman," never as an equal even though greatly admired.

The academic is not likely to find many persons with educational training comparable to his in a typical agency. Furthermore, the agency's hierarchy of authority is not always related to amount of education. The academic gains rank and privilege chiefly through education. Agency staff do not constitute an established professional group, and there is no great attempt to increase educational levels of new entrants as a step towards professionalism (Hughes, 1958).

Two surveys, one under the auspices of the present project and using a wide range of regional, state, and Area Agencies on Aging (AAA) staff (Bicknell, 1975) and one utilizing a sample of AAAs (Tobin, Davidson, and Sack, 1976), illustrate the role of education in the agency on aging. In Bicknell's sample of 73 persons, all administrative heads, specialists, field representatives, and planners, only 4 percent held the doctorate and fewer than 60 percent held any degree past the baccalaureate. In the study of AAAs, which did not differentiate among levels of graduate degrees, nearly half of the directors had had graduate training, many in professions in which the master's is the normal, if not terminal, degree. Staff lower in the cadre would be expected to have less education. In the Tobin, Davidson, and Sack study about 70 percent cited career experiences as the most important part of job preparation, and only 8 percent considered their formal education as most important.

The academician in consultation almost always has the doctoral degree;

furthermore, as education stretches towards the doctorate, more and more specialization is typical, so that general knowledge and professional scope become less and less important. On the contrary, flexibility of orientation and preparation is the norm for agency staff. In the area of social work, for example, 80 percent of direct service positions are held by persons without degrees in that field. A considerable body of research details the fact that such positions "are manned with equal or greater frequency and without demonstrably different effects by untrained social workers as by MSW-trained social workers" (Loewenberg, 1970).

The academician has difficulty relating to differences within staff because identification lies in the task more than in the credentials to perform it. Freeman (1971) points out that the academic always wrestles with problems of pomposity and arrogance. Furthermore, the academic is far removed from the complex of needs and resources always being fine-tuned by the agency. Although academics recognize their isolation and decry it, they tend to believe that depth and rigor in any field gives them authority over any mass of variables (Moravcsik, 1973). When academicians attempt to interpret laboratory findings for life situations, there is always emphasis on the mastery of the "laboratory" and the superficiality in the "life."

The academic, particularly one trained in a research discipline, tends to think in terms of variables, of abstract phenomena derived from human experience but not representative of human sentience, always set in a matrix of other variables. The agency person is interested in the human being and his surroundings. The researcher who enters the service agency is in a highly vulnerable position. He is accused of not really understanding what he is studying and of being insensitive to the subtle nuances of another's situation. The researcher is cautious, and the practitioner and the researcher may not agree on what is subject to scientific control. The academic is often short on relevance (Koch, 1971; Silverman, 1971); some social scientists admit that they have erected a model of man which leaves out environment, behavioral and social influences, and organismic history and adhere to the variables which can be adequately controlled in the laboratory (Bronfenbrenner, 1974).

On the other hand, administrators when not themselves scientists are lacking in understanding and are sometimes contemptuous of scientific methods and applications. McCony (1960, p. 35) noted that often policy makers expect too much: "An answer that cannot be found from the data available, a prediction when none can be made, an analysis made in too little time, a firm black and white answer when the evidence is not

Charles Taylor 19

conclusive and only alternatives based on different assumptions can be given.''

STYLE: VALUES AND OBJECTIVES OF INSIDERS AND OUTSIDERS

Clearly related to cognitive orientations are matters of values and objectives; in a word, style. Halmos (1973, p. 300) has pointed out that personal service orientation is "personal, global and synthesizing rather than analytical, manipulative and fragmentary." The research scientist is as interested in raising questions as in answering them; at no time is an issue closed. Schrader (1963) has suggested that many persons seriously question whether the scientific endeavor is even suitable to answering questions of human factors, even though it has been the touchstone of progress for physical and biological questions. Such resistance is not cognitive but practical. Science makes few breakthroughs, either from diligent work or serendipity. Kuhn (1962) used the concept of "paradigms" to explain why scientists tend to concentrate on increasingly specialized research. The agency cannot point to work well-done, progress being made, the situation well in hand. What counts are clearly recognizable decisions and clearly obvious results. Making sense of sound evidence is still the responsibility of the practitioner; the researcher does not necessarily know how to make sense or how to account for the facts he generates (Phillips, 1973).

Not everyone feels that the scientific approach is necessary or appropriate to agency life. Polansky (1971, p. 1098) states: "The practitioner involved in trying to help clients is at most a scientist coincidentally. He does not value knowledge for its own sake, and this stance seems quite appropriate."

What accounts for these two appositional points of view and value systems? One major explanation is the relationships between their day-to-day life and the period of communication and consultation which is entered into. The agency person in that situation continues to perform his cyclic activities; his duties and responsibilities are not changed in the relationship. However, the activity or skill offered to the agency by the academic is only a small part of his everyday life. Even in the best universities, research must be teased out of the daily routine and becomes almost an avocation, highly rewarded professionally but self-motivated, self-engineered, and self-scheduled. This absence of "ritualism" (Merton, 1957) in the academic's life allows him to adopt long time frames and partial anticipatory goals. Considerable stimulus comes from the fact that such activities are also part of a social network, in which one's personal skills mesh with those of others whose career goals are dependent on some collaborative output. Research is certainly not business as usual; it proceeds at an internally determined pace, with progress being made at stages which cannot be predetermined. There are few outright winners for effort spent, but there are no clear losers either.

Furthermore, only his peers are competent to judge the work of a scientific researcher. Academic and scientific work is "refereed" more for adequacy of methodology than for usefulness of outcome. This is not so for the agency, where the review mechanisms are many. Several hierarchies of evaluation include: the legitimizers and/or financial supporters of the agency; the recipient or client for whom the service exists; other agencies parallel to or superior to the agency; public media; and the larger public that is more or less aware of the agency and its functions. These many evaluations lead to a feeling that the enterprise is being monitored, not for demonstrable elements of goodness but for elements of style, timeliness, political influence, etc.

Of course a sense of development and fruition is often denied to the agency by the constraints of constant deadlines imposed from outside the system. "The pressures of unpredictable responses often to questions which are alien to the life and thought of the staff often lead to decisional urgency that cannot await developments of 'proper' information. This is one of the many identifiable sources of strain between the 'intellectual' (the scientist or other professional) and the manager in administrative organizations. The expert is not accustomed to the 'terrible immediacy' of administrative decision and when asked for advice based on reliable knowledge does not welcome the additional note, 'We needed it yesterday'" (McCony, 1960, p. 69).

This model of activity in which there is literally no discretionary time leads to what Harshbarger (1974) has called "turbulence." The academic, coming from an atmosphere in which cyclic disposition of duties along orderly dimensions may eventually lead to a blurring of a time ordering, is likely to label inefficiency or at least lack of careful administrative planning as the cause of the agency's temporal disorder.

In addition to the setting, there are problems of vocabulary and general communication. The academic tends towards polysyllabic and esoteric vocabulary, but the agency has its own jargon and surplus meanings. Especially in the early stages of a relationship, when some jockeying for advantage is to be expected, misunderstanding of vocabulary can be a serious deterrent to effective communication.

Probably greater strain is imposed by not having the opportunity to communicate. McCony (1960, p. 34) commented that, "Low morale among experts . . . is well-known. It comes much more, I am convinced, from their feeling of not being consulted than from any other reason. The expert yearns to be as effective and integral as opportunities will provide, but in practical terms the needed and wanted affiliation which the agency had envisioned simply does not emerge in the pressure of day-to-day demands."

Usually the expert is called on to expand an area in which the agency is weak and the administrator would benefit if it were possible to ruminate and gain some greater measure of expertise, if nothing more than the appreciation of what such technique could bring to the agency. The staff members lower in the hierarchy are aware of the time pressures imposed on the administrators and often protect them from what is seen as the invasion of the outside expert.

A rich literature (for example, Roe, 1953; Hudson, 1966; McClelland, 1971) leads to the inescapable conclusion that persons from different occupations and professions, or even from different specializations within a given profession, have sharply divergent value systems. It is not certain whether the differences arise because occupations shape people and their values or people with certain value systems seek and find entry into different occupational slots. At any rate, these differences emerge early in the work life and continue to manifest themselves (Silverman, 1971).

Scientists, according to McClelland, (1971) are best differentiated from nonscientists by their inability to deal effectively with human power and aggression. They retreat into symbols and abstractions, seek out dependable laws of nature, and avoid intimate personal contact. Hudson and Jacot (1971) showed that attitudes towards power are highly related to area of occupation among educated persons; scientists are very "prickly" people.

Research on the kinds of persons who work in and manage agencies is less well-developed, probably because of even greater variability than exists in the research sciences. From Hudson's (1966) point of view, persons whose work is related to or who have positions in agencies that operate in the human behalf are likely to be more oriented to rationality about people and less to rationality about things and ideas. Certainly, no one could survive in the bureaucratic maze of the agency without a strong feeling that the work would eventually in some way benefit the target population. Still, Tobin, Davidson, and Sack (1976) provide evidence that persons from many disciplines are found in duplicate work roles in the field of aging. But they also make clear that the field of study does affect how the director, at least, approaches his work. Some persons were more firmly attached to management values than human values. One important point is that the higher the education and the more scientific the goals of the profession, the more likely the agency manager is to seek and accept outside help (Polansky, 1971).

AMITY AND RESOLUTION

Bennis et al. (1974) have stressed that eventual good will is anticipated when the behavioral scientist meets the organization. Indeed, the good will fosters grandiose visions of dramatic breakthroughs, "utopian hopes . . . that all their day-to-day organizational concerns will be extirpated" (Bennis et al. 1974, p. 397). Behavioral scientists, however, are not above touting their wares. Both parties get trapped in a false dream.

Creating a working relationship between the two types of persons is not easy. Demone and Harshbarger (1974, p. 99) make us aware that "competition, prejudice and distinct boundary maintenance and domain protection are more common than collaboration and cooperation."

The rigid boundaries which inhibit free flow of communication and good will come more from inexperience with cooperative ventures than from any reservoir of ill will. Rapaport (1971, p. 161), in speaking of social work consultation, where participants in both sides of the arrangement come from the same educational pool, noted that "it is becoming increasingly clear that social workers are moving into consultation with new services and new social work careerists whose value base, goals, technical competence and personal styles are greatly at variance with the professional culture. The role of the expert and objective, more distant, less active consultant is dysfunctional in such settings. A more collaborative approach to consultation, with greater emphasis on a role and socialization model may be needed."

This project was developed with the understanding that whatever strains and inefficiencies occurred in the relationships that evolved, the enterprise would be valuable for both academics and agencies. Pooling the considerable experience and dedication to older people was expected to set a pattern for both expanded and more pointed and efficient ways of benefitting the elderly. That unifying dedication *was* more important than the discrepancies and had the effect of developing relationships which are still continuing.

Friendship and respect are only mildly infringed on by vocational differences. More and Suchauer (1976), in studying professionals from various health-related disciplines, ranked along levels of power, found that "though occupational prestige predicts the assertiveness, intelligence and responsibility of occupational 'images,' it does not distinguish the likeabilty or congeniality."

The values of the enterprise certainly gave many agency personnel a glimpse of the riches of experience, education, and dedication of the academic community. For some of the academics, the chance to learn the variables, the limitations, and the resources of agency life opened up a vision of new efforts needed for the field and helped to form a resolution to aid in creating a genuine interface with agencies on aging.

REFERENCES

Beisser, A., and Green, R. 1972. *Mental Health Consultation and Education.* Palo Alto, Calif.: National Press.

Benveniste, G. 1972. *The Politics of Expertise.* Berkeley, Calif.: Glendenary Press.

Bennis, W. G.; Malone, M. F.; Berkowitz, N. H.; and Klein, M. W. 1974. Can the behavioral sciences contribute to organizational effectiveness? In *A Handbook of Human Service Organizations,* ed. H. W. Demone, Jr., and D. Harshbarger. New York: Behavioral Publications.

Bicknell, A. T. 1975. An approach to co-ordination of education and careers in gerontology. Unpublished report to the Gerontological Society.

Bronfenbrenner, U. 1974. Developmental research, public policy, and the ecology of childhood. *Child Development* 45:1–5.

Bucher, R., and Strauss, A. 1961. Professions in progress. *American Journal of Sociology* 66:326–33.

Demone, H. W., Jr., and Harshbarger, D. H., eds. 1974. *A Handbook of Human Service Organizations.* New York: Behavioral Publications.

Freeman, J. L. 1971. Psychology as science. *Social Research* 38:710–31.

Ganesh, S. R. 1978. Organizational consultants: A comparison of styles. *Human Relations* 31:1–28.

Golton, N. 1968. The social work entrepreneur and practioner development. *Proceedings of the Seventh Annual Conference of the Advocates of Private Practice.* Bakersfield, Calif.

Halmos, P. 1973. Professions today and tomorrow. In *The Professions and Their Prospects,* ed. E. Friedson. Beverly Hills, Calif.: Sage Publications.

Harries-Jenkins, G. 1970. Professionals in organizations. In *Professions and Professionalization,* ed. J. A. Jackson., Cambridge: Cambridge University Press.

Harshbarger, D. 1974. Turbulence and resources: The bases for a predictive model of interorganizational communication in the human services. In *A Handbook of Human Service Organizations,* ed. H. W. Demone, Jr., and D. H. Harshbarger. New York: Behavioral Publications.

Hudson, L. 1966. *Contrary Imaginations.* London: Schocken.

Hudson, L., and Jacot, B. 1971. Marriage and fertility in academic life. *Nature* 229:531–33.

Hughes, E. C. 1958. *Men and Their Work.* Glencoe, Ill.: Free Press.

Koch, S. 1971. Reflections on psychology. *Social Research* 38:669–709.

Kuhn, T. S. 1962. *The Structure of Scientific Revolutions.* Chicago, Ill.: University of Chicago Press.

Lippitt, R., and Lippitt, G. 1978. *The Consulting Process in Action.* La Jolla, Calif.: University Associates.

Loewenberg, F. M. 1970. Toward a systems analysis of social welfare manpower utilization patterns. *Child Welfare* 49:252–53.

McClelland, D. 1971. On the psychodynamics of creative physical scientists. In *The Ecology of Human Intelligence,* ed. L. Hudson. London: Peter Smith.

McCony, J. L. 1960. *Science and Public Administration.* University, Ala.: University of Alabama Press.

Merton, R. K. 1957. *Social Theory and Social Structure.* Glencoe, Ill.: Free Press.

Moore, W. E. 1963. *Man, Time and Society.* New York: Wiley.

Moravcsik, M. J. 1973. The universal intellectual versus the expert. *Minerva* 11:109–12.

More, D. M., and Suchauer, R. W. 1976. Occupational situs, prestige and stereotypes. *Sociology of Work and Occupations* 3:169–86.

Nottingham, J. A. 1973. Can community psychology afford to be only "scientific"? *Professional Psychology* 4:421–28.

Oleson, V., and Whittaker, E. W. 1968. *The Silent Dialog: A Study in the Social Psychology of Professional Education.* San Francisco, Calif.: Jossey-Bass.

Phillips, D. L. 1973. The present and the future. In *The Professions and their Prospects,* ed. E. Friedson. Beverly Hills, Calif.: Sage Publications.

Polansky, N. A. 1971. Research in social work. *Encyclopedia of Social Work.* New York: National Association of Social Workers.

Rapaport, L. 1971. Social work consultation. *Encyclopedia of Social Work.* New York: National Association of Social Workers.

Rhodes, W. C. 1974. Principles and practices of consultation. *Professional Psychology* 5:287–92.

Roe, A. 1953. Psychological study of eminent psychologists and anthropologists and a comparison with biological and physical scientists. *Psychological Monographs* 67.

Schrader, R. 1963. *Science and Policy.* New York: Macmillan.

Silverman, I. 1971. Crisis in social psychology: The relevance of relevance. *American Psychologist* 26:583–84.

Tobin, S. S.; Davidson, S. M.; and Sack, A. 1976. *Effective Social Services for Older Americans.* Ann Arbor–Detroit, Mich.: The Institute of Gerontology.

3. Negotiating the Research Contract: Terms of the Agreement

M. Margaret Clark and Julio L. Ruffini

WE are concerned here only with the particular kind of applied geron-tological research in which the *client* is the agency or program being studied by the academic researcher. We do not present a generic state-ment of the negotiation of contracts for all types of research, or even for all types of applied research. We do not address issues in cases where the client may be somebody other than the agency or program under study, nor do we address problems associated with situations where graduate students are placed with agencies for training purposes. In these and other situations, the problems and responses to those problems will differ from the framework of this paper.

These guidelines are designed to establish a framework for discussion of a range of problems which, while finite conceptually, have, in real set-tings, many permutations and subtle distinctions. While much of this discussion may not seem new to many sophisticated scholars, our experi-ences with a number of applied gerontological research projects convince us that seemingly obvious guidelines are by no means adhered to, and that many blunders are committed precisely because of failure to specify clearly the terms of agreement during negotiation of the research contract. In case after case either insufficient attention or time is devoted to a thorough specification of the crucial issues, so that important projects are embarked upon with very little mutual understanding of the nature of the research; or, even if considerable attention is given to negotiation of a common set of assumptions, lack of congruence of perceptions on the part of agency staff and researcher is still common.

We address a number of the most significant aspects that need to be clearly and precisely dealt with during the research contract negotiation: goals of the research, role of the researcher, allegiance and loyalty, accountability of the researcher, and ethical considerations.

GOALS OF RESEARCH

To preclude later misunderstandings, it is crucial that the research goals be clearly understood and agreed to by the researcher and the agency.

25

While agreements as to the goals of the project and the procedures for attaining them are possible, researchers and agency staff should be aware of a number of factors which could create problems.

Goals must be clearly stated and capable of being achieved in the time allotted. It should be understood that the goals of the researcher and agency staff may differ. Some projects considered valuable by the researcher might prove to be burdensome to the agency's hard-pressed staff. The researcher must consider that the procurement of some kinds of data might jeopardize the agency's mission and expend more cost in terms of effort, time, and money than would be saved as a result of the study: in terms of efficiency, for example.

Researchers often think in terms of the ideal, maximum research and obtaining data that would be theoretically significant and generalizable. But a maximum research effort may not be what the agency desires; it may want answers to some fairly specific questions. If those questions are of limited theoretical value, the kind that could be answered by staff, the researcher may not be interested.

Agreement between agency staff and the researcher as to what is mutually useful research is the crux of the research contract. What is useful to both must be understood. Staff should be aware, or should be made aware, that applied research can be of enormous interest to the researcher if it has some broader significance, if, that is, it can be applied to situations beyond the particular context. Frequently agency staff are so concerned with obtaining answers to pressing questions that they are not very receptive to generalizable research.

Personnel in new agencies are often overworked with organizational and management problems, budgetary and record-keeping functions, concern with needs assessment, and beleaguered by politics, so that they have no time to establish research priorities. They can use almost any research results, they say to the researcher.

In such a situation it is the researcher's responsibility to ensure that the appropriate agency staff seek a mutual definition of the research goals. If this is not done, it is not really applied research. That is, it is not research that is oriented toward problem-solving but is focused on whatever the researcher thinks is interesting.

No researcher should undertake a project that he cannot complete given the resources available. One constraint is time: What are the time limitations and what can be done within that period? Many researchers, while allowing sufficient time for data collection, often fail to allow time for analyzing, reporting, and disseminating their findings. This too often

results in procrastination in report writing and a poor reputation for researchers.

Failure to provide a product for the fee paid has not been adequately discussed among academic researchers. Often, such failure occurs because researchers on the trail of promising data cannot bring themselves to halt their search for more information. There is always the temptation to collect just a bit more data or to do a few more cross-tabs. By the time the data are collected and analyzed it is time for the researcher to embark on other projects. It has been said that "Unreported research has never been done." Until the report is published the research cannot be considered complete.

Even in the best circumstances, of course, researchers may collect more data than can be analyzed, because it is not always known which lines of inquiry will prove to be dead ends. In basic research, establishing the null hypothesis may be useful; in applied research it is almost useless. It is usually not helpful to agencies to report negative findings obtained in blind alleys—that no difference or relations were found, that it is not known if other procedures would have been better.

Clearly, then, the researcher must be certain his project can be accomplished. This does not mean, however, that the completed project will necessarily be the one originally envisioned. Serendipity is one of the more appealing aspects of social research. We begin by looking at one question and discover that while we have no answer for it, we have stumbled upon the answers to other questions which may be even more significant.

An example from the senior author's research may illustrate the point. Her study of culture and aging, which began as a study of self-esteem and self-image, showed that what informants were discussing had less to do with their image of themselves than with the values they used to make those judgments. Thus, a reasonably good values instrument was discovered in a study designed for other purposes.

This does not mean that the researcher has gone astray. It merely means that if he focuses on one set of important questions, he may obtain answers to other closely related questions. Focused research need not be narrow. Not only must the project be one that can be accomplished, it must also be one of interest to the researcher. The development of a laundry list, while possibly useful to an agency, is not enough for the researcher, who seeks interconnected sets of data with broader meaning.

For these reasons, it is important that the terms of the negotiated agreement include some means for mutually redefining research goals during the course of the project. If, as the work proceeds, it becomes clear that the goals are unsatisfactory, there should be some mechanism for renegotiating others. This is best accomplished by establishing a cut-off point, a date several weeks into the project, when there can be stocktaking, analysis of the progress, and, if necessary, decisions about modifying the goals.

At that time, a number of facts may become clear: the goals were too ambitious; the original questions are no longer the most interesting; the desired information is too costly; the allotted time is inadequate; the results would be damaging to the agency or to the population it serves. So, while it is crucial to have at the outset a mutually understood agreement, that agreement need not be rigid or overly specific. Initially the agreement may be flexible and tentative, with the understanding that there will be a future renegotiation of goals.

In fact, negotiation of research goals may be an ongoing sequence of discussions and interim mutual understandings. The first goal would be to have the researcher look over the agency while the agency staff looks him over. The point is that although individual and changing considerations enter into negotiations about research goals, the ultimate set of goals has to be determined by negotiation and be mutually arrived at and agreed upon. The researcher sets the goals alone only at his own peril.

This does not mean that there cannot be multiple goals—some for the agency and others for the researcher. The researcher may wish to develop a data base for the solution of a particular problem while that data base may be useful to the agency in considering other problems the researcher is not contracting to study. Thus, there may be other uses of data or different analytic goals that lie beyond the particular contract.

The agreement might state that the researcher will provide certain information in an agreed form, while he is free to use the experience and data for other goals. Or the researcher may wish to analyze the data in a different way for some future theoretical problem. This would be agreeable to the agency so long as its goals are met during the contract period, and the researcher's particular interests are pursued either outside the contract period or without imperiling the agency goals.

ROLE OF THE RESEARCHER

The role of the researcher, while clearly spelled out and understood by all appropriate agency staff, must retain some flexibility. The researcher must avoid becoming another staff member. Here the anthropological role of friendly stranger may serve as a useful model. It is impossible to work toward a set of program goals as a staff member and at the same time evaluate or study the effort made to achieve those goals. Even if the research concerns a program conducted by the agency, rather than the agency itself, the researcher cannot function effectively as a staff member.

He needs access to information and personnel which may be cut off to him as a staff member, and he must have immunity from the normal bureaucratic procedures required of staff. Involvement should proceed only so far as necessary to understand the dynamics of the program. To a certain extent, the researcher should remain an outsider looking at the system from an external vantage point.

The researcher's time and energy are not efficiently utilized as a staff member. In applied medical social science, there have been a number of instances in which health professionals with research training, or in the process of obtaining it, have attempted to perform the professional and research roles simultaneously. This is often extremely complicated because of the difficulty of working concurrently within two disparate perceptual frameworks. It is not only a matter of conflict but a matter of attention—of being able to attend to the complexities of two systems while being part of both at the same time.

An example is the physician who, as part of his social science training, studied the community clinic where he was a volunteer physician. He found it impossible to reconstruct the daily events in terms, for example, of role relations between nurses and patients while he was taking blood samples or examining patients. He had to attend to business, which occupied so much of his mind that he was unable to attend to the task of perceiving social interaction.

The researcher should develop a role that allows him to stand outside the normal activities of the program staff while being able to observe the dynamics of that program. This is truer for the observational studies of the field researcher than for someone engaged in survey research or interviewing with structured questionnaires. Whatever the research method, the optimal research role is that of a friendly stranger.

It is necessary to reconcile the clearly defined research role with flexibility of role. As the research progresses it may become clear that too much or not enough role distance has been allowed. Just as there must be a mechanism for renegotiating the research goals, there must be a mechanism for renegotiating the role of the researcher. We cannot over-emphasize the importance of an ongoing dialogue between the researcher and the contact person who represents the agency in negotiations. This has to be not constant, not continuous, but ongoing, continual interchange. Meetings need not be daily, not even weekly, but it is desirable, especially in the early stages, to discuss progress and renegotiate the contract if necessary, or to reestablish previous agreements.

ALLEGIANCE AND LOYALTY

Meetings are useful from another standpoint. They serve as a feedback mechanism so that concerns of the different parties may be addressed. The agency head, for example, may become alarmed at what he believes the direction the research is taking. Without frequent dialogue the agency head may not understand what the researcher is doing or why. He might, for example, be concerned that the researcher is talking to agency clients and be alarmed that his authority and the agency's performance are being undermined.

This brings us to an important matter. Many problems have arisen in applied research because researchers and agency staff have often failed to view themselves as a problem-solving team having a common set of goals. There are a number of models of interaction between agency personnel and applied researchers. In recent years many programs have come under attack by researchers, and a confrontational model has developed. Such a model can be useful in calling attention to abuses or weaknesses of a system. Such a stance, however, is doomed to failure in the kind of applied research under discussion here.

The role of critic should not be undertaken by the researcher under contract to study an agency. This does not mean that the researcher is obliged to tell the agency head only what he wants to hear. The purpose of the applied research is to provide the agency with useful information.

The negotiation of the research contract should, therefore, include a consideration of how data which identify program flaws or weaknesses will be utilized or made public. Particular settings and situations call for different kinds of agreements. However, the researcher always owes it to the agency to inform it first about the nature of any critical data.

ACCOUNTABILITY OF RESEARCHER

To whom is the applied researcher responsible? This again is not an either/or question. There is a joint or multiple responsibility. The researcher is responsible to the demands and ethics of his discipline. He is also expected to provide a product for the people who are paying for a product. The researcher is responsible to the agency to provide the staff with a reasonable set of working relationships and to involve them in defining the research goals.

This does not mean that the researcher is not independent. He cannot be expected to punch a time clock as do staff members. The researcher has to work within certain time constraints, however, as he has to fit his schedule to the schedules of the staff members he hopes to interview or observe. The availability of staff as well as agency equipment is a matter of negotiation and should be clearly defined. Even such matters as access to telephone, postage, typing, Xeroxing, etc., have to be delineated.

ETHICAL CONSIDERATIONS

Confidentiality

It is essential in negotiating the research contract that the research goals be related to the ability of the researcher to proceed in an ethical manner. The researcher cannot disclose confidential material, even within the agency, except in very general terms. Sources of information must be protected. This is especially true when the researcher is analyzing organizational structure or internal management relationships. The powerful as well as the powerless must be protected. We know that employees who are in relatively powerless positions must be protected against those who could dismiss them or who could deny them promotions or other benefits, but we often forget that agency administrators are also entitled to protection of their confidentiality. Administrators have the right to say to the researcher, "These are my hidden agenda items. I don't want people in the agency to know about these."

At the same time that the researcher protects his sources he must defend his right to generalize from the data, by rendering the data anonymous. This is very difficult when a small organization is being studied. Which kinds of information can and cannot be sought must be negotiated at the outset.

This brings us back to the discovery of weaknesses during the contract period. This can be a difficult question, as an example may demonstrate. A researcher is hired by an area agency to look at a nutrition program and discovers some irregularities in purchase of food. Perhaps it is not being purchased economically due to preferential letting of food contracts, ignoring competitive bidding procedures. What is the researcher to do? Blow the whistle on the agency? The researcher has to make a distinction between his role as a researcher and his role as a citizen. He owes it to the agency to point out his findings. The irregularity may be inadvertent, may be due to the act of a single staff member, or may be the result of a subcontractor acting without the agency's knowledge. The researcher should proceed in good faith and assume that public servants are innocent until proven guilty. If there are abuses they can be corrected if brought to the attention of the appropriate staff members.

What if, at a later time, the researcher discovers that the abuses still exist? Does the contract buy his eternal allegiance and loyalty? If the information was obtained during the term of the contract, confidentiality applies, and the best the researcher can do is to publish his findings while rendering the agency anonymous. If, however, the irregularity is discovered after the contract period has expired, by the researcher in the role of citizen, it should be considered new information and not subject to confidentiality. The likelihood of these kinds of dramatic ethical situations is not very great, but they do occur.

There have been cases in which a matter of confidentiality has had to take precedence over some public issue. In such instances the researcher's first rule of ethics is probably the same as that of the physician: do no harm. The researcher cannot always avoid sins of omission, but he can try not to *commit* any harmful acts. This is a very complex issue, of course: at which point does taking no action become the moral equivalent of taking harmful action? The researcher should, first, protect his sources. The entire research enterprise will crumble if people cannot trust researchers to protect their anonymity.

Ownership of Data

Ownership of data is another matter to be negotiated. The researcher must have a copy of his data if he is to analyze and report them. The agency, then, cannot maintain control over the only copy of the data, beyond the access of the researcher. The researcher's responsibility to publish the theoretical aspects of the material would certainly necessitate access, especially since most of that theoretical analysis and writing will occur after the contract period.

On the other hand, the agency must also protect itself. It is entitled to anonymity and to protection against confidential material falling into the wrong hands. The agency is justified, therefore, in requiring that the data, if they are to be removed from the premises, be rendered anonymous by the deletion of names or other identifying information.

The researcher often forgets that he does not have exclusive rights to the data; the agency also may have a right to the data and to publish them. If materials are developed through the cooperation of the agency, a data bank utilizing some of the agency's resources, for example, the researcher cannot simply take the data. The terms of the agreement should include a provision for processing the material in duplicate.

Clearly, however, confidential information that identifies individuals cannot be disclosed. On the other hand, in research involved in needs assessment, for example, the agency might want access to the raw data. In most instances, however, agencies are content with a final summary report.

The agency has the right to withhold information from the researcher. Some documents may be entirely withheld or may be shown to the investigator without granting him permission to keep or copy them. Access to agency documents is a matter for negotiation. A distinction has to be made between research materials which have been developed by the agency and are being analyzed by the researcher, which are the property of the agency, and materials that are developed by the researcher during the course of the contract work, and to which the researcher has a right. Whoever develops material has a right to control that material.

CONCLUSION

Social research is becoming less and less an activity of the lone academic scholar. Studies conducted as part of an applied enterprise rather than as purely scientific investigations are becoming more important. In certain fields, such as industrial sociology and psychology or applied anthropology, applied research has been conducted for some time, and a substantial literature exists documenting the problems involved in such research.

In an interdisciplinary field such as gerontology, however, applied research is relatively new, and the attention devoted to problems in applied gerontological research settings has been relatively slight. Gerontologists must recognize that more and more gerontological research will take place in applied settings and that guidelines, even if only tentative on one hand, and seemingly obvious on the other, need to be developed, refined, and continually modified in keeping with ever changing conditions. This chapter is meant to contribute to such a needed development. It is our firm conviction that numerous catastrophes, harmful to researchers and practitioners alike, may be avoided by the type of preventive measures discussed here.

4. Case I. Sample Surveys: A Tool for Needs Assessment

David P. Fauri

EDITOR'S NOTE: The case study by David Fauri illustrates clearly the problems and pitfalls for an academic researcher who is working in the "real world"— a state government agency on aging. Fauri's assignment resulted from the federal mandate that the state agency must prepare a state plan and the plan must include an assessment of the needs (income, housing, transportation, etc.) of the older population, particularly those persons in greatest need: low income elderly and minorities.

Fauri developed a detailed model for a sample survey, including a precise timetable for the steps in the survey process. However, he encountered problems, and his plan was not carried out. This case illustrates the crucial interorganizational relations between federal bureaucracy and state agency. Although needs assessment surveys were mandated, plans for their implementation were ambiguous.

Fauri's experiences are instructive for the intern or consultant working in a public agency. He points out some of the areas in which "outsider" and "insider" should have a clear and probably a written agreement: general objectives, time schedule, need for regular communication, attention to the content of communication, avoidance of office politics, and a statement of expectations of both parties.

PLANNING for a needs assessment survey of older Americans in the state of Tennessee was undertaken during the summer of 1975 to help the Tennessee Commission on Aging (TCA) respond to an apparent federal mandate for a needs assessment survey in each state. This project was identified as appropriate for a gerontological consultant as the commission had not previously conducted a needs assessment and did not have staff with the necessary experience and technical training.

The following describes the background to undertaking such a survey of elderly persons and outlines the rationale for developing capability for such work through a limited model project and the phases of such a project. Problems preventing implementation of the project are identified. Finally, the process through which a consulting academic brings ideas and knowledge to the operating level of state government is explored.

This work was undertaken as one of two major projects during a three-month period. Sponsorship was provided the Gerontological Society under contract with the Administration on Aging (AOA). The other project was organizational structure revision for the commission. The

consultant, while not having had experience in Tennessee state government, had worked in a central office of a state welfare department and had earlier experiences with municipal and federal governments.

BACKGROUND

The requirement for state agency involvement in "status and needs assessment of older Americans" was mandated as an element of the yearly state plan, and the Tennessee Commission on Aging responded by hiring an outside consultant to design a project. The mandate was:

The State Plan shall provide that the State Agency, in consultation with the National Clearinghouse on Aging, shall undertake or arrange for the regular collection of data on the needs of the elderly throughout the state. The data collected shall include such areas as:
  (1) Income;
  (2) Physical and Mental Health;
  (3) Housing;
  (4) Employment;
  (5) Nutrition;
  (6) Social Services;
  (7) Transportation; and
  (8) Any other subject area considered appropriate by the State Agency.

The data collected must identify the location, special needs and living conditions of those older persons found to be in greatest need in the state for the purpose of determining the population of older persons that will be given priority in the utilization of the funds available. In this effort special attention shall be given to the needs of low income and minority older persons in the State. The State Agency shall take such steps as are necessary to move toward the development of a system that will provide for the systematic storage, retrieval, and analysis of such data and other data made available from the Administration on Aging and for the dissemination of such data to other public and private agencies and organizations having programs affecting the elderly in the State and the public at large (Federal Register, 1973, p. 28046).

The plan developed for a model project status and needs assessment survey was intended to make it possible for the TCA to develop a continuing needs assessment system providing for regular accumulation and utilization of data on the status and needs of elderly Tennesseans. The project defined the steps necessary to conduct a model or pilot in one of Tennessee's nine Development Districts—the Development Districts being contiguous with the state's nine Area Agencies on Aging (AAAS). The intent was to assist the commission in seeking expert assistance for project management and in monitoring progress.

The commission was not staffed to conduct social survey research and was not likely to acquire resources to allow it to conduct such research. It was staffed adequately to establish and monitor outside contracts. These were key conditions and constraints to the project. The consultant specified items to be included in contract formulation, including services required, support facilities, and a time frame. The plan also called for weekly project evaluation and review by a project manager.

The greatest difficulty in planning a status and needs assessment survey was the absence of a statewide organization specializing in social survey research with an on-staff capacity to complete all survey steps. Efforts were made to identify organizations that had such potential capabilities, but state government had meager resources for this work. Only one department of state government had undertaken a major project of this type; the Department of Health was engaged in a study of the health status of Tennesseans. Three staff persons were hired for this three-year project, but only one remained with the research. Delays and high costs pointed to the wisdom of contracting specialized research talent outside of state government.

The plan did not examine the philosophy and conceptual foundation of needs assessment research as the commission's interest in the topic was already established. Materials produced for technical assistance by the AOA (HEW, 1975) present briefly the conceptual framework, and a publication by the Center for Social Research and Development (1974) summarizes the philosophical and conceptual issues.

RATIONALE FOR A MODEL PROJECT

The consultant recommended that the TCA conduct a model or pilot needs assessment project instead of a statewide needs assessment. Key factors contributing to this recommendation follow:

1. The commission had not previously conducted social survey research, and its staff did not possess experience in this area.

2. Tennessee had no social survey research institute or similar organization with major statewide social survey experience.

3. Social research is expensive, especially when conducted by individuals and organizations not possessing staff for sophisticated activities such as interviewing, computer programming, data analysis, and survey design.

4. Tennessee is complex geographically and in terms of cultural diversity, and this increased the problems of state coverage.

5. The AAAS, which might have provided assistance and local support for the survey, varied significantly in staff resources and capabilities.

6. The quality of the survey results should be high, given the expense, the projected use of resulting data in planning and programming of future services, and the projected use of data for measuring the impact of the commission's programs. By using a pilot project to perfect the instrument an increase in the quality of the eventual statewide survey was anticipated.

7. Congress and the AOA endorsed the concept of needs assessment research but did not set arbitrary deadline dates for full implementation, recognizing that most state and area agencies lacked experience in this kind of activity.

MODEL PROJECT PHASES

Six major project phases were identified for the model, and each was divided into from two to five specific events. The six project phases were preplanning, contract formulation, survey design and planning, data collection, computer application, and data analysis and evaluation.

An Event List (table 4.1) and Flow Diagram (fig. 4.1) divided the six phases into detailed steps. This was a simplified modification of the PERT (Program Evaluation Review Technique) approach to the planning and management of new projects, based on aspects of the PERT system which were directly applicable to this project and which required no special instruction in the finer details of PERT methodology, particularly its more complex statistical prediction and control techniques. The Event List identifies major tasks to be completed. The Flow Diagram displays the Events in logical order, as circles. The arrows connecting the circles represent Activities which would require the expenditure of resources, time, and energy in order to complete the Events. No Event can be considered complete until all previous Events connected to it by Activ-

Table 4.1. Event List for a Model Project Status and Needs Assessment Survey of Older Americans in the State of Tennessee

Event no. (completion date)	Event
1. (Sept. 15)	Resources identified include: —funding sources (Title XX, Model Projects Funds) —potential primary contractor for project management (private or not-for-profit research organizations, university social research groups, gerontology research groups)—potential secondary contractors for specific subcontracted services (social scientist with expertise in gerontology, interviewers, interview trainers, computer facilities and software support [programs and programmer], social statistician)
2. (Sept. 30)	Tennessee Commission on Aging pilot project manager identified
3. (Sept. 30)	Request for proposal and invitation to general meeting issued to all potential primary contractors.
4. (Sept. 30)	Pilot AAA identified
5. (Oct. 15)	General meeting held
6. (Nov. 14)	Proposals by potential primary contractors submitted
7. (Nov. 26)	Funding committed
8. (Dec. 1)	Primary contractor selected
9. (Dec. 31)	Project manager and direct support staff contracted (An individual with social survey research experience and/or a gerontologist with social survey research knowledge plus an administrative assistant/secretary)
10. (Jan. 30)	Detailed survey analysis planned
11. (Feb. 2)	Social statistician contracted
12. (Mar. 1)	Cluster sample selected
13. (Mar. 15)	Interview trainers contracted (persons with social survey interview background *and* training skills)
14. (Mar. 15)	Interviewers contracted
15. (Mar. 29)	Interviewers trained
16. (May 29)	Interviews completed (including telephone control, follow-up on selected interviews)
17. (June 1)	Computer facilities and software support contracted (including continuing access to data beyond project termination)
18. (June 28)	Questionnaire data transferred to computer-readable input form (cards, optical scanner, or magnetic tape) and verified
19. (June 30)	Computer output (data printout) obtained
20. (July 16)	Preliminary analysis of output completed
21. (Aug. 2)	Second computer run completed (if indicated as necessary by preliminary analysis)
22. (Aug. 16)	Final analysis of output completed
23. (Aug. 31)	Evaluation of pilot survey and plan for statewide implementation completed

ities are completed. A time frame from September 15, 1975, to August 31, 1976, was proposed. Event Completion Dates within this frame were tied to each Event on both the Event List and Flow Diagram.

This approach is extremely valuable in charting complex new work, involving a number of interrelated individuals and organizations. Those providing specialized services can use the plan to see where and when their work fits into the total project. When displayed as large wall charts, the Event List and the Flow Diagram are valuable for project management and monitoring.

Phase 1—Preplanning (Events 1–4)

This phase included the background research and development work plus preparation on the part of the commission's staff to involve outside organizations in the formulation of a contract. Potential financial resources available for funding the project included uncommitted model project funds of the Tennessee Commission on Aging and funds from Title XX of the Social Security Act. Potential contractors were identified and contacted. It was suggested by the consultant that these persons be invited to a meeting on the project. It was also suggested that the commission executive director appoint one staff member as the project manager to serve as liaison with the contractors and monitor project implementation. During this phase a Development District and AAA in which the survey could be conducted was to be identified. A Development District in close geographic proximity to contractors would reduce costs. The final selection would take into consideration the willingness of the area planner in the district to work on such a project and the ability of the commission's district field representative to become involved.

Total cost was not treated in detail. Potential contractors were expected to examine the AOA documents and to obtain necessary information to calculate cluster sampling costs for the specified Development District. Survey procedure was specified in these documents. The Tennessee Department of Health hired their own researchers and conducted a statewide random sample survey at a cost of $35.00 per interview. A standard random sample interview unit cost in urban areas was $10.00 to $12.00. Cluster sampling is more expensive per interview unit (and is required by the survey design received from AOA) as it requires seeking out interviewees within the given geographic sample area. Total model project costs in the range of $20,000 would be possible; for example, 650 interviews were required, and the Development District selected included

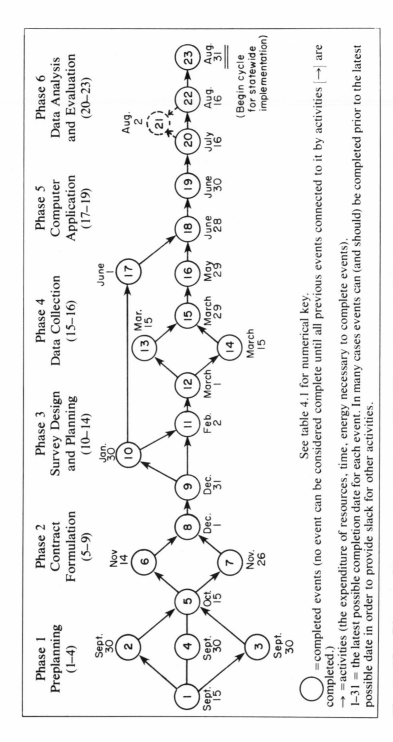

Fig. 4.1. Flow Diagram of Events and Activities in a Model Project Status and Needs Assessment Survey of Older Americans in the State of Tennessee

both rural and urban areas. This would suggest statewide implementation the following year would cost $100,000, with economics of scale applied and efficiencies learned through the conduct of the model project. These were merely rough projections, and the model project experience would provide more definite data.

Phase 2—Contract Formulation (Events 5–9)

A general meeting of interested contractors was called to discuss specifics of proposal preparation. Proposals would be submitted one month after this meeting. Funding would be clarified in preparation for selection of the final contract and the primary contractor. By the end of the calendar year, the contractor would have hired a project manager and support staff. (The contractor's project manager would have primary operating responsibility. The commission's project manager would carry this job as only one of his or her responsibilities, monitoring the project and serving as liaison with the contractor.) The commission, through its project manager, would be prepared to work with potential contractors as they prepare their proposals. Organizations or individuals conducting the model project would be in very good position to conduct the statewide needs assessment survey. Final proposals not selected were to be considered for subcontract roles.

Phase 3—Survey Design and Planning (Events 10–14)

Although the AOA materials provided the basic methodology and questionnaire information, the project staff would have to devote considerable time to designing the data analysis, locating interviewers and interviewer trainers, and drawing the cluster sample. Cluster sampling requires a high level of skill, and a social statistician or demographer would be required for assistance in ensuring statistical validity for the sample, particularly if the contractor's project manager did not possess this ability. Extreme care would be necessary in drawing the sample as interview data validity would be dependent on proper sampling technique.

Phase 4—Data Collection (Events 15–16)

Data collection involved locating and interviewing elderly persons in their residences. Possible sources of interviewers included local university programs in sociology, social welfare, social work, and gerontology; professional interviewers living in the area and located through other survey research organizations; elderly persons identified through the AAA; and recent college graduates seeking employment. Acceptance of the interviewer by the elderly had to be considered. Generally, elderly persons are more likely to accept an interviewer into their homes if the interviewer is known to them or is an older person. AAAS could be of assistance in preparing individuals to grant interviews. The AOA provided an interview training manual along with the questionnaire. The persons selected to do this training needed training skills and familiarity with characteristics of elderly persons and social survey interview techniques. Checks of interviewer reliability on a small sample of interviews were to be conducted by telephone, asking the respondent to verify answers given on the questionnaire. In some cases, this might have required face-to-face contact when telephone service was lacking or not a satisfactory means of communication.

Phase 5—Computer Application (Events 17–19)

Data processing would require access to computer facilities and to the Bio-Medical Data (BMD) package. It might have been possible to utilize the Statistical Package for the Social Sciences (SPSS) computer program rather than the BMD package, although the AOA materials (Utilization Manual) recommend the BMD package. The primary contractor would be able to utilize the one most economical and efficient in obtaining the level of analysis specified in the AOA Survey Guide. Computer programming assistance would be required and obtained on a subcontract basis if the project manager and staff did not have the capability. In addition, services for transferring data to computer readable form (cards, tape, or optical scan forms) would be needed. The AOA questionnaire was precoded so that key-punching or optical scan forms could be taken directly from it without a separate coding operation. It was recommended that the primary contractor have access to computer facilities and the appropriate canned program; the state computer facility was not recommended because its use involved a complex series of bureaucratic steps and procedures which would result in delay.

Phase 6—Data Analysis and Evaluation (Events 20–23)

This phase represents the culmination of the model project and includes analysis of the data and the evaluation of the needs assessment survey process in preparation for statewide implementation. The data analysis would be guided by the work done during Phase 3 (Survey Design and Planning). Provision was made for a second computer run after the preliminary data analysis in the event problems were encountered or data manipulation at this point would give more meaningful or statistically significant results. The evaluation would include an assessment of the model project and a projection of this experience for purposes of planning a statewide status and needs assessment survey and would involve the primary contractor's project manager as well as the TCA project manager and other staff. The state plan for the following year could reflect the undertaking of the statewide project, and appropriate funding could be sought well in advance if the model project proved successful.

IMPLEMENTATION PROBLEMS

This needs assessment project has not been implemented. However, the TCA did meet one of its major objectives through this undertaking in its demonstrable willingness to explore needs assessment research in the state. This interest apparently was adequate to meet the concerns of the regional AOA representative and to show needs assessment activity in the state plan for 1975/76. The state agency was thus able to meet the environmental pressure for such activity through this consultant's development of a plan for a model project.

The following factors prevented implementation of the plan for a model needs assessment survey.

1. The state agency staff members did not have survey research experience. Other responsibilities precluded this consultant from remaining on the project. If this had been possible it is likely the model project would have been conducted.

2. It was not possible to hire a project manager or a researcher on the state agency staff due to a hiring freeze then in effect in state government.

3. Shortly after this report was submitted, the commission became involved in controversy concerning the selection of new citizen members of the commission, and this resulted in the delay or tabling of a number of projects which might have been reviewed and implemented.

4. There was a change in the regional AOA representative as-

signed to the state. The new representative knew less about needs assessment and did not encourage it.

5. The state agency appeared to feel that the planning accomplished by the consultant would meet any inquiries from the regional level concerning progress. The plan was available to meet inquiries and to refer to in the yearly state plan for utilization of federal monies.

6. In carrying out the assignment, the consultant was unable to generate commitment to or enthusiasm for a needs assessment survey. The state agency staff would have preferred the consultant to complete the survey. This was impossible, within the framework of a few weeks' time, and the staff was not interested in carrying on the project without the presence of someone with "expertise" in this type of work.

7. Throughout the project planning, the expressed federal mandate for needs assessment activity at the state level was not fully communicated or interpreted by Washington AOA to the regional offices. The regional office in turn was of little assistance in furthering state activity for needs assessment. The state agency was thus in the position of knowing activity was expected but also of not having explicit standards concerning the quantity and quality of activity. Not wishing to bring additional work into an understaffed office, the state agency did not pursue these questions. This consultant in making inquiry of the regional and central offices found that AOA had not clarified the matter of needs assessment and that organizational commitment to it was lacking.

With a lack of clarity on the issue apparent at the federal level and with the state agency understaffed both in number of employees and in research capability, the problem of implementation is not surprising. In fact, the decision to use the external resources of the Gerontological Society consultant to show some needs assessment activity was a highly rational organizational strategy. Unfortunately, it did not result in acquiring improved data for program planning and decision-making in the state agency and the AAAS.

TRANSFERRING INFORMATION AND KNOWLEDGE

The foregoing suggests the state agency achieved the goal of demonstrating activity toward a needs assessment without actually having to commit its resources. This met the ambiguous federal mandate, and the state agency would thus consider the consultant's work at least partially successful. In this case, however, the transfer of information and knowledge from the academic consultant to the agency was less than successful. The model needs assessment survey was not undertaken, and the agency did not acquire, either on its staff or through contractual relationship, increased expertise in needs assessment or project management. Further, the agency did not develop a system for developing and using in its program planning the needs assessment data on a continuing basis, and this was a major intent of the federal mandate.

Consultants can justifiably be used to meet short-term organizational goals, and this can result in benefits for both the organization and the consultant. Unfortunately, the intended organizational objectives and the role of the consultant may not always be clear. In this case, the consultant attempted to prepare a plan to allow the organization to conduct a needs assessment. This was done with the understanding that the organization intended to conduct a needs assessment survey in the near future. The agency, for reasons previously mentioned, did not pursue this course of action. It would likely have done so only if the consultant had remained to manage the project.

This case provides a good example of some of the pitfalls encountered by academics consulting in government agencies. Some general guidelines for maximizing the contributions of consultants in similar situations will be enumerated with the intent that they will contribute to successful relationships between gerontological agencies and consultants.

1. The organization and the consultant should agree on objectives for the consultant's work. Of course, the consultant must recognize that the agency may be engaged in negotiations and accommodations which might be termed administrative politics and which would be going on whether or not the consultant were present. In such situations, the consultant can do little else than attempt to become aware of these processes and determine whether his efforts should be continued, depending on the projected results and their value to the agency and its clientele. In most cases, it would be expected that the consultant would attempt to do his best and produce as good a product as possible within the constraints of a

political process unless he had serious question about ethical aspects of the potential uses of his product.

2. The time element is a critical factor. Consultations are usually time-limited because of fiscal constraints or project deadlines. Short-term consultations are most appropriate for highly technical work which does not involve program, project, or organizational development but rather involves situations in which the consultant provides certain technical expertise such as knowledge of statistics or computers or perhaps a specific clientele. When the consultant is asked to engage in or assist in program or project development, longer term consulting arrangements are usually desirable. Frequently, the consultant's request for a long-term relationship with an agency, e.g., one or two years, is viewed as an attempt to provide a secure income for a considerable period. While this may be true in some cases, both parties should recognize that maximum benefit is apt to accrue if the consultant is allowed sufficient time, not only to provide technical assistance and planning for programming but also to aid in carrying out and perhaps even in evaluating the plan.

3. Communication between consultant and agency is crucial. Normally a consultant seeks access to both the technical and the top management levels of the organization. Organizations are usually receptive to such arrangements if they are convinced it will help produce the desired results. The terminology of academic consultants and agency employees often varies, with the consultant's vocabulary reflecting technical and specialized terms relating to his field of specialized training and research methodology. The agency employees' terminology often reflects bureaucratic terms and code words and pragmatic applications of currently popular concepts. The consultant must realize the psychological impact of what may appear to be sophisticated terminology relating to quantitative methodology or specialized and abstract terms. Of particular note, the academic gerontologist may refer to and use research findings and concepts to which agency employees have not been exposed, and he must use this information in a manner which is seen as helpful to and assisting employees. Frequently, such knowledge and information may have a negative impact if it is used to buttress the consultant's position and substantiate his expertise.

4. In a related vein, the consultant and, if possible, the agency need to recognize the dual pressures the consultant faces in seeking

agency acceptance. On the one hand, he has the status attached to academic persons. This may be reflected in the consultant's being introduced as "Doctor" even when others in the agency are introduced by their first names, and it may be reflected in his being addressed as "Doc" rather than by his first name. On the other hand, there are pressures and expectations for the consultant to be a member of the agency team and to acquire bureaucratic terminology and behaviors which would lead to acceptance. There is no easy formula for handling this potential role conflict, but awareness of it and willingness to consider methods of dealing with it in a given situation can be extremely useful.

5. The consultant should be prepared to share his work in progress with agency employees. He should also attempt to share early drafts of reports or proposals for discussion. This should be done unless it is threatening to persons within the agency or there are specific guidelines or contractual arrangements which prohibit it. Sharing information reduces the mystery about what the consultant is doing and what he is likely to recommend and facilitates acceptance of the work.

6. The agency should attempt to open the organization fully to the consultant by inviting him to board meetings at the institutional level and staff meetings at the management level. Most agencies recognize that such access is necessary to familiarize the consultant with the agency's methods of operation. If such access is not offered consultants should request it and state the reasons for the request. If necessary, agreements can be reached which would limit the consultant from discussing outside of the agency the proceedings of such meetings.

7. The consultant should make every effort to stay out of office politics and personal feuds, unless he is involved in organizational development efforts which are aimed at increasing the effectiveness of working relationships. Generally, engaging in relationships which are going to identify the consultant as supportive of a particular person or camp in disputes will only hamper his effectiveness and the acceptance of his work. Avoiding such situations is not difficult if the consultant is able to indicate that he is not familiar enough with the situation to state an opinion. Of course, it is possible that a consultant will be brought into an agency to assist a party in a particular power struggle. Item 1, above, relates to such possible situations.

8. The importance of a well-drawn contract cannot be overemphasized. To avoid misunderstandings and disagreements, the expectations of the consultant and the agency must be clearly stated in a contract or letter of agreement in which many of the items listed above might well be included. While time spent in drawing up such a document may appear to be wasteful, because the agency is not receiving consultation during this period and the consultant is not receiving compensation, it should be remembered that this time expended at the outset will likely prove advantageous in terms of a better relationship and product.

Consultation by the academic gerontologist in governmental agencies has great potential and can be rewarding and beneficial to both parties. The consultant, in addition to earning compensation, can develop better understanding of the implementation of gerontological programs and related research questions. This, of course, can further both his teaching and research interests. For the agency, such consultation offers assistance in meeting organization goals and in bringing knowledge and technical expertise into program planning and evaluation and agency administration. The third party benefiting from such relationships is the consumer of services provided by or through the agency. The consultation offers opportunity for merging academic knowledge, research findings, and technical expertise with the administrative and planning mechanisms of program planning and delivery agencies with a potential result of increased and improved programs and services.

REFERENCES

Center for Business and Economic Research. 1972. *A Study of Needs of Senior Citizens in Tennessee*. A report prepared for the Tennessee Commission on Aging. Knoxville, Tenn.: The University of Tennessee.

Center for Social Research and Development. 1974. *Analysis and Synthesis of Needs Assessment in the Field of Human Services*. Denver, Col.: University of Denver.

Federal Register. 1973. Title 45—Public Welfare, Chapter IX, Administration on Aging, Department of Health, Education, and Welfare, Part 903—Grants for State and Community Programs on Aging. Vol. 38, No. 196, Thursday, October 11, 1973. Washington: U.S. Government Printing Office.

Forcese, D. P., and Richer, S. 1973. *Social Research Methods*. Englewood Cliffs, N.J.: Prentice-Hall.

U.S. Department of Health, Education, and Welfare. 1975. Office of Human

Development. Administration on Aging. *Assessing the Needs of Older Americans (Survey Guide, Utilization Manual, Questionnaire, Interviewer Training Manual)*. Washington: U. S. Government Printing Office.

Webb, K., and Harty, H. P. 1973. *Obtaining Citizen Feedback: The Application of Citizen Surveys to Local Government*. Washington: The Urban Institute.

5. Case II. The Realities of Needs Assessment: Rural Oregon

Elizabeth W. Moen

EDITOR'S NOTE: Elizabeth Moen's experience involved an intensive exposure to older rural Oregonians. Her assignment was to study and consult concerning a needs assessment survey, which is a federal requirement of regular statewide planning. Her close-up view of a small number of older Oregonians leads her to question the value of a traditional survey approach to needs assessment.

Many of the older persons Moen met were too proud to ask for assistance or even to learn about programs for which they had real needs. Their attitudes and behavior may have been strongly influenced by situational and cultural factors or a combination of both period and cohort effects. We do not know whether future cohorts who are now aging will feel the same way about governmental programs because they will have had different experiences and lived in a different period.

The reader must be aware of the cohort issue and the effects of the historical period when reading this study, and must remember that Moen's sample was small. Indeed, her careful and detailed assessment of unmet needs indicates one difficulty faced by program planners and administrators dealing with careful facts based on a small sample. How does one utilize and integrate information about a small subgroup in planning for a whole state like Oregon where the needs of about 300,000 persons must be considered? Qualitative studies of this kind are particularly valuable because they may disclose new dimensions and perceptions that are often lost in the surveys carried out with structured questions.

THE Oregon State Program on Aging (OSPA), like such agencies in all other states, faces the complex and difficult task of determining the needs of its older residents in order to develop effective service programs. My project as a summer fellow of the Gerontological Society was to assist OSPA in determining the needs of the elderly and in developing programs for the delivery of services to them. The project had both methodological and substantive goals: to procure information that would aid in the design of the sampling procedure and the questionnaire for a formal needs assessment survey; to gain some understanding of why many of the elderly do not use the available services; and to make recommendations for changes in delivery that might lead to greater acceptance.

The success of a survey depends not only on the sampling procedures but also on the design and administration of the questionnaire. It is important to know enough about the study population to determine whom to question (i.e., how the sample should be stratified), what to ask, and how to ask it. Thus, the study could be characterized as an exploratory effort to gain qualitative information on the situation and attitudes of the elderly of Oregon.

The research was carried out mainly in small towns and rural areas, because OSPA felt it knew less about the needs of the elderly living in nonurban areas and also believed the nonurban elderly are more reluctant to accept help. In addition, these areas generally have a higher proportion of elderly residents than do urban areas. Although the rural condition is ". . . a crucial determinant of the total configuration of needs which must be met in the delivery of services to aged consumers" (Smith, 1975, p. 63), participants in one conference have concluded that the rural aged generally have been ignored by sociological research (Powers, Keith, and Goudy, 1975; Smith, 1975). OSPA had good reason to be concerned about needs assessment methodology and service delivery. Both are being scrutinized and criticized, and questions are being raised about the adequacy and validity of data obtained through formal surveys and social indicators (Bild and Havighurst, 1976; Kendig and Warren, 1976; Bagley, 1977; Bignam, 1977; Streib, 1978). According to Binstock and Levin, the results of intervention efforts to cure social ills have not been good; in the U.S. ". . . the record of ineffective performance has begun to accumulate at a staggering and frustrating rate" (1976, p. 511).

Why isn't the service strategy for the elderly more effective? A major problem is lack of knowledge; much of the failure of intervention is due to ". . . theoretical and empirical inadequacies in our capacity to develop and design effective methods of social intervention" (Binstock and Levin, 1976, p. 511). The gap between the development of knowledge and its translation into services appears to be sizable in the case of the elderly. Research in gerontology has received relatively minor federal support (especially in intervention-relevant areas); there is no well-developed theory in social gerontology; and existing intervention strategies have not been empirically verified (Estes and Freeman, 1976; Beattie, 1976). The knowledge/service gap is even greater for the rural elderly. There is a paucity of adequate data with policy-making implications, and while there are models of service delivery to the urban aged population, comparable rural models are virtually nonexistent (Powers, Keith, and Goudy, 1975; Smith, 1975).

Poorly administered services are also thought to inhibit acceptance by the elderly. Certainly, as we found in Oregon, lack of knowledge, red tape, insensitivity, and strict eligibility requirements do discourage potential clients (Beattie, 1976). Even service providers are now questioning the effectiveness of traditional service approaches (Wagner, 1977).

While much of the problem of low acceptance is in the design and administration of services, much more attention has been given to the providers of service than to the clients. In the July 1977 Federal Administration on Aging grant proposal guidelines, nearly all of the "researchable questions" asked "What is wrong with the delivery system?", not "What are the elderly thinking?" If the reluctance of the elderly to admit need and accept help involves their own attitudes and beliefs, their own perception of welfare and social services, and their own idea of what is appropriate behavior, then research should be directly concerned with the elderly themselves. This was the starting point in planning the summer fellowship.

I spent several days becoming acquainted with services and programs and discussing the project with the regional directors who were to make the initial contacts. I was also invited to the quarterly meeting of the area agency directors where the project was described and discussed further, and several directors volunteered to host it; i.e., to make the contacts which would enable me to meet a variety of older people in their areas.

During the field work I was accompanied by Thomas Moen, a professional photographer and co-author of the report, "What Do the Elderly Want?" A secondary goal of the research was to study use of photography as a means of communication and as a research tool in the social sciences. Both the OSPA and the Gerontological Society were very supportive of this effort.

Our work took place in a variety of settings: Portland, the largest city in Oregon with a metropolitan population of about one million; La Grande, a small city of 10,500; and five towns ranging in size from eight houses to 1800 people. We visited a number of senior centers where we ate lunch and talked informally with the participants, meal site directors, nutritionists, cooks, bus drivers, and volunteers. We also talked with agency directors and outreach workers in welfare and senior services.

The contract with OSPA was negotiated very easily because our goals were very similar. The director of OSPA was very hardworking, knowledgeable, and compassionate. The field work was pure joy. The dedicated service workers, delightful elders, and magnificent countryside made a very special "real world."

FIELDWORK

Our first goal was to select a heterogeneous group of participants for in-depth interviews who would help us learn which social and demographic characteristics of the elderly are associated with particular needs. The characteristics included sex, marital status, socioeconomic status, physical ability, type of housing, geographic location, and age. We met some of those who participated in interviews at the meal sites or senior centers, but those who did not receive services, who were physically disabled, or who were geographically isolated were introduced to us by caseworkers and outreach workers.

We interviewed 25 people—16 women and nine men, including two married couples. A number of them participated frequently in senior activities and utilized services for the elderly. Some took part only in congregate meals and were quite opposed to any other services, while others did not attend meals and received no form of assistance except Social Security.

The ages of the respondents ranged from 57 to 96. Eight were married, 12 were widowed, four divorced, and one never married. Education ranged from none to college graduate, but the majority had eight to 12 years of schooling. All were retired, although a few had part-time jobs, sold their handwork, or did odd jobs. Some had worked in white-collar positions but most had a rather checkered work history, and it was very difficult to characterize their occupational status. Their work was distinguished by its difficulty and undependability. Moreover they had to develop a variety of skills in order to remain continuously employed.

Most of the participants had very modest incomes with Social Security the main source. A few had a pension or received income from property, and a few received Supplemental Security Income (ssi). At one extreme was a woman who lived on $66.90 a month, and at the other extreme was a woman who was able to pay $8,000 for medical care in 1975, and expected to do so again in 1976. Housing ranged from a comfortable new two-bedroom home to a one-room shack without plumbing or electricity. The respondents displayed a full range of physical conditions, from vigor to complete disability, but most had some physical complaints and a number could get about only with difficulty. Within their age range, the degree of disability did not appear to be correlated with age.

INTERVIEWS

We had met most of the people prior to going to their homes for the interviews and explained that we worked for the Gerontological Society, a group interested in the well being of the elderly. We told them our purpose was to learn about their life experiences and what it is like to be old in this country at this time.

The interview can be described as a directed conversation. We had a mental list of topics and often steered the conversation to these areas or probed for more information at certain points. We tried to cover the same material with each subject, but since this was an exploratory study, the interview was sufficiently unstructured for the subject to introduce or dwell on topics of importance to themselves. Each interview lasted three to four hours and usually involved two sessions.

At first we were concerned that the participants might be so intimidated by all of our equipment that they would not allow us to record or photograph but everyone agreed without persuasion and signed release forms for both. In fact, we discovered that the simultaneous use of the camera and tape recorder aided rather than hindered the interviews. The equipment provided an initial topic of conversation, and we got the impression that using the recorder and cameras reinforced our statement that what they had to say was important and actually encouraged their speaking. Some people just sat before the microphone and told their life story without a bit of prompting. A number of people were camera shy, and in these cases the photographer would wait until they felt at ease. In every case the interview seemed to benefit from the presence of two people; the interviewer drew attention away from the camera, but at the same time the camera seemed to be stimulating and to encourage greater expressiveness.

RESULTS

Needs Assessment

We concluded that the needs of the elderly cannot be adequately determined by direct methods; i.e., a formal, highly structured survey would not produce the necessary information. Most of the expressed needs were revealed during the course of conversation, although in response to a direct question, the need had often been denied. Below are examples of the failure of direct methods.

Direct questions.—People with obvious physical disabilities were quite willing to talk about related problems and needs, but beyond that, little information was volunteered. Direct questions related to income, health, social contacts, daily maintenance, transportation, etc. generally received negative responses.

Suggestion list.—Since people were reluctant to volunteer information, we also showed them a list of all services available to the elderly and asked them to name those they would like to use. Generally nothing was named other than that which was already being used.

Contingency planning.—Since many people denied having any immediate needs, we also tried to ascertain if they would use services if their situation were to change. We asked questions such as, "If you could no longer do housework (chores, pay bills, drive, etc.) what would you do?" If they did not volunteer an answer we would ask if they would use a special service such as homemaker, chore service, ssi, or transportation. But most people were unwilling or unable to imagine themselves in another situation and could not respond.

Projection.—Finally, we tried describing other people in similar situations and asked if they thought these (fictitious) persons needed assistance, what kind, and if they ought to accept help. Most said they could only speak for themselves and not for others. But when we described needy people who refused assistance, even those who were most adamant about not accepting help themselves indicated it is fine for others who are *truly* in need.

Had we not visited their homes, or just limited our time and conversations to a formal questionnaire, we would have concluded that Oregon's elderly have few needs. It was only through the establishment of friendly relationships (not probing questions) and prolonged conversation that a clearer idea of their situation emerged, and that needs, anger, and despondency were revealed. These revelations have continued through correspondence with a number of the participants.

Even when a person seemed to be quite open with us, there was still a gap—often quite large—between his own expression of need and our assessment of his situation. And if we did view him from a different perspective, did this mean that the needs we perceived were any less real or urgent?

Major Concerns of the Elderly

Despite their reticence, the elderly expressed certain major concerns strongly and repeatedly. People were most concerned about being able to maintain their independence, especially in their own home, and to stay out of a nursing home by any means possible. Unfortunately many felt they had only two options: manage entirely on their own or enter a nursing home.

The elderly have mixed motives for wanting to stay in their homes. Many were deeply rooted there and in their neighborhoods. Others were not particularly attached to their home but owned it or were allowed to live there rent-free. For many who do not make rent or mortgage payments, it was a question of survival; their incomes did not allow additional expenditures. As prices increase and the elderly are less able to cut costs by doing their own maintenance, gardening, or sewing, their fears and anxieties increase. Most respondents see the nursing home as their only option, which makes them even more determined to stay out.

We were puzzled about their attitudes, for if nursing homes are perceived to be in nearly everybody's future, then why is there such a fear of them? Why would energies be organized around staying out of them? The obvious answer to us—poor quality of care—was only one aspect of their concern. A nursing home is a symbol of rejection by one's family or of one's complete physical and mental deterioration. There is a deep fear of being sent to a nursing home before this deterioration has occurred, for then it is seen as a degrading and dehumanizing experience. "I'd go crazy there." "There's nothing to do." "They just sit there." After going to a nursing home (a very nice nursing home) and witnessing the blank stares of all of the people who were *just sitting there,* we could appreciate the fear of being sent to such a place.

Desired Assistance

The need for assistance in obtaining health care, transportation, employment, and fuel was frequently expressed by the elderly, and such assistance would certainly enhance their feelings of independence.

Health care.—Reliable medical and dental care and help with medical, dental, and pharmacy bills were mentioned most often. Nearly everyone indicated a lack of confidence in or distrust of physicians. Everyone told of an unfortunate incident with diagnosis or treatment, or an outrageous bill. Even those with health insurance, Medicare, or Medicaid have had difficulty paying their bills, and many described Medicare or Medicaid as a fraud. In the words of one 78-year-old woman, "Medicare doesn't pay anything. The whole hospital system is a great big graft . . . they just want to pauperize you before you die." And those who are paying the nursing home bills for a spouse or parent, like this woman, are truly being pauperized.

The elderly want better health care, a higher level of assistance, and a more rational plan for assistance that would cover their greatest needs and encourage the provision and use of preventive services.

Transportation.—Those without transportation find it difficult to maintain their independence and are enthusiastic about special transportation services. But these services are especially problematic for nonmetropolitan areas. There is no public transportation and Senior Centers are not able to fill this need. Not enough money is available for cars, buses, drivers, or even gas, and there are too few riders to fill the requirements for the subsidies that are available. In order to meet the needs of the elderly in low density areas, subsidies and regulations about passenger-miles would have to be adjusted.

Employment.—Many of the elderly could solve their own problems if they had more money, and many would rather work than accept assistance. Those who are able to work resent that they cannot help themselves, that they cannot find jobs, that ceilings are placed on the amount of money they can earn, and especially that they are forced to retire merely because of age. They are also aware that these restrictions do not apply to everyone. One said, "Congressmen and big shots get pensions and earn all kinds of money, while those on Social Security are cut off . . . it's not fair. . . ."

Job substitute programs such as Green Thumb and Senior Aides are welcomed for they provide benefits far beyond the small salary. Participants told how good it is to feel useful, to be able to help others, and to have the chance to meet people. One man told of sitting alone for five years, "down in the dumps," and so lonesome he would "pretty near go crazy." He had become so weak from inactivity that he would fall just going the short distance to his mailbox. Through the Senior Center he joined the Green Thumb program and became a driver's aide. Since then his physical condition and mental outlook have improved enormously. He feels he is doing something important, he has something to occupy him four days a week, he has made friends, and he has a bit more money. Unfortunately, there are not enough positions funded for the number of people who would like such jobs even though the cost of these programs is small compared to the returns—work is accomplished, a person is rehabilitated, and future expenses for hospitalization or welfare may be avoided.

Fuel.—The high cost of fuel for heating is another major cause of anxiety. A number of people used wood because it was the cheapest fuel available, but wood presents serious problems, for even if it is delivered, it must be split and carried. Many of the elderly can no longer perform these tasks and must depend on someone else to do them. For some, the wood chopping assistance provided by some Senior Centers is enough, but for others, a subsidy for fuel and conversion from wood to another fuel source is badly needed if they are to remain independent.

EXPLANATIONS

Our attempts to learn about the needs of the elderly yielded puzzling results. They were reluctant to admit the need for any assistance, yet they were deeply concerned about a common set of problems—problems that could be solved or alleviated by services already in existence. But these are the very services that the elderly say they don't need. The "nonacceptor syndrome" may even be so strong that it leads to denial of need even though services are being used, refusal to use services for which a need is expressed, or even denial of acceptance of assistance that is actually being given.

Acceptors and Nonacceptors

The nonacceptor syndrome can be partially explained in terms of relative deprivation. Need is a relative concept, and while our view was of their present condition, their view encompassed their past as well.

Many of Oregon's elderly people are immigrants or children of immigrants. They came from families with limited means and opportunities and were subject to discrimination (Higham, 1971; Wheeler, 1975). Because of their level of education they had access only to low paying jobs with few benefits and remained in the lower job levels throughout their working years. Economically, some of the elderly are as well off or even better off now than they have ever been. Their income is higher (and if not higher, at least more reliable), and they have more material comforts and fewer obligations. "I've had it rough," said one woman who was receiving SSI and had been below the poverty level for years. But she, and others, also believes ". . . old people have never had it this good" and wishes her mother could have had what older people have today. Similarly, a study of the elderly in New York found, "The reverse of fortune, not life-long inadequacy or deprivation, causes a person to seek help in his later years" (Blenkner, 1962, p. 308).

The nonacceptor syndrome may also be partially explained by a lack of knowledge about services and confusion over eligibility, or the belief that the costs of application (red tape, forms, trips to welfare offices, and transportation problems) are not worth the meager benefits. But whether or not services are used, a sharp distinction is made between services for the elderly and services for the poor. Like the residents of Bethnal Green (Townsend, 1957), many would rather spend their last penny of savings than get welfare assistance, and some would starve before admitting they need help. As one man told us, "The word, 'welfare' is taboo to old people. They will go without necessities . . . they should call it something else." This seems to be the heart of the problem: old people do not want to admit they are poor, do not want to be thought of as poor, and do not want to be associated with poverty programs. Thus, to fully complete the puzzle—to understand why the rural elderly will not admit needs or use services—it is necessary to understand how welfare is defined and why it is taboo.

The Acceptor/Nonacceptor Continuum

The first step in understanding why people do not use services is to determine who does use them. To clarify the analysis, we devised an acceptor/nonacceptor continuum (fig. 5.1). At the acceptor end, the extreme type is the "unworthy chiseler," he who seeks out and uses any and all services, even when he does not need them, or could do something on his own to alleviate need, or will even cheat to gain services. At the extreme of the nonacceptor end is the "super proud," he who is truly in need but will not accept help from any source. (The terms "super proud" and "unworthy chiseler" come from desciptions of such types made by the elderly themselves.)

In figure 5.1 the five horizontal lines represent the range of acceptance of the more usual forms of assistance available. If they are arranged from those most readily accepted to those least readily accepted, they seem to form a Guttman scale.

1. *Earned Assistance:* Social Security and pensions, i.e., programs to which the recipient has contributed at least part of what he will receive. This is the most readily accepted form of assistance.
2. *Mutual Assistance:* Bartering and aid from friends, neighbors, and family, which is usually accepted with reciprocation in mind.

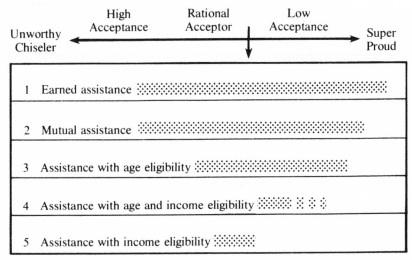

Fig. 5.1. The Acceptor/Nonacceptor Continuum

3. *Assistance Based on Age Eligibility:* Programs and services available to all senior citizens, i.e., reduced-fare movie or bus tickets.
4. *Assistance Based on Age and Income Eligibility:* Programs for the elderly with limited means, e.g., homemaker or chore service. The acceptance of these services appears to depend on whether they are perceived as welfare or senior programs since the patterns of attitudes and use were not as consistent as with other modes of assistance.
5. *Assistance Based on Income Eligibility:* Services commonly called welfare which label a person as poor. These are the least readily accepted.

In addition to rejection by the potential user, there may also be normative rejection by the service provider. We encountered only one such case. A person seeking assistance was considered to be ineligible and was excluded from systems of mutual aid and the Meals on Wheels routes. This sort of informal screening may be an important factor in service delivery.

The individual most eager for help had a ready explanation for why others refuse it: "Them that needs it should have it." She thought that people who won't accept help ". . . don't really need it . . . they probably have money in the bank or someone to help them. It's got to be that way." Since this conclusion differed from our observation that some people who need help are unwilling to accept it, we regard the area of the continuum of most interest here to be the rational acceptor—those who at one time were nonacceptors of varying degree but who have moved along the continuum to the point where they are willing to accept any form of help when needed. They have sought and found a rationale for acceptance, which is often based on the idea of mutual aid or the feeling that this assistance has been earned and is not given grudgingly. One woman received ssi, food stamps, rent reduction, and a housekeeper because, "People want to give help. It comes from the heart"; but when she goes to lunch at the senior center she ". . . wouldn't think of not paying." Another woman would not get help at first; she ". . . never asked the County or anybody for anything." She felt she had earned Social Security but not food stamps; she was eventually convinced that she deserved the stamps because she had worked a long time and paid taxes.

Why Welfare is Taboo: Cohort Analysis

Having seen how welfare is defined, we then sought to understand why it is thought to be unearned and taboo. Why, as de Beauvoir (1972, p. 241) asked, do ". . . older people have the feeling that they are begging and many cannot bring themselves to do it?"

Relative deprivation has been suggested as a partial explanation for the insistence of the elderly that they do not need help. However, this does not imply that the elderly are a homogeneous group. Although many have shared circumstances similar enough to result in the feeling that "they never had it so good," an examination of age cohorts reveals that they have also had very different experiences.

We noticed differences between the younger elderly (60–75) and the older elderly (76 and above), but it was not until parents and their children were interviewed that we fully appreciated that it is as ludicrous to combine those aged 60 to 90 as it would be those aged 20 to 50. In doing so, age loses all analytical and theoretical value.

Two of the most resistant people we met were women over 80 who would take part only in congregate meals and use transportation services solely for that purpose. They were both adamantly opposed to food stamps or any other form of welfare even though both qualified and could

Table 5.1. A Brief Social and Economic History of Ten-Year Age Cohorts Born 1880–1930

| Date | Age Cohort in 1976 | | | | | | History |
| | Older Elderly | | Younger Elderly | | Future Elderly | | |
	87–96	77–86	67–76	57–66	47–56	37–46	
1900	20	10	0				
1910	30	20	10	0			Workmen's Compensation Act
1920	40	30	20	10	0		World War I, rural prosperity Economic prosperity except rural area "Old Age Relief" programs in some states Strong anti-union activities
1930	50	40	30	20	10	0	Depression New Deal, new attitudes about poverty Federal works programs Social Security Act and unemployment compensation
1940	60	50	40	30	20	10	World War II Postwar economic boom
1950	70	60	50	40	30	20	Korean War Farm labor covered by Social Security Self-employed farmers covered by Social Security

Table 5.1—Continued

| 1960 | 80 | 70 | 60 | 50 | 40 | 30 | Recession
General economic prosperity
Senior Citizens Housing Act
Older Americans Act |
| 1970 | 90 | 80 | 70 | 60 | 50 | 40 | Vietnam
Stagflation
Supplemental Security Income |

use the assistance. We talked to the 65- and 70-year-old daughters of one; both were in favor of food stamps and one talked of applying for them. We also talked to the 66-year-old son of the other woman. He not only favored welfare assistance to the needy, but was irate because his mother was doing without necessities rather than accept help.

Kammerman (1976) studied eight countries and found that age 75 demarcates the younger and older elderly. She concluded that, ". . . if there is a chronological age that provides a social policy beacon in the area of social gerontology it is probably age 75. All countries reported that at the very least there are two generations of aging, with 75 being the dividing line" (1976, p. 530; see also Neugarten, 1974, 1975).

We examined the history of several cohorts of elders in an attempt to provide some insight as to why welfare is taboo for the more advanced elderly but may be less so for the younger elderly. Table 5.1 is a brief economic and social history for ten-year age cohorts born between 1880 and 1930, and who were 46–96 years old in 1976. The interpretation of the effects of their backgrounds refers only to the kinds of people studied in Oregon—the rural working class. As table 5.1 shows, the older elderly started working at the beginning of this century. Although this was a period of violent struggle for the rights of labor there were few unions and they did not have much power. Salaries were very low and Workmen's Compensation was about the only benefit available. The agricultural sector prospered during World War I, but farmers did not share in the generally good economy of the twenties. The depression hit the older elderly in what should have been their peak earning years when they had families to raise and mortgages to pay. They were too old to benefit very much from the post–World-War-II boom, and the illnesses resulting from long years of substandard living and working conditions often wiped out what financial recovery they did make. Prior to 1930 the poorhouse, characterized by "insufficient and unfit food, filth and unhealthful discomfort" (Shanas et al., 1968, p. 106), was about the only form of public assistance available to the needy, and the older elderly were too old to gain maximum benefits from Social Security and other such programs introduced during the 1930s.

The older elderly have had a most difficult life and have been socialized to a culture and ideology which stressed individualism and promised rewards to anyone who worked hard. They worked under exploitive circumstances and yet believed that anyone who refused to work or asked for assistance was a chiseler. And now, even when they are old, sick, disabled, and poor, much of which is a result of their work history, they feel ashamed at the thought of accepting help. "I've never asked for anything in my life," or "I always made my way through," were frequent comments. They are left without morally acceptable remedies for their deprivation. Oregon's elderly working class feel somewhat cheated, for they believe they "built this country" and "suffered for it" and yet know others have much higher retirement incomes.

The younger elderly may represent a transition in attitudes toward welfare. The depression occurred during their early working years, and, because of their age, they were more likely than the older elderly to be influenced by the change in attitudes toward labor and poverty that took place during the New Deal. Economic failure was widespread during the depression and could no longer be blamed on the individual as it had been previously. Now it was seen as a failure of society, resulting in many social welfare programs. The government also developed a more positive attitude toward unions as evidenced by the National Industrial Recovery Act of 1933. With the right to organize, union membership increased, and collective bargaining brought higher salaries and more benefits. The post–World-War-II economic boom coincided with the strengthened position of labor and the most productive years of the younger elderly. Consequently, while they tend to be in a better financial position than the older elderly, they also appear to be less reluctant to admit need and seek assistance. This has also been shown in a study of urban and rural men in which those over 75 had less income but felt less economically deprived than those aged 60–64, who had higher incomes but felt more deprived (Youmans, 1977).

The working life of the future elderly began after the depression, and they have mainly known only the more favorable attitudes toward labor and social welfare programs. They have generally experienced continuously greater prosperity and are accustomed to a fairly high standard of living. Thus, when they retire they may be even more likely to see themselves as needy and expect services and assistance. In fact, since the future elderly are more educated and more politically aware, they may demand a much higher level of assistance than is presently available to the elderly (Uhlenberg, 1976).

Generalizations and Rural-Urban Differences

Bourg (1975) has noted there is still a tendency to reify the rural-urban continuum. Rather than making comparative studies, and searching for commonalities, students of one area assume that opposite results will obtain for the other area. Consequently, in assessing the generalizability of our findings and explanations beyond the rural working class, it is necessary to consider whether a rural or urban location influences the needs of the elderly and their attitudes toward assistance.

Urban areas can provide a greater variety of services at a lower per capita cost (Williams, Youmans, and Sorensen, 1975). There is also a proportionally larger pool of volunteers in urban areas. Although rural and urban residents share common needs, each also has unique problems. For instance, rural residents who do not have access to a car are more likely to need special transportation assistance than are urban residents, while urbanites may be more likely to need nutritional assistance since they may be less able to grow, process, and preserve their own food. Since urban employment has been more stable, has paid more, has offered more benefits, and has been less debilitating than rural employment, one's current level of needs may vary directly with time spent in rural areas in the past, rather than reflecting only the current residence.

Rural or urban residence appears to have a greater influence upon the type and level of needs of the elderly and the ability of an area to deliver services, rather than on the attitude of the elderly toward accepting these services. We were impressed by the consistency of our data regarding the attitudes of the elderly toward assistance with the findings of previous research on urban and rural elderly in the U.S. and other countries (e.g., West, 1945; Townsend, 1957; Blenkner, 1962; Shanas et al., 1968; and studies described by de Beauvoir, 1972, and Philblad, 1955). Very similar attitudes about assistance were expressed by Portland's working class participants and observed by the service personnel and volunteers. Thus, it may be argued that the reluctance to admit need and to use services is more a function of social class than of a rural upbringing or current rural residence, and that the findings of this study and their interpretations may apply to both urban and rural elderly who have experienced life and work histories similar to those of Oregon's rural elderly.

IMPLICATIONS AND EVALUATIONS

While this study cannot be used for its original purpose of designing a needs assessment survey, it has been widely disseminated and is being used for other purposes. Two hundred copies of the illustrated report, printed and bound by OSPA, were distributed by the agency as far away as New Zealand. The report was also reprinted as a special issue of *The*

Pioneer, the quarterly magazine of OSPA. More than 3000 copies were distributed, some of which are being used in the training of social service and field workers in Oregon and as resource and staff development material for OSPA. The agency also requested a series of pictures and captions to be mounted for an exhibit. A report on the project has also been published in *Social Problems* (Moen, 1978).

The director of OSPA at the time of the project informed me that the agency will not be doing a needs assessment survey. Instead, it will request funding from the legislature on the basis of current programs and reports from local service agencies. According to the former director, the report is not used as a lobbying tool, but, "We would say that the $1800 investment in publication . . . has been well worth doing in terms not so much of immediate tangible outcomes but in terms of recurring and long lasting intangible and tangible outcomes in our state."

My feelings about the project are mixed, but I think the conclusions do have theoretical, methodological, and policy implications. Coming from an exploratory study, however, these implications must be tested and evaluated further. I would feel more confident if we had been able to spend time with more people.

The implications for social gerontological theory can be summarized as follows

1. Among the elderly, the younger elderly are more likely to perceive need and utilize services than are the older elderly.

2. When services are ranked from the most to the least acceptable, from Earned Assistance to Assistance Based on Income Eligibility, the younger elderly are more likely than the older elderly to utilize the less acceptable services.

3. Within age cohorts of elders, the reluctance to admit need and use services is more a function of social class than of rural/urban residence in that the working class has the most conservative attitudes and behavior.

4. Perception of need and attitudes toward services are results of cohort effects and age/period interaction, rather than of aging itself. Therefore, as the current younger and future elderly grow older, cohorts at each age will feel needier, be more willing to accept assistance, and have a more positive attitude about government intervention.

5. Since each successive cohort of elderly will be more educated,

and since the proportion of elderly in the population will increase, there will be greater group consciousness, and they will become more politically active in their own behalf.

The empirical evaluation of these ideas would involve the testing and development of social gerontological theory, especially the life-course perspective. But to test life-course hypotheses it is also necessary to test hypotheses based on developmental and present-time perspectives, thus showing the relative importance of age, period, and cohort effects. Such research would also have implications for other social gerontological perspectives, e.g., by following cohorts over time, the degree of social engagement or "disengagement" by the elderly would be recorded, and testing an hypothesis about group consciousness would also involve testing Rose's Subculture theory. From a methodological viewpoint our project was unsuccessful because the only advice we could give OSPA about a formal needs assessment survey was "don't do it." We concluded that if all the needs of individual elders are to be ascertained, it may be necessary to do more than just ask them. Service workers may have to form close relationships with them, contact friends and family, and even make an arbitrary diagnosis of their condition. Streib (1978) has raised the question of whether this approach might not lead to invasion of privacy or raise false hopes and unrealistic expectations for assistance that legislators or taxpayers might not support. I suspect that any method of needs assessment that involves a potential recipient could raise hopes, but the issue of privacy as well as informed consent is very important.

On the positive side, the project may have saved the state a great deal of money, for a careful needs assessment survey may cost up to $100,000 (see Fauri, chapter 4). Another potentially positive methodological outcome is that the elderly rank services according to acceptability, which appears to be dependent upon the universality of eligibility, the degree of contribution by the recipient, and the labelling of the recipient as poor. If the elderly are as consistent in their ranking as they appear to be, then modes of assistance should form a Guttman Scale. If such a scale were verified in subsequent research then it would provide a fairly simple method for estimating potential service utilization, and it could provide some fairly clear-cut guidelines for the design of assistance programs.

Policy implications are found in the earlier discussion of the areas of greatest concern: health care, transportation, employment, and fuel, which are all obvious unmet needs. We also made some more general recommendations about services that might lead to higher utilization or, better yet, ultimately enable the elderly to help themselves. These recommendations are summarized below.

Expansion of outreach.—It appears that the success of senior services ultimately depends on the outreach program and the outreach worker. Senior citizens need to know what is available, need a clear understanding of programs and services, and need to feel they are wanted as participants. Yet it is the outreach program which seems to have the most limited resources and personnel. In fact, one senior agency we visited had a position designed solely as outreach, and this was only a half-time, low-salaried job.

We also observed that all outreach workers are low-paid women. Why do these important positions have such low priority? Why are there so few outreach workers? Why do they have such limited budgets? Why are their salaries so low? (It also seems that the closer one works with the people, the lower the pay.) And why are they all women? It is important to involve men in these services since a major reason older men give for not coming to meals or other activities is that they seem like women's clubs. Is this a classic case of "women's work"? Outreach positions should not be pin-money positions: these jobs require the best people available of both sexes. I am not suggesting, however, that raising the status and salary of the position should be accompanied by imposition of stiff eligibility requirements. This is not a question of education as much as of empathy, energy, enthusiasm, and warmth.

Alternatives to welfare.—To raise the level of acceptance, alternatives to welfare must be sought or the people's concept of welfare must be changed. A major obstacle to obtaining welfare assistance is that formal application must be made, i.e., one must not only admit needing help but also ask for it publicly. This may be too high a price to pay for people who are determined to remain independent. Welfare assistance might be more acceptable if it were channeled through senior services or if it were more like senior services, which sometimes are delivered without being requested or are obtained by paying a small fee. Again and again we were told how important it is to pay something for the congregate meals, even if it is only a few cents. One woman explained that if meals were free, ". . . fewer people would come. It works both ways—the poor want to do what they can."

Poverty prevention.—Many of the problems of the elderly do not arise suddenly at age 65. They are the result of economic crises for which this country has few programs for prevention or assistance. Aside from employment problems, the major economic crises are usually precipitated by medical bills and could be prevented by reform of the health care system. Severe illnesses often occur in middle age, taking all savings and placing people in debt. One woman told us that her husband had been hospitalized for five years, and in order to pay his bills she lived on less than $60 a month for a long time.

Revamping the welfare system to include preventive programs might remove much of the current stigma and might reduce costs in the long run. One woman who had tried to prevent a crisis told us bitterly, "Welfare wouldn't help me when I needed it and so I lost my home, my holdings, my eyesight, and my career. . . . I'm part welfare now. . . . They made me that way."

Senior self-help and organized bartering.—The elderly are reluctant to seek help, but they also realize that if they asked for everything they need, the current system could not handle the additional burden. Since it is most desirable not to need services at all, we concluded that it would be advisable to develop alternatives. A number of the elderly in rural areas were involved in reliable systems of bartering and help. Each person we talked to possessed a number of skills that were not being fully utilized. Why not capitalize on their desire for independence, their willingness to help, and their dormant skills by matching needs with skills and by organizing assistance networks. The fear of being a burden might be reduced if there were a definite possibility of assistance reciprocation. These networks could include people of all ages and need not exclude the disabled for they can contribute companionship. In the critical area of transportation it would be especially beneficial to find younger people who would barter rides for services.

Contingency planning.—Many of the elderly have absolutely no plans for the future. They do not know what they would do if their finances or health were to get worse or if their spouse were to die. Most just leave their fate up to God or a nursing home. Precrisis counseling for the elderly could be a very valuable program, presenting options to the nursing home, enabling them to learn about services, and perhaps making it easier to accept help when it is needed.

WHICH REAL WORLD?

A basic tenet of sociology is that there is no "real world." Instead, there are groups of people with different histories, circumstances, resources, opportunities, and perceptions. To reduce the complexity of so many worlds, we often create stereotypes about their residents. Even the fellowship program, in my opinion, perpetuated stereotypes about academics and bureaucrats.

One major similarity between academics and bureaucrats is their isolation from manual workers, the elderly, children, minorities, and the poor. Instead of becoming acquainted with the people they study and serve, they often rely on stereotypes. It was not until the field work in Oregon that I could fully appreciate how inaccurate and harmful such images could be. The stereotypes and simple explanations did not fit. It was a powerful lesson which was reinforced this summer when I had the opportunity to interview coal miners, construction workers, ranchers, and farmers of all ages.

I have tried, in subsequent writing and teaching, to convey the strength of our elders and the rationality of their attitudes and behavior. The slide show we produced has been especially effective in helping students understand the situation of older people. The field work in Oregon has not only affected my own understanding of the elderly, but it has also changed my approach to research. As a demographer trained in the tradition of logical positivism and survey research, I was not convinced previously of the value of qualitative data and ethnographic methods. Now I believe that both perspectives should be used in tandem and that before researchers treat their "subjects" as census tracts, standard deviations, or regression coefficients, they must first get to know them as real people. I hope the Gerontological Society continues to provide the opportunity to do this—it is money well spent.

REFERENCES

Atchley, R. C., ed. 1975. *Rural Environment and Aging*. Washington: The Gerontological Society.
Bagley, S. 1977. Personal communication. National Institute on Aging, Bethesda, Md.
Beattie, W. M. 1976. Aging and the social services. In *Handbook of Aging and the Social Sciences,* ed. R. H. Binstock and E. Shanas. New York: Van Nostrand Reinhold.
Bignam, J. 1977. Personal communication. Regional AOA, Denver, Col.
Bild, B. R., and Havighurst, R. J. 1976. Senior citizens in great cities: The case of Chicago. *The Gerontologist* 16:3–88.
Binstock, R. H., and Levin, M. A. 1976. The political dilemmas of intervention policies. In *Handbook of Aging and the Social Sciences,* ed. R. H. Binstock and E. Shanas. New York: Van Nostrand Reinhold.
Blenkner, M. 1962. Social work with the aging. In *Social Welfare and the Aging*, ed. J. Kaplan and G. Aldridge. New York: Columbia University Press.
Bourg, C. J. 1975. Differentiation, centrality and solidarity in rural environments.

In *Rural Environments and Aging,* ed. R. Atchley. Washington: The Gerontological Society.

Burkhardt, J., and Lewis, J. 1975. *The Older American Status and Needs Assessment Questionnaire.* Bethesda, Md.: R.M.C. Research Corporation.

de Beauvior, S. 1972. *The Coming of Age.* New York: Putnam.

Estes, C. L., and Freeman, H. E. 1976. Strategies of design and research for
intervention. In *Handbook of Aging and the Social Sciences,* ed. R. H.
Binstock and E. Shanas. New York: Van Nostrand Reinhold.

Higham, J. 1971. *Strangers in the Land.* New York: Atheneum.

Kammerman, S. B. 1976. Community services for the aged: The view from eight
countries. *The Gerontologist* 16:529–37.

Kendig, H. L., and Warren, R. 1976. The adequacy of census data in planning and
advocacy for the elderly. *The Gerontologist* 16:392–96.

Moen, E. W. 1978. The reluctance of the elderly to accept help. *Social Problems*
25:293–303.

Moen, E. W., and Moen, T. H. 1977. What do the elderly want? Salem: State of
Oregon. (Reprinted in *The Pioneer,* Winter, 1977, 1–27.)

Neugarten, B. L. 1974. Age groups in American society and the rise of the
young-old. *Annals* 415:187–98.

Neugarten, B. L. 1975. The future of the young-old. *The Gerontologist* 15:4–9.

Philblad, C. T. 1975. Culture, life style and social environments of the small town.
In *Rural Environment and Aging,* ed. R. C. Atchley. Washington, D.C.: The
Gerontological Society.

Powers, E. A.; Keith, P.; and Goudy, W. 1975. Family relationships and friendship. In *Rural Environment and Aging,* ed. R. C. Atchley. Washington, D.C.:
The Gerontological Society.

Shanas, E.; Townsend, P.; Wedderburn, D.; Friis, H.; Milhoy P.; and Stehouwer,
J. 1968. *Old People in Three Industrial Societies.* New York: Atherton.

Sheppard, H. L. 1976. Work and retirement. In *Handbook of Aging and the Social
Sciences,* ed. R. H. Binstock and E. Shanas. New York: Van Nostrand
Reinhold.

Smith, S. H. 1975. Reaction. In *Rural Environment and Aging,* ed. R. C. Atchley.
Washington, D.C.: The Gerontological Society.

Streib, G. F. 1978. Needs assessment of the elderly in northern Florida. In
Improving Quality of Health Care for the Elderly, ed. J. W. Brookbank. Gainesville: University Presses of Florida.

Townsend, P. 1957. *The Family Life of Older People.* London: Routledge and
Kegan Paul.

Uhlenberg, P. 1976. Changing structure of the older population of the U.S. during
the twentieth century. *The Gerontologist* 17:197–202

Wagner, D. 1977. Review of *Natural Helping Networks. The Gerontologist* 17:180

West, J. 1945. *Plainville U.S.A.* New York: Columbia University Press.

Wheeler, T. C., ed. 1975. *The Immigrant Experience.* New York: Penguin.

Williams, A. S.; Youmans, R. C.; and Sorensen, D. M. 1975. *Providing Rural
Public Services.* Corvallis: Oregon State University Agricultural Experiment
Station.

Youmans, E. G. 1977. Attitudes: Young-old and old-old. *The Gerontologist*
17:175–78

6. Case III. Cross-Cultural Consultation: Challenge, Commitment, or Commuted Sentence?

Michael A. Allen

EDITOR'S NOTE: One of the most striking, enriching, and complicating characteristics of the United States is the diversity of the racial, religious, and ethnic origins of its people. Like other agencies of the federal government, the Administration on Aging (AOA) has attempted—not always successfully—to deal with special populations, ethnic minorities, rural residents, and persons with low incomes. American Indians in the Southwest meet all of these criteria. It is necessary to understand the difficulties involved in formulating policies and administering programs to meet needs arising from ethnic status. Indians are members of tribal groups (nations) many of which have solemn, long-standing treaties with the U.S. government. The belief in tribal sovereignty often leads Indians to feel they should be treated differently from other Americans who live in rural areas and are poor. The claim to nationhood also poses difficulties for state and local government administrators.

Arizona offers a clear example of these issues because Indians constitute a substantial segment of the population and are scattered over a vast geographical area. Allen presents a detailed description and analysis of the situation involving the Bureau of Aging and a number of tribes in Arizona.

THIS case study is an abbreviated record of some of the challenges, pitfalls, and rewards involved in consultation on cross-cultural American Indian aging issues. The consultant's role was to evaluate the efforts of the Arizona Bureau on Aging (BOA) in implementing the Older Americans Act (OAA) on ten of the 18 Arizona American Indian reservations. The objective was to develop and discuss the following five topics: the social context and issues during the consultation; the author's motivation for entering aging consultation-internship and process of involvement; the process of defining the consultant's role in relation to the director of the BOA; the impact of the social context on the consultation role and interpersonal relations; and the outcomes of consultation-internship efforts and experience.

SOCIAL CONTEXT AND ISSUES

Approximately 196,900 (9.6 percent) of the residents of Arizona at the time of the study (1974) were 65 years of age or older; the number of

Table 6.1. Reservation Populations
Age 65 and Over

Reservation and Tribe	No. Age 65 or Over	Tribal Total Population	%Total Population 65 Years or Older
Ak-Chin			
Papago	6	266	(2.2%)
Camp Verde			
Yavapai, Apache	5	94	(5.3%)
Cocopha			
Yuma	26	360	(7.2%)
Colorado River			
Mohave, Chemehuevi	130	1,567	(8.3%)
Fort Apache			
White Mountain Apache	230	7,200	(3.2%)
Fort McDowell			
Mohave, Apache, Yavapai	25	340	(7.3%)
Fort Mohave			
Mohave	15	387	(3.9%)
Gila Bend			
Papago	18	273	(6.6%)
Gila River			
Maricopa	569	8,331	(6.8%)
Havasupai			
Havasupai	22	363	(6.1%)
Hopi			
Hopi	498	6,567	(7.6%)
Hualapai			
Hualapai	32	870	(3.6%)
Kaibab			
Paiute	5	153	(3.3%)
Navajo			
Navajo	5,553	77,979	(7.2%)
Papago			
Papago	535	7,703	(6.8%)
Quechuan	62	856	(7.2%)
Salt River			
Pima, Maricopa	90	2,780	(3.2%)
San Carlos			
Apache	174	5,097	(3.4%)
San Xavier			
Papago	54	732	(7.5%)
Tonto/Payson			
Apache	2	65	(3.7%)
Yavapai-Prescott			
Apache	5	94	(5.4%)
Total	8,083	112,077	(6.6%)

Source: 1973 Bureau of Indian Affairs Labor Statistics

Arizona American Indians aged 65 and older on reservations was approximately 8,083 or 6.6 percent of the reservation population (table 6.1). (The latter represents 4.1 percent of the total persons in Arizona aged 65 and older.) The lower percentage of American Indian population over 65 is due to the fact that many of the Arizona reservations are similar to underdeveloped nations in which recent medical technology has decreased infant mortality and thus increased the proportion of young people. Therefore, on several Arizona reservations 50 percent of the population is under age 18. It has been stated that the life expectancy of American Indians is less than that of white Americans. However, at 45 and older, the gap between the two groups diminishes. Actually the author observed and spoke with several American Indian elderly who were reportedly in their eighties and nineties and who seemed to be in unusual physical and mental health. There may be some factor of natural selectivity operating in that those elderly who survive infant diseases, teenage accidents, and beyond middle years are exceptionally resilient individuals.

There were at least three areas in the social setting which complicated the consultant's efforts to evaluate AOA impact on American Indian elderly: problems with the data collection process, because American Indian individuals questioned the right of the consultant to request and publish or publicize tribal information; the request for direct funding from the federal government by American Indian communities in order to bypass the state aging structure; and the policy of self-determination among the American Indian communities.

Problems of Data Collection

Data collection is becoming increasingly difficult for non-Indians who seek to obtain information concerning the Indian community. First, the traditional values and religious structures of many such communities support a tendency to view knowledge and information about their concerns as private matters rather than as topics of public information and consumption in the dominant Anglo culture. This private/public dichotomy in a sense parallels the Indian view of the traditional sacred/secular worlds.

Second, their reticence to divulge information is due to prior experiences in which they have entrusted an "outside" research consultant with information and later read reports based on that information which they deemed insufficient or misrepresentative of the American Indian community perspective. Thus, rather than relying on outside sources to portray their viewpoints, more "modern" Indian communities have developed their own data collection procedures. Another motivation for more self-reliance in obtaining data is the Indians' growing sophistication and awareness that data may mean financial support for social programs. Most American Indian communities were well aware of "headcount," or per capita, need and minority status as priority criteria for allocation of AOA funds in 1974. They wish to retain control over this information.

A third reason for reticence may be a defensive posture due to either semantic confusion or the fact that the information is just not available. The consultant may receive the "silent treatment" due to traditional values of privacy, or distrust, or insufficient knowledge. Such nonresponse becomes discouraging to the inexperienced interviewer, especially when a minimum of explanation is offered concerning the silence. Thus, neophytes as well as experienced consultants may become frustrated, anxious, and impatient, which creates further distrust in the community—and a vicious circle of more misunderstanding and more misinformation evolves.

Even table 6.2 of this study became controversial. The source of the data in table 6.2 is the Bureau of Indian Affairs (BIA). However, BIA officials admit this table is not based on an actual count but is a projection based upon a probability formula. Yet, when the consultant requested information from the tribes concerning the number of residents over 65, only two of the ten tribes stated that they really had the means to gain such information. Several tribes were starting to develop data systems in 1974. Such scarcity of information leads to conflict between tribes and the older population and also greatly weakens the planning, implementing, and evaluating of AOA programs on reservations. Many American Indian representatives (and, for that matter, Anglo advocates and constituents) view needs assessment procedures and research as too costly and time-consuming for what they *perceive* to be already known in a general way by working with the people. It certainly is often more difficult and costly to obtain information on a reservation than in urban communities due to geographic distance, reduced systems of communication, and the American Indians' lack of understanding of attempts at precision in research methodology.

Request for Direct Funding

The most important historical and contemporary issue in American In-

Table 6.2 Distribution of Reservation
Population 65 Years and Older

Reservation and Tribe	No. Age 65 and Over	Area Square Miles[a]	One Individual Per "X" Square Miles for 65 and Over Population
Ak-Chin			
Papago	6	34	7.3
Camp Verde			
Yavapai, Apache	5	1	.2
Cocopah			
Yuma	26	1	.04
Colorado River			
Mohave, Chemeheuvi	130	353	2.7
Fort Apache			
White Mountain Apache	230	2,601	11.3
Fort McDowell			
Mohave, Apache, Yavapai	25	39	1.6
Fort Mohave			
Mohave	15	37	2.5
Gilda Bend			
Papago	18	16	.9
Gila River			
Maricopa	569	581	1.0
Havasupai			
Havasupai	22	5	.23
Hopi			
Hopi	498	3,863	7.8
Hualapai			
Hualapai	32	1,550	48.4
Kaibab			
Paiute	5	188	37.6
Navajo			
Navajo	5,553	14,014	2.5
Papago			
Papago	535	4,334	8.1
Quechan	62		
Salt River			
Pima, Maricopa	90	73	.8
San Carlos			
Apache	174	2,898	16.1
San Xavier			
Papago	54	111	2.1
Tonto/Payson			
Apache	2		

(Continued)

Table 6.2—*Continued*

Yavapai-Prescott			
Yavapai	5	2	.4
Total[b]	8,021	30,701	3.7

a. *Arizona Statistical Review.* September 1971, p. 48.
b. Quechan and Tonto/Payson population and reservation size not included.

dian social programs is the unique relationship of Indian communities to the federal government. The Indians and their representatives believe that the Older Americans Act is another example of the growing tendency of the federal government to pass responsibilities to the states for improving the situation of the tribes. The American Indian communities, in turn, have repeatedly recommended revision of Section 303, Part A, and Section 612 of the Older Americans Act of 1965 as amended November 1970, to *no longer require tribes to go through the state level of government.* (White House Conference on Aging, 1971, p. 3) Thus, the Arizona tribes are requesting a national office on Indian elderly.

Such an office would perform the following functions: Review proposed programs at the congressional level in a more equitable and immediate manner; advocate on behalf of the tribes the receipt of support and the monies from agencies other than HEW for elderly program funds (i.e., HUD, Manpower, Transportation, etc.); and earmark and allocate funds to various tribes, based upon an agreed grant formula.

Although the request for a national office on Indian elderly was made at the 1971 White House Conference on Aging, the Older Americans Act, as amended in 1973, designates the tribe as a "unit of general purpose local government" (Federal Register, 1973, p. 28044). This concept would regard a reservation as a political "*subdivision of the state . . .* whose authority is broad and general and is not limited to only one function or a combination of related functions" (Federal Register, 1973, p. 28044).

Desire for Self-determination

Thus, a controversy arose from differing legal and cultural definitions, in addition to a desire for self-determination. The Arizona tribes wished to evaluate their own needs and deal only with the federal government; they would not negotiate with an intermediary less sovereign than themselves, that is, the state of Arizona and its BOA. Yet there were countervailing activities operating. The Older Americans Act supported the Intergovernmental Cooperation Act (1968) requiring American Indian tribes, as political subdivisions of the state, to follow reorganization procedures on local plans—a coordination process which was reinforced by A–95 procedures which most American tribes did not officially recognize, yet followed in a "sense of cooperative spirit." Also, the division of the state into six planning and service areas (Arizona Executive Order 70–2, 1970) fostered animosity and created cumbersome planning procedures in dealing with state and tribal matters. The tribes were requested to recognize and coordinate their operations with the state government and also to coordinate activities with regional subunits of the state—the Councils of Government (COGS), where four of the six Area Agencies on Aging (AAAS) were established. Most American Indian communities believed this was illegal and were irritated and humiliated by the requirement to cooperate with the state level of government and also by the mandate to cooperate with the COG's AAA for project approval and funding. Only two tribes (White Mountain Apache and Colorado River) sent "observers" to COG on a regular basis. Many of the Indian leaders perceived tribal representation at the COG as "token" representation with few returns. They felt it seemed to sanction a process they regarded as illegal and time-consuming. Thus, the 1973 revision of the Older Americans Act, Title III, which tried to reinforce statewide comprehensive planning and also increase the role of the AAA, resulted in minimal involvement by Arizona's American Indian communities.

The BOA, AAA, and American Indian governments are in a bureaucratic and political dilemma. On the one hand, there are political pressures and national sentiment to serve minority low-income aged persons, especially American Indian communities in Arizona. On the other hand, there is the problem of carrying out statewide comprehensive planning with a community that insists on self-determination, and does not recognize the official state-AAA planning structure.

To placate the political pressures to serve minority low-income aging, the BOA director (in 1973) allocated supplementary Title III funds to begin three reservation nutrition programs. There was an immediate outcry from all sectors of the Anglo population. Many Anglo advocates, providers, and constituents of urban areas had suffered reductions in program budgets or had not received any funding after formally applying and dealing with the "cumbersome" BOA needs assessment procedures.

Thus, the Anglo outcry was, "Why should the American Indian communities receive funds, when they had refused to participate in the proposal planning process required of others?"

Based upon the 1973 experience, plus stronger guidelines from Washington which supported state "comprehensive" planning, the BOA director took a "hard-line" position in his 1974 planning philosophy. He stated that the American Indian governments must formulate lucid, well-defined proposals with attainable and demanding objectives and must participate in the state planning process. The reply from the American Indian community was outrage and criticism of the state structure and an appeal to the federal level of aging structure for direct funding.

One such appeal transpired at a 1974 spring regional gerontological meeting (in Arizona) in which representatives of two American Indian communities "buttonholed" the commissioner on aging, who assured the communities funds from the federal supplementary aging budget. This assurance was flaunted at the BOA director, who felt that the commissioner on aging had made a mockery of the state comprehensive planning procedure which was the intent of the 1973 revision of the Older Americans Act. Furthermore, the director felt that the actions of the commissioner had totally undermined the Arizona effort to coordinate American Indian communities in the prescribed planning process. However, the two tribes subsequently received the funds they requested.

It was this climate and social setting that motivated the director to seek a gerontology consultant under the auspices of the Gerontological Society's Summer Intern Program.

MOTIVATION OF THE CONSULTANT AND PROCESS OF INVOLVEMENT

As assistant professor of sociology at Northern Arizona University, the author had numerous opportunities to become involved in planning and providing research for the local COG. The COG, with its AAA staff of two individuals, served a geographical area that included three American Indian reservations and was as large as Pennsylvania. In addition, there were numerous local agency and advocacy councils on aging located in the university community, which served as the county seat and Regional-Federal Social Service Center for northern Arizona. The author had originally intended to apply for the summer consultation to evaluate the impact of the state system on aging upon the status of the *rural* older adult residents of Arizona. He felt that such an evaluative research project was necessitated by numerous federal AOA guidelines and programs which were inherently inconsistent with application of rural resources to the needs of rural older adult residents. The summer internship was to provide an opportunity to develop short-term evaluative research on the relationships of the Older Americans Act objective, federal-state interpretation, program implementation, and the program impact on Arizona's rural elderly.

In May 1974, shortly after the internship was awarded, the author and the director of the Arizona BOA attended the Gerontological Society workshop. It became immediately apparent that both parties perceived different priorities within the consultant-internship role, particularly in the substantive area. The director gave highest priority to developing evaluative research on state aging programs and relations with the 18 Arizona American Indian communities rather than to the more general area of rural aging, which was the prime interest of the author. He documented political pressures and conflicts among the AOA-BOA-AAA and the American Indian communities which he viewed as disruptive to the entire state planning on aging and implementation procedures. He noted at least three reasons for giving the American Indian situation highest priority: the demand for direct funding, the rumor that the commissioner on aging had agreed to fund two Arizona tribal governments directly from AOA supplementary funds, and the difficulty in monitoring and evaluating Indian nutrition programs. At this point, he was seriously considering terminating an American Indian congregate nutrition program, although he acknowledged that such a termination would be considered politically unwise, might create further American Indian criticism, and would probably result in a squeeze from AOA, as it would reflect on the Older Americans Act 1972 revision emphasis on minority, low-income nutrition programs.

Although the author recognized the challenge and the necessity for intervention in cross-cultural and American Indian aging programs, he had serious doubts as to whether such a task could be accomplished during a short-term summer consultation. The author was well aware that his role would largely be that of a "troubleshooter" in a setting of controversy and confrontation. In such situations, few consultants have been able to consult, communicate, and commit energies toward resolution of issues without charges being raised concerning their integrity and credibility. There would also be little possibility of actually resolving such complex issues as legal sovereignty, control of social service, or direct federal funding of American Indian programs. These issues would require more time and resources than those available to a powerless consultant, who would probably be considered an "outsider."

In spite of these doubts, the consultant and the director came to a mutually agreeable, though not totally satisfactory, accommodation on the role and program objectives. The American Indian aging program would receive the highest priority. Second, rural aging issues would be addressed via observing aging programs and interviewing elderly residents at intermediate points between sites of reservation research.

In return for emphasizing the American Indian aging issue, the director agreed to a "hands off" and "no-holds-barred" policy to assure that the research would be candid and properly describe the Indian communities' perspectives, criticisms, and objectives. Every effort was to be made to obtain a representative viewpoint of the various concerns of the American Indian communities by interviewing their leaders, their elderly, the providers of the program, staff representatives of government social agencies (i.e., BIA and Public Health Services [PHS]), and American Indian coordinating and advocacy groups (Affiliated Tribes of Arizona, Inc., and Indian Development District of Arizona).

The interview sessions were to emphasize at least five basic areas. (1) What are the needs of the Indian elderly on the reservation? (2) How appropriate are the guidelines of Title III of the Older Americans Act in effecting programs for the aged on the reservation? (3) How appropriate are Title VII guidelines for providing a successful nutrition program on the reservation? (4) What recommendations can be offered on how Older American legislation may be changed to meet more effectively the needs of the reservation elderly and the general Arizona American Indian community? (5) Are there any specific comments or recommendations concerning the performance of the Arizona BOA and its staff in relation to reservation elderly?

DEFINING THE CONSULTANT'S ROLE: RELATIONS WITH THE BOA DIRECTOR AND STAFF

The director was very receptive to the consultant program and made every effort to support it. He viewed a successful consultation as including research and recommendations depicting American Indian, state, and federal positions and providing a basis to formulate alternatives in planning and funding programs for the Indian elderly. The BOA director took several actions to assure a successful consultation.

1. The director had an initial discussion with the consultant and was always available for meetings to review and question objectives or motivations and possible covert-overt political and cultural ramifications of the assignment.

2. The director provided open access to all files and information during an orientation period and throughout the consultation.

3. The director assured the consultant open communication channels. No subject dealing with the topic of investigation was deemed taboo.

4. The director introduced the consultant to his staff and clearly identified the consultant's role and the significance of the effort to the agency. He requested full staff cooperation, including candidness, and, if necessary, criticism of the BOA and its director, their superior.

5. As an additional means of motivation, the director assured the consultant that if the returns on the effort were significant (even if the results were critical of the BOA), there would be public hearings and a publication of the results.

With the role well-defined and the assurance of cooperation, the consultant felt more confident and encouraged that he could intervene in the issue without agency backlash. The "free-hand" status also reduced the common dilemma in consultation—that the final results must be compromised to assure favor with the hiring agency.

6. At the spring preparatory workshop, the director had brought numerous materials as briefs for the first week of orientation, discussion with staff, and evaluation of BOA structure. Thus, the first week of internship was an effective orientation and coordination effort.

This first week of the consultantship included individual in-depth discussions with the staff concerning their roles, the Older Americans Act and its application in Arizona, their roles with American Indian aging programs, their views of Older Americans Act application to reservation elderly, and their attitudes toward the American Indian community and individuals. It was apparent that the all-Anglo BOA staff were well-intentioned, well-meaning individuals who, however, were unfamiliar with American Indian cultures. They were also perplexed, confused, and becoming resentful that in public meetings and on-site evaluations they were criticized by American Indian representatives for "properly applying D.C. guidelines." The general sentiment was that the staff would rather write off the "American Indian problem" and instead assist the Indian communities in negotiating directly with the federal or AOA bureaucracy. The staff felt the writers of federal policy and guidelines should at least familiarize themselves with the difficulties of implementing guidelines to American Indian reservations.

RELATIONS WITH TRIBAL LEADERS

During the first week, the consultant tried to formulate a seven-week itinerary including appointments with representatives of American Indian leadership, BIA, PHS, and American Indian elderly on the reservation. This effort posed three logistic problems.

From the outset the consultant had been concerned with differences in demeanor and *time* values between the Anglo and reservation cultures. The American Indian community resents outside researchers visiting their reservations for a very brief period and then leaving as instant experts acting as authoritative figures in providing public pronouncements on Indian affairs. Often such information is superficial and serves to support myths about the community.

Second, the quick and pragmatic Anglo orientation toward research may imply to the American Indian community that its culture is simple and plastic—a "see through" culture. Although aware of this conflict, the consultant could schedule only three or four days for *each* of the ten reservations studied. Thus, the same Anglo time-frame demands severely limited his ability to develop rapport and obtain the confidence of the American Indian subjects.

Last, the consultant wished to be considered a neutral person, trying to develop individual, group, and community perspective. However, he was immediately associated with the "foe," the state bureaucracy on aging, which seemed to undermine his integrity and his efforts to attain the American Indian perspective. Association with the Gerontology Society would have been preferred, although it might have been difficult to familiarize the Indians with the purpose of the society. Another possibility would have been association with the AOA, but this would have created a different set of problems. Thus, the pressure of the Anglo-short-time "hustling"-oriented structure for interview sessions combined with a social setting based on distrust of Anglo officials on aging thwarted a tight research-interview itinerary.

The following example reflects the difficulties that may evolve in interpersonal relations between a consultant and an American Indian representative due to time pressures, unfamiliarity, and distrust while trying to discuss significant issues immediately. The author had followed all the acceptable Anglo procedures for making an appointment with a chairman of a particular Arizona Indian community. There was the introductory telephone call and the arrangement of a mutually agreeable appointment, a follow-up letter, and a final reaffirming telephone call two days prior to the agreed appointment date. When the author arrived, he was told to wait in the outer office until the chairman was available (a phenomenon later reported by tribal chairmen as a process all too familiar to American Indian leadership meeting with state and federal officials). The consultant dutifully waited for three hours while American Indian individuals who arrived after the consultant gained audience with the chairman. The chairman finally appeared only to state the hour of day was more suitable for lunch than a meeting. We would, therefore, confer after the one-hour lunch break. After lunch, the chairman finally invited the consultant to his office, where he fumbled through his stack of letters and requested that the consultant once again state his purpose. It was apparent that the chairman knew where the introductory letter was located, yet he desired to hear in person the presentation of purpose. The consultant repeated his presentation, noting that his objective was to gain information from leadership and older adult American Indians concerning *their* needs and *their* views on how relations may be improved with state and federal bureaucracies concerning social service programs for the Indian elderly. The consultant emphasized that this was an opportunity for an American Indian community to present *its* perspective and that the consultant would record and make every effort to present them truthfully in a final report. Each person interviewed would receive a copy of the report and have the right to rectify any perceived misrepresentation and generally criticize the effort.

After this short presentation, the experienced chairman, in his sixth decade, sat back in his swivel chair, stared at the consultant for long silent moments, then retorted: "You remind me of a story my father once told me! There was a fox. One day while he was walking along a path, he saw this large raw, enticing piece of meat. The fox circled and circled the meat smelling and viewing it from all angles. Yet the meat appeared and smelled tainted." The chairman continued, stating that he felt the consultant was as the meat—enticing but tainted! A two-hour discussion ensued concerning the issue of credibility between American Indian communities and government representatives. Toward the end of the conversation, the chairman admitted he had been "burnt" by entrusting government

agency representatives with information which was misused and ultimately disrupted his community. After another 15 minutes of verbal
sparring, the chairman agreed he felt more enticed but was still reticent
about the research on aging. He dismissed the meeting with the statement
that he would require another evening to consider the matter. The next
day he agreed to discuss the aging issues of his community, and a very
informative and open session resulted.

Although the above is an extreme example of cross-cultural distrust,
even the more trusting American Indian leaders and elderly were hesitant
about sharing information until there had been a discussion to evaluate the
consultant's sincerity and integrity in accurately expressing the American
Indian perspective. In addition, leaders were reassurred that the individuals interviewed would receive a copy of the report and the invitation to
react via criticizing, clarifying, and/or complimenting it.

Outcomes of Consultantship

Underscored in this effort is the consultant's belief that his responsibility
is to depict and clarify discrepancies between parties in a controversial
setting. It is hoped that such a function will result in further discussion
among the parties as to the source and impact of such differential viewpoints. Thus, the disclosure of discrepancies was one outcome of polling
93 individuals concerning their perception of American Indian elderly
needs. Table 6.3 indicates a diverse perspective between American Indian
representatives and the Anglo agency representatives. Although the sample is too small to be representative, there are indications for an open-
ended reservation needs assessment model to determine difference in
values, priorities, and/or perception as to the needs of the American
Indian elderly. This information may also be a forewarning to planners on
aging to closely review sources as well as results of needs assessment, as
many BIA and PHS sources have been called before Washington, D.C.
committees to give their viewpoints on American Indian affairs. Such
Anglo representatives have every right to their viewpoints and to be
expert witnesses, yet they should not generalize on behalf of the American Indian perspective. One can pose this question for planners: If you
had the data from table 6.3 (and assuming a larger and representative
sample), how would you plan aging monies for American Indian elderly in
Arizona?

Table 6.4 also depicts diversity among American Indian communities in
values, priorities, and perceptions concerning the needs of elderly. Too
often, a single policy and guideline is created because of collective re-

Table 6.3. Needs of American Indian Elderly from Perspective
of Reservation Residents and Staff
of Supportive Agencies

Need	# Reservation Residents Perceive Need N=61 (100%)	# Supportive Agency Staff Perceive Need N=32 (100%)	Total N=93 (100%)
Home maintenance and repair	30 (49%)	10 (31%)	40 (43%)
Home visitation	26 (43%)	8 (25%)	34 (36%)
Transportation to social agencies and stores	26 (43%)	6 (25%)	32 (34%)
Direct funding	26 (43%)	1 (3%)	27 (29%)
Transportation for fuel and water	25 (41%)	5 (16%)	30 (32%)
Increasing food costs and increasing poor diets	18 (29.5%)	6 (19%)	24 (26%)
Nursing or convalescent home on reservation	14 (23%)	16 (50%)	30 (32%)
Gerontological training	13 (21%)	8 (9%)	16 (17%)
Assistance with bureaucratic forms	9 (15%)	2 (6%)	11 (12%)
Employment assistance	3 (5%)	1 (3%)	4 (4%)
Financial assistance	3 (5%)	4 (12%)	7 (7%)
Reduce age for eligibility to Older American's Program	3 (5%)	2 (6%)	5 (5%)
Nutritional education	2 (3%)	2 (6%)	4 (4%)
Legal assistance	2 (3%)		
Alternatives to nursing home (foster & day care homes)	1 (1.7%)	2 (6%)	3 (3%)
More staff	1 (1.7%)		1 (1%)
Earlier information on legislation	1 (1.7%)		1 (1%)
Health education	1 (1.7%)		1 (1%)
Medical storehouse (crutches & wheelchairs)	1 (1.7%)	1 (3%)	2 (2%)
Health care		2 (6%)	2 (2%)

sponses; however, it may ignore diversity within the American Indian aging populations. For example, the issue of direct funding elicits a tremendous range of responses—from zero to 100 percent in different tribes. A key question to ask decision-makers on aging is: How would you alter your plans or implement your programs if the information on perceived needs was available to you (given more representative size of sample, but same results)?

The consultant's final report and BOA publication covered the diversity

Table 6.4. Perceived Needs by Tribe Leaders

Need	Colorado River	Gila River	Hualapai	Hopi	Navajo	Papago	San Carlos	Salt River	White Mt. Apache	Yavapai-Prescott
Nursing & convalescent home on reservation	5 (63%)	1 (17%)	1 (20%)	—	—	2 (33%)	1 (25%)	—	2 (66%)	1 (100%)
Direct funding	4 (50%)	6 (100%)	1 (20%)	3 (75%)	6 (46%)	2 (33%)	1 (25%)	2 (100%)	—	—
Nutrition-meals program	3 (38%)	—	—	—	—	3 (50%)	—	2 (100%)	1 (33%)	—
Home repair & maintenance	3 (38%)	5 (83%)	—	4 (100%)	9 (69%)	2 (33%)	2 (50%)	—	2 (66%)	1 (100%)
Home visitation	3 (38%)	2 (33%)	2 (40%)	3 (75%)	9 (69%)	6 (100%)	2 (50%)	2 (100%)	1 (33%)	—
Transportation (fuel and water)	—	4 (66%)	—	3 (75%)	9 (69%)	5 (83%)	1 (25%)	2 (100%)	1 (33%)	—
Reduced age eligibility	1 (20%)	—	1 (20%)	—	1 (7%)	—	—	—	—	—
Employment assistance	1 (20%)	—	—	—	—	—	—	—	—	—
Transportation (agency and store)	3 (38%)	3 (50%)	2 (40%)	3 (75%)	9 (69%)	5 (83%)	1 (25%)	2 (100%)	1 (33%)	—
Assistance with bureaucratic forms	—	3 (50%)	—	—	1 (7%)	2 (33%)	1 25%	—	1 (33%)	—
Legal assistance	—	2 (33%)	—	—	—	—	—	—	—	—
Gerontology training	—	1 (17%)	—	2 (50%)	4 (31%)	2 (33%)	—	—	1 (33%)	—
Decreasing food costs	—	—	2 (40%)	—	6 (46%)	—	—	—	—	—
Foster home	—	—	—	—	—	—	—	—	—	—
Medical storehouse	—	—	—	—	—	—	1 (25%)	2 (100%)	—	—
Financial assistance	—	—	—	—	—	—	—	1 (50%)	1 (33%)	—
Health education	—	—	—	—	—	—	—	1 (50%)	—	—
Day care center	—	—	—	—	—	—	—	—	—	—
Gerontology staff	—	—	—	—	3 (23%)	—	—	—	—	—
Earlier legislation information	—	—	—	—	2 (15%)	—	—	2 (100%)	—	—
Housing	—	—	—	—	—	—	—	2 (100%)	—	—

of needs, direct funding, the political sovereignty-direct funding issues, combined with recommendations to the federal, state, and American Indian bureaucracies. The consultant felt free to "step on everyone's toes" or to support the position that all parties responsible for American Indian aging programs had to reevaluate their positions. Every effort was made to depict all viewpoints, note alternative areas, and describe the possible ramifications of each measure. An example of such information and form provided in the report is the following statement on direct funding.

Representatives from the ten tribes participating in this study listed the following alternatives in order of priority, for funding, monitoring, and evaluating.

Aging Programs:
First Choice: Direct funding from Federal Office on Aging.
Second Choice: Funding to the representative Indian organization who in turn would fund, evaluate and monitor tribal aging programs.
Last Choice: Continue to be funded through state structure which shifted in 1974 from state Bureau of Aging to the Six Area Agencies on Aging (i.e., status quo).
All of the above choices have varying advantages, disadvantages, and probabilities of becoming established.

Direct Funding:
Presently there are strong indications the federal government does not wish to deal with 18 different Arizona reservations with diverse conditions, plus opening the "floodgates" to all remaining tribal governments across the nation.

I. One recommendation by a tribal representative, as an alternative to the present system, has been to formulate a national office on Indian elderly. Such a plan would require amendments to the present Older Americans Act to release the Commissioner on Aging from "responsibilities" to another agency. Direct funding also requires a formula on how to administer funds to various tribes and how such funds will be accounted. For example, should funding to tribes be accounted against total aging funds allocated to the state, in this case, Arizona?

II. Representative Indian Organization:

It has also been suggested that the *Office of Native American Programs* (ONAP) with national and field representatives on each reservation could become a grantee for the tribes of the nation. Each tribe would have a representative on ONAP board which would formulate allocation formula, monitor, and evaluate Indian programs. The perceived advantage of the Indian administered program would be a better understanding and appreciation of American Indian lifestyles and values. Such an understanding should provide more harmony in administration, planning, monitoring and evaluation, than in the present state structure. One disadvantage of any additional middle agency administration is that some of the funds will be absorbed for administrative costs of the Indian agency. Also there is the question of creating a formula for allocating funds which is acceptable to all tribes.

Two other Arizona based tribal coordination agencies have been suggested: *Arizona Affiliated Tribes Inc.*, and *Indian Development District of Arizona*. Both organizations include representation from all the Arizona tribes. All the tribes have tentatively agreed to join such a confederation and make efforts to agree on a formula to allocate funds, except the Navajo. The Navajo will not support or join such an administrative level outside the sovereignty of the tribe because of their larger numbers and cultural differences.

The Arizona Seventh Planning District

The formation of a seventh planning or COG district would afford the Arizona tribes direct funding. However, there are two financial disadvantages: 1) Again there would be another administrative level which would absorb program funds. 2) If the allocation of funds is continued on a per capita basis, the tribes would receive fewer funds than presently allocated. Also, the likelihood for the political development of a seventh planning all-Indian COG district is quite remote, as previously mentioned. The planning districts were formulated by executive order (governor); the present governor has refused any alternative to such planning districts as was illustrated in the case of Santa Cruz County. Also, there is the question of whether the Navajo tribe would support or join a seventh district.

State Agency Funding

As a last resort, the tribal representatives would accept funding through the state structure. The tribal representatives noted that there could be ramifications if a tribe agreed to enter state assistance as the federal government would "write off" the tribes due to receiving state aid—though it may be minimal aid in aging program areas. Thus, the tribes are reticent to accept state aid or enter into state agreements unless there is a clear understanding between the tribe and federal officials concerning the state-tribal agreement.

If none of the tribally desired funding alternatives evolve, there are some measures which should be assumed by state aging officials to improve relations and understanding between tribal officials and state aging officials. Greater thought should be given to clarifying the granting, monitoring and evaluation process of tribal aging programs. Also, further consideration should be given to enlarge the State Bureau of Aging, and if possible, hire qualified tribal employees to become State Bureau field representatives on reservations.

I. RECOMMENDATIONS TO TRIBAL LEADERSHIP AND PEOPLES
  A. Alternatives to State Funding of Tribal Aging Funds:
    1. The tribal leadership of the Arizona tribes should combine efforts and analyze the three alternatives or others and make recommendations to the task force of the Arizona Advisory Council on Aging (see recommendation #3 to state and federal officials)
    2. Send tribal representative and/or communique to the forthcoming federal Senate hearings on the renewal of the Older Americans Act.

II. RECOMMENDATIONS TO STATE AND FEDERAL OFFICIALS
  A. Alternatives to State Funding of Tribal Aging Funds:
    It is recommended that:
    1. The Arizona Advisory Council on Aging formulate a task force to further investigate the three alternatives to state funding, monitoring, and evaluation of tribal aging program.
    2. Upon completion of the task force recommendation, the Arizona Advisory Council should recommend their conclusions to the Governor, state and federal congressional leaders, to support the recommendations at the federal hearings on the Older Americans Act.

At the suggestion of the bureau director, this discussion and the final report was presented before the Governor's Advisory Council on Aging. The American Indian representative attending the council seriously questioned why the report was not *first* presented to an American Indian symposium. The report was later presented at two additional university locations and at an American Indian symposium.

As may be expected, those in attendance at such hearings and symposia accentuated the portion of the report that depicted their perspective and were disturbed by those segments critical of their own viewpoints. However, the backstabbing practices of the past were avoided, and the American Indian elderly issue and the roles of various vested interests did become more clearly focused and lucid in the opening discussions.

The report was well received by the BOA director and staff, though it was critical of the agency's practices and structure. However, the report did lend credence to the dilemma of the state BOA and suggested that AOA authorities reevaluate inconsistent practices and policies, such as "direct funding" versus comprehensive planning. The consultant recommended two additional American Indian staff (one each for northern and southern Arizona tribes), who would be more familiar with Indian cultures and facilitate more effective BOA-tribal relations and coordinate aging program planning, monitoring, and evaluation.

Since the report was issued, there have been *some* positive changes focusing on American Indian aging. In 1975, *one* BOA staff position was created, and an American Indian individual was hired to perform the coordinating role with the Indian communities. Also, another effort to clarify the national trends and interests in American Indian aging was initiated via the first national American Indian aging symposium held in Arizona. Several COGs are presently accepting grant proposals, and in return the Indian communities are allowing AAA staff to serve as consultants to assist in the monitoring and evaluation processes.

However, these efforts are just superficial adjustments to maintain some continuity within the state delivery system. They do not really deal with the macrosystem changes necessary to resolve at least two issues: direct funding and participation-accountability in providing American Indian aging programs. Thus, there are still many viable questions which are inherent in the OAA as administered by the AOA, state BOA, and AAA and which suggest "major" restructuring of the Older Americans Act and thereby aging planning and delivery structure.

OUTCOMES TO CONSULTANT

There were numerous outcomes for the consultant as an academician and individual interested in the older American and his/her efforts to retain a dignified lifestyle. In the role of a student or an intern, the author was able to gain greater insights into and appreciation of the complexities in structure and decision-making involved in formulating services for the aging. The all too common situation of funding numerous aging needs with limited resources requires the administration planner to be creative, hard-nosed, practical, and yet empathetic. The in-fighting and structural concerns (policy, guidelines, objectives, etc.) have given the author a greater awareness and an understanding of how easily the staff at any level of bureaucracy may lose sight of its major objective—to provide the older adult with the means to meet with dignity the daily requirements for living.

Another concern is the "buck passing" that is all too apparent in the bureaucratic structure on aging; this phenomenon is ironic in an age of "accountability." It was common in discussing hard issues to hear the AAA staff blame the BOA and, in turn, the state blame the "feds." This ploy is especially utilized to redirect hostility of the aging constituency to another sector and to emphasize that greater decisions are made and control held at the next level of blame. There may be some inherent validity in such propositions; yet, how does the lower level of bureaucracy assist the constituency in directing their concerns to the next level of bureaucracy in efforts for constructive change rather than operating in a disarming and disorienting fashion? Also, each level must be accountable for some functional outcome or there is no reason for its existence. Each level of the structure on aging should reexamine its responsibilities and possible weaknesses. What would be the cost of being candid with their constituents rather than running popularity contests for aging constituencies or covering up their own fallibility at the expense of the next level of bureaucracy? Such candor would be refreshing, would lend credibility to the system, and would elicit respect from the aging constituency.

The author appreciated the opportunity to confront and observe the creativity of human thinking and the resultant diverse perspectives in a cross-cultural setting. Too often in planning and policy formation, diversity in life-style is minimized, yet diversity is a reality. The consultant achieved greater sophistication in interviewing, interpreting, and recording differing viewpoints effectively and with integrity. In this case the author has taken the position that the role of the consultant in a controversial setting should be to document and reflect the diverse viewpoints. Then, as an added contribution, the consultant synthesizes the controversial perspectives through formulating alternative recommendations. He has the responsibility of commiting his viewpoints and expertise, as a neutral third party, by indicating positive and negative ramifications of each recommendation. Thus, the consultant serves as recorder, synthesizer, and agent of change. In the last role, he should not be an active advocate but a provider of recommendations which the parties in the controversy must accept or reject.

To be candid, another personal outcome was frustration. After an intense two-month experience and preparation of the report, a consultant who is concerned with the research issue desires more than a minimal or courtesy response to his efforts. The consultant was appreciative of the attempts of many individuals in the state to publish and provide numerous and formal hearings. Yet, the tenor of the hearings was largely threefold: *curiosity* and amazement were the attitudes of those less informed on the contemporary status of American Indian elderly; *complimentary* reaction from those who enjoyed the presentation or appreciated the information, yet were powerless to create change; and *condescending* individuals who were providing the consultant with a pat-on-the-head rather than on the back, or those who felt powerless and resigned to failure. The last were those who felt the research report was interesting and/or informative *but,* "Mark my words, little will be initiated and your report will be just another addition to the bureaucratic pile gathering dust." Unfortunately, that is too often the case, a statement made with critical and not cynical motivation. The author noted results and changes at the AAA, BOA, and American Indian governmental levels, yet the jury is still out at the AOA level. To my knowledge, there has been minimal AOA effort regarding the American Indian elderly and the administrative concerns noted here.

This cross-cultural consultation was a challenge to the author's communication skills, personal values and ethical structure, and professional research knowledge. There were also numerous encounters which required patience, perseverance, and humility in noting personal errors in judgment. From such challenges the consultant gained some appreciation of the enlarged commitment required to effect any change in structure which would assure better services to Arizona American Indian elderly and all older adults.

REFERENCES

Allen, M. 1967. "Need Achievement Among Senior Male Navajo High School Students." Master's thesis, Normal, Illinois.
Allen, M. 1975. *A Profile of Needs and Recommendations for Implementing Aging Programs on Ten Arizona Reservations: A Summer Study 1974*. Phoenix: Bureau of Aging, Arizona Department of Economic Security.
Federal Register, 1973. Chap. IX. Administration on Aging. Vol. 38 (196), Thursday, Oct. 11, p. 28044.

Foster, G. M. 1969. *Applied Anthropology.* Boston, Mass.: Little, Brown, and Co., Inc.

Rossi, P. H., and Williams, W. eds. 1972. *Evaluating Social Programs: Theory, Practice and Policies.* New York: Seminar Press.

Weiss, C. H. 1972. *Evaluation Research: Methods of Assessing Program Effectiveness.* Englewood Cliffs, N. J.: Prentice-Hall, Inc.

White House Conference on Aging. 1971. Recommended for action: The Elderly Indian.

Wholey, J.; Scanlon, J.; Duffy, H.; Fukumoto, J.; and Vogt, L. 1973. *Federal Evaluation Policy: Analyzing the Effects of Public Programs.* Washington: The Urban Institute.

7. Case IV. Interagency Relations and the Aging Network: The State Unit on Aging and AAAs in Kansas

George R. Peters

EDITOR'S NOTE: Peters highlights the complexity of the administrative structure which delivers services to the elderly. Using data from interviews with agency staff, he describes and analyzes the organizational constraints on the Area Agencies on Aging and the Kansas State Unit on Aging. He shows a keen sense of the complicated rules, roles, relationships, and resources, which crisscross in sometimes contradictory ways, and he notes the importance of communication or, more precisely, the lack of it and the differing perceptions of persons in several levels of the organization.

Peters finds that almost all of the individuals involved—regardless of their rank or organizational location—are strongly committed to serving the elderly. Such dedication to this common goal may be a major reason that the agencies operate as efficaciously as they do. However, despite the strong commitment to service, there are often inefficiencies, staff turnover, and ambiguity in operation of directives. The author concludes that change in structure is the key to better operation.

Peters also points out that little attempt is made at job orientation and training. Persons who work in agencies dealing with the elderly are not expected to have a knowledge of gerontology.

The problems described in this study may be found in service agencies dealing with other clients. Problems may occur at the state level because many of the staff are young and at early stages in their careers.

The author hints that the difficulties encountered by aging organizations are partly the result of the newness of these organizations. Young agencies and organizations may have problems somewhat different from those of older established agencies, which may suffer from complacency and rigidity.

AS a summer 1976 Gerontological Society research fellow I completed a study of relations between the Kansas State Unit on Aging (KSUA) and the ten state area agencies on aging (AAAS). In this chapter the background and conceptual framework of the study and outline procedures used are described, and a preliminary and largely descriptive overview of results is presented. I depart, however, from the usual mode of the research report which reduces to a statement of problem, procedure, results, and conclusion. Those elements, while essential to an understanding of the work I completed, fail to sensitize the reader to equally important issues of why I proceeded as I did and the difficulties encountered. An attempt is made to relate aspects of the work milieu and the decision-making processes of the research. In their present form data analyses should be regarded as preliminary.

The focus is on problems existing in the KSUA and AAAS and in the relations between the agencies. Thus, the primary concern is with the organizational structures developed to deliver programs rather than with the programs delivered. That focus is necessary, albeit somewhat narrow. It is necessary, since I am convinced that the types of organizational problems discussed below have hindered the effectiveness of the Kansas aging network in meeting its mandates. It is narrow, however, since the reader could conclude that the interests of older Kansans are not being served and that nothing of merit is occurring in Kansas. Such conclusions are unwarranted. Nutrition projects, senior centers, transportation services, etc. are operating, thriving, and increasing in importance. Kansas, as many states, has experienced difficulties in implementing programming and services for its older citizens. Such problems were anticipated by Hudson (1973, 1974). In a sense Kansas represents a case study in the problems of developing structures to implement comprehensive public policy in behalf of the elderly.

Officially, my work began June 1, 1976; in fact, it started nearly two months prior to that date. The fellowship was for the summer. I submitted my report to the society in October 1976. In a sense the project has not yet ended; since the official completion of the study I have maintained ties with the KSUA and the AAAS in a number of capacities and have extended the work to a study of area boards and county advisory councils. I now appreciate more fully orientation statements to the effect that a major aim of the fellowship program was to build ongoing relations between fellows and agencies.

BACKGROUND

Before applying for the fellowship I met with Dr. A. Bramble, Director, Services for the Aging, who indicated interest in having a fellow work through the state office. We agreed that were the fellowship awarded I would design and complete a research project of mutual interest to the KSUA and myself; several possible projects were discussed. When the fellowship was awarded, we met again and agreed that the study would focus on the relationships between the KSUA and state AAAS and ways of improving them.

Bramble pointed out that relations between the agencies were less than optimal. Such a milieu, we agreed, was detrimental to effective programming for the aged. He provided illustrations of events which placed the KSUA and AAAS in an adversary relation, given a lack of clearly defined and delineated divisions of responsibility, labor, control, lines of authority, channels of communication, and definition of the roles of the agencies in the aging network.

We agreed that I would assume full responsibility for the design and conduct of the study. I was introduced to the state staff and was assured of full cooperation from the KSUA. The promise of cooperation was met although difficulties, discussed later, arose as the study progressed. Dr. Bramble agreed to "let the chips fall where they may," as long as results were reported accurately and fairly. Similar expressions of support were extended by AAA directors and staff.

The first three weeks of the study were spent in and around the KSUA office, where I familiarized myself with state staff and KSUA office procedures, conceptualized the study, and developed instruments and a procedure for implementation.

THE STUDY

It became clear that to understand relations between the KSUA and AAAS necessitated reference to the broader network as well—e.g., federal, regional, and local units—and to the legislation that created the units as they currently exist.

Conceptual Framework

The study was conceptualized in terms of three interrelated considerations: the positions of State Units on Aging KSUAS and AAAS in the Administration on Aging (AOA) vertical system, particularly as these relate to the 1973 amendments to the Older Americans Act (OAA); the organizational impact of the mandates of OAA and the apparent model of organization and planning from which the legislation emanated; and propositions drawn from the organizational literature.

SUAS *and* AAAS *in the* AOA *vertical system.*—The 1973 OAA amendments introduced a "new" approach to implement the objectives of the act.[1] This approach was intended to "encourage and assist" state and local agencies to develop "comprehensive and coordinated" service systems by entering "new cooperative arrangements with each other and with providers of social services." By the amendments, AAAS were created. The intent of the amendments was the development of a coordinated network of direct and supportive services to meet the mandated goals of the OAA. As Howenstein, Miller, and Tucker (1975) point out, however, "a dimension remaining unclarified in the OAA and AOAS guidelines and regulations is *how* the direct service and supportive services networks are to work." They suggest two reasons for the lack of specificity. First, it provides individual states and AAAS with the opportunity of developing structures tailor-made to local situations. Second, while it is generally agreed that existing systems are relatively ineffective, no one seems to know what kinds of new arrangements will work. SUAS and AAAS then were placed in an organizational structure and mandated activities; but, not only did they have to negotiate for new kinds of service systems, but they had to conceptualize them first.

In Kansas, at least, the result was the movement of large amounts of money into a state with a history of minimal systematic and broad-based planning for aging services.[2] With dollars and mandate in hand, but an inadequately developed organizational structure, the state proceeded to create AAAS. As in many states, AAAS were designated on the basis of one-at-a-time assessments of the organizational and political resources and histories of their Public Service Agencies (PSAS) (Steinberg, 1976).

Actions were taken in the midst of severe time pressures to produce. They inevitably produced stress, initially upon the KSUA, and ultimately upon the newly created AAAS. Often this resulted in an almost necessary practice of hasty and ritual token compliance with regulations from assessment guides. In those early stages, and to some extent today, changes in regulations, sudden announcements of additional federal monies, and the inability (or capacity given inadequate resources) of either the KSUA or fledgling AAAS to conceptualize or implement an integrated statewide policy or planning effort made the development of a coordinated system of direct and supportive services network difficult.

The impact of AAAS legislation of the OAA organizational model.—A related consideration is the impact of the OAA legislation on SUAS and AAA activities and the apparent organizational model upon which that legislation rests. The OAA proscribes tasks for both SUAS and AAAS which ostensibly define the agencies' roles and which are linked by language like *coordination in the areas of planning, assessment resource development, and service delivery.* Apparently not recognized is that the multiplicity of activities and tasks mandated often produce difficulties, considering the limitations and constraints of funding and staffing. Given their stage of development, many SUAS and AAAS found some of their mandated charges to be in conflict with one another, or with the interests of agency or area project demands, particularly where mandates were translated into tasks to be accomplished simultaneously, without placing them in some order of relative importance.

As Hudson (1974) points out, the Title III amendments provided for an integrated administrative program under which goals and resources are congruent and where certain target populations are designated for priority attention. Simultaneously, AAAs are expected to serve variously as catalysts, organizers, planners, and advocates in order "to make existing services more effective and accessible to the elderly, and to marshall and expand existing resources on behalf of the elderly to the maximum extent possible." The intended outcome is to attract resources in addition to those available through Title III appropriations in order to reorient existing service systems, to tap additional resources for purposes of improving and inaugurating new services, and to increase access for persons to all of these. In large measure, however, SUAs and AAAs have been told what to do, with little advice as to how to proceed.

The OAA legislation—and particularly the 1973 Title III amendments—is premised on a goal model which provides a basis for rational planning in the aging network (Hudson, 1974). The model represents an attempt at developing "comprehensive planning" for aging within the vertical domain of the OAA which spans administrative and organizational space from the federal to the local levels (Hudson, 1973). Implicit in any goal model is the empirical proposition that the major criteria for determining the allocation of resources—including human resources—is their functionality for the goal. The model assumes that activities, procedures, and allocations not tied to goals impair effectiveness and are either dysfunctional or minor aberrations to be resolved. It also assumes that actors in the system will be preoccupied with goal attainment.

The strength of the model lies in its emphasis on goal attainment. Nevertheless, a number of students (e.g., Etzioni, 1960; Warren, 1971; Hudson, 1974) have cited the model's weaknesses and question its validity in terms of the accuracy of its assumptions about the motives of relevant actors. The model assumes too simplistic a view of motivation which ignores the possibility of differential definition of goals, goal maximization and achievement, and multiple motives of actors. Further, the model largely ignores the possibility that differential placement of actors in a system, contextual variables—both social and political—and historical factors influence perceptions of resources, needs, objectives, and action steps quite aside from the motives of actors and the intent of stated goals, and that these will strongly influence actions. Essentially, the rational planning model is nonbehavioral. In its concern for goal attainment, the model views actors as instruments to be used for goal attainment, asking "for what" are resources, actors, and procedures to be used. The question "by whom" is infrequently raised. Yet, ultimately the acts of people produce outcomes in the aging network. By ignoring behavioral determinants, the goal model lacks any realistic ability to account for the actors' diverse and rich range of activities—many of which occur as planning, program building, and serving older people. In sum, the major shortcoming of the goal model is its dubious connection with the "real world" problems faced by actors.

Hudson (1974) outlines elements of an alternative to the goal model which emphasizes the behavior of actors in a social system and provides a more viable basis to account for actions in AAAS. His approach is relevant to SUAS and to relationships between SUA and AAAS. He points out, "The amended Older Americans Act calls on the area agencies to perform one role which is essentially administrative: overseeing the development of support and gap filling services. At the same time it charges them with tasks which are, in fact, quite different: drawing in outside resources and making planners and providers more responsive to the needs of older persons. To the area agencies conceptualized in system terms, these may appear not only as separate, but largely incompatible, alternatives." Although SUAS and AAAS are mandated to build and develop gap-filling and support services—which Hudson calls the linkage network—within the framework of AOA and state guidelines and to mobilize resources and redirect other service systems, they must and will decide on the priority of the two charges. Decisions may or may not be congruent or even compatible with the full mandates of the OAA, but they will in all likelihood be determined by the actors' perceptions of organizational needs and sources of support in the AOA system.

By approaching aging agencies as social systems, as Hudson suggests, one's interpretation of behavior in an agency differs from that afforded by a goal model. For example, it becomes necessary to view organizational activity in the context of environmental constraints, including the position the organization occupies vis-à-vis other organizations and agencies in the environment, the position the organization wishes—and perhaps is mandated—to occupy in relation to those organizations and agencies, and the degree of dependence upon or interdependence with other organizations and agencies.

The first task of any organization is to survive. Hudson suggests this should lead suas and aaas to emphasize building the linkage network, given their dependence on the aoa vertical system and their somewhat ill-defined role in it. Activities are directed toward "carving out a policy space," defining a group domain, and identifying and legitimizing a place in the structure of authority, responsibility, and power. The agencies must do that to survive, but also to establish a viable basis for conducting activities more closely related to the interests of the aged.

Hudson argues that aaas will not mobilize resources and redirect other services beyond compliance with federal and state regulations and monitoring. Lacking a strong organizational base, a sense of identity, and accumulated power sufficient to enter joint ventures on their own, or at least equal on terms, with others, aaa participation carries great risk but little potential payoff. To the extent that joint ventures are undertaken, they are likely to be highly limited, utilizing only the marginal resources of partners; thereby, through asking for little, little can be asked in return. Or, cooperative efforts may assume a token form, giving an impression of joint efforts when, in fact, goals are displaced by an agenda in which minutia, discussion of procedures for interrelating, and carefully defining the terms of the agreement insure that cooperative efforts will not occur. Or, agencies may agree to cooperative ventures but effectively select only nonthreatening and positive endeavors in which commodities—money, clients, or functions—are divided among participants, insuring that each gets a piece of the action. Or, agencies may enter joint arrangements in order to preserve their autonomy from one another and, in the name of developing comprehensive and coordinated services, preserve their "turf."

Similar comments apply to suas who also are mandated as planners and as coordinators of integrated service delivery systems. In a sense, their work is even more strenuous, given the administrative task of overseeing the development of aaas.

The above does not mean that agency persons have rejected the goals that established the organization. Neither should it be inferred that personal commitments to such goals are meaningless. Rather, the approach emphasizes the context in which actors must function in attempts to meet goals and delineates some of the constraints on presumably goal-directed behavior.

Inputs from the organizational literature.—The ksua and aaas were viewed as organizations created to achieve certain objectives and consisting of sets of persons, differentially located within the organizations, who must interact with one another and with others (e.g. older people, community groups, governmental agencies, etc.) external to the organization to achieve those objectives. The concern was not only with whether objectives were or were not achieved, but also with how people in the aging network went about achieving—or not achieving—them. My approach focused on identifying patterned actions and interactions of and between people and the underlying attitudes, perceptions, beliefs, motivations, habits, and expectations which support patterns of action. Patterns of action within and between the KSUA and AAAS comprise what Haas and Drabek (1973) call an organizational performance structure. I desired to study the performance structure of the agencies by examining who does what; how the organizations are maintained; who communicates with whom about what; who makes what decisions; how activities are coordinated, maintained, sanctioned, and managed; how the organizations adapt to their environments; what conflicts exist between persons in the organizations, what are the sources of conflict, and how are conflicts resolved? These factors were considered within the framework of the formal and informal rules governing behavior in the organization, interpersonal relations in the aging network, and the resources available to the organizations.

PROCEDURE

Several early decisions determined the strategy and procedure of the research. First, I would personally visit each of ten AAAS, in addition to spending time at the state office, and in opposition to bringing AAA directors into that office for data gathering purposes. That decision had several bases. It was consistent with the conceptual frame of the study which viewed the KSUA and AAAS as components of the aging network who by federal mandate must interact; as containing persons located in different organizational positions in the network who often hold varying, if not conflicting, perceptions of the proper role of the two agencies; and which persons, by the reports of others (Hudson, 1974; Steinberg, 1976; Howenstein, Miller, and Tucker, 1975) and by KSUA and AAAS staff, have experienced difficulty in their organizational relations.

Thus, respecting "turf" problems, I believed the quality of the data would be enhanced by an on-site data gathering procedure. Greater insight into problems would be gained by hearing of them in context. I also wanted to meet the people who comprise the aging network in Kansas and to observe facilities and operations. I was later told by AAA staff that to date I was the only person who has visited every AAA in the state.

Second, and with a minor exception, an unstructured, depth interview technique was employed as the major data gathering device.[3] Accordingly, I defined a number of topic areas around which a series of sensitizing questions would be asked of all respondents. This permitted me to obtain responses to a somewhat standardized set of questions but maximized opportunities for respondents to answer in their own words and in terms of their perceptions. It also allowed me to probe when responses were either unclear or in need of elaboration.

Interviews were taped. At the close of the interviews, respondents completed a brief questionnaire containing a series of checklist items and statements related to problems and tasks of AAAs and other compounds of the aging network. The items were adapted from several studies (Howenstein, Miller, and Tucker, 1975; Steinberg, 1976; Tobin, 1976).

Third, although interviews comprised the major data generating device, other procedures were also employed. The following data sources, implicitly, also summarize my activities.

1. Interviews with state staff and state administrative officials
2. Interviews with AAA directors, staff (where relevant), and selected project personnel
3. Interview with HEW regional representative
4. Interviews with selected AAA board members
5. Access to files, correspondence, reports, state and area plans, memos, etc.
6. Attended a Governors Advisory Committee meeting; interviewed the chairman of that group
7. Attended state staff meetings
8. Observed an AAA assessment conducted by state staff
9. Observed two AAA board meetings and committee sessions
10. Attended the bimonthly AAA directors-state staff meeting
11. Observed the first meeting of AAA board chairpersons

I anticipated problems in establishing my independence from the state office and AAAs and in achieving a rapport with state and AAA staff. These concerns were largely unwarranted. My identification with the Gerontological Society and my function as a researcher were accepted. In regard to rapport, I spent the first three weeks of the fellowship observing in the state office, getting to know the state staff informally, becoming familiar with office procedure, and conceptualizing the study. One indicator of the success of this procedure was the rapidity with which casual conversations turned to issues of substance on aging problems in Kansas. A fortunate coincidence in timing and my participation in the First Kansas Governor's Conference on Aging allowed me to present to the AAA directors the rationale for the study and the need for their participation and to respond to their questions. Contacts with several persons strategically located in the aging network helped establish my credibility and the importance of the study to the AAA directors. Follow-up telephone calls to each director further clarified questions about the study and their necessary part in it.

Because I was aware of the already busy schedules of the AAA and state staff and knew of the frequent requests made of them to participate in studies, I was concerned about the seriousness with which they would view my proposal. Could they spare the necessary time, and would they willingly provide the in-depth information sought? My fears were unfounded. I was successful, in part by reason of the procedures described above. Beyond that, however, I sensed that I was welcomed as someone who came not to judge or evaluate them, but rather to listen to their views on developments in aging, which were given willingly, freely, and typically with surprising bluntness.

I experienced some difficulty in maintaining my researcher role. As mutual familiarity developed, I was occasionally sought out as consultant, dispenser of "expert" advice, and occasional confidant. I had to decide whether to become more intimately involved in the network, thereby potentially influencing the data outcomes, or to maintain the stance of observer. The dilemma is an old one for researchers. Either choice would result in observer effects. I opted to become involved, with the proviso that during the course of the study I would not allow myself to "take sides."[4] To what extent the data outcomes per se were affected by my choice I am not sure, although I believe that the results reported are accurate.

I had wanted to include HEW regional personnel and AAA board members in the study to a greater degree than I was able. Further, I had hoped to initiate contacts with the surrounding states to develop a comparative framework for my analysis of the Kansas data. Time constraints of the fellowship allowed for minimal collection of information from board members and the regional office and did not permit establishing contacts with the surrounding states.

The foregoing describes the procedure followed. It does not specify certain difficulties experienced during the study and others which emerged in response partially to the work and partially to undercurrents of change in the network which I sensed but did not fully appreciate until much later.

In retrospect, it is clear that the research expectations of the KSUA and AAAS differed in some fundamental ways from my own. I conceived and presented the study as an examination of selected elements of the aging network, their organizational structure and relationships. The agencies desired outcomes providing immediate input into programs and problems and to strengthen their positions vis-à-vis one another. The several desired outcomes are not inherently inconsistent, given sufficient time to conceive and carry out a study frame placing them into a set of ordered outcomes possessing different time priorities. Unfortunately, the time constraints of the fellowship did not allow for such a strategy. Despite fairly frequent informal discussions about the study's progress in which desired results were reiterated, and, I believe appreciated, at no time was a formal written agreement developed. Rather the work proceeded by a "gentlemen's" agreement. We were all "gentlemen," but with somewhat different priorities.

Difficulties arose when my report to the society was completed. That report, although presented as preliminary and for only limited distribution prior to revision, aroused considerable hostility at the state level. I had understood that only the KSUA director would receive a copy and that two copies would be forwarded to the Gerontological Society. Further, that I would distribute personal "not for citation" copies to those who had provided data. That would be followed by a joint session of AAA and state staff in which rebuttals could be presented, misinterpretations clarified, and plans made for a final revised report to be widely distributed. Rather, several days prior to leaving for the Gerontological Society meetings in New York I was asked to come to a special meeting of the state staff for purposes of discussing the report. Upon arrival, I learned that the report had been duplicated and distributed to the staff. Further, several had written critical responses to the study and stated their criticisms in the meeting.

I chose not to debate the issues raised by the staff. I reminded them that the report was preliminary and that I believed the meeting should have included AAA staff, who also had contributed to the study but had not yet received the report. Beyond that I listened to the criticisms. Given the tense atmosphere and the fact no one from the state level would be present at the Gerontological Society meetings, I decided to keep my remarks on the project to a minimum while at the meeting of fellows.

Two issues were of concern: I felt that I had an obligation, before making the study public, to provide opportunity for response to all who had provided data, and I was concerned that AAA staff would feel their trust had been violated. Indeed, several, upon learning of the above events, initially were angered. I was also concerned that my ability to conduct future research of this type would be jeopardized.

The situation was even more difficult, given the political atmosphere in which it occurred. As the study progressed I discovered strong statewide support for moving the KSUA out from under its umbrella agency by creating a new department or agency. Although the elements of a statewide grass roots movement were present, it appeared unlikely that such an action would occur given opposition at the executive level of state government. Late in the fall of 1976, however, those supporting the creation of a department exerted strong and coordinated pressures on the state legislature. In the spring of 1977 a bill creating a new state Department on Aging was passed and sent to the governor, who approved it.[5]

The experience sensitized me to the delicate balance between research, application, public policy, ethics, and change. There was a positive response to the idea of and need for research on agencies, but I was reminded of how differences in defining research and, more important, its outcomes, can affect the research process. I was, and am, confronted with ethical concerns of how—or if—to report on certain sensitive issues. Were the work to be repeated I would seek more feedback on conceptual and study design issues than either time or my own inclinations permitted then.

RESULTS

This is a preliminary statement of results, containing primarily data obtained from AAA directors and selected staff and KSUA staff. The emphasis is on problem areas as perceived and reported by staff as these relate to AAA/KSUA relationships. This emphasis should not infer that programming efforts are devoid of positive outcomes. Indeed, there are effective and fruitful programs in the state. Nonetheless, programming is hampered by a series of problems.

Organizational Constraints in the Kansas Aging Network

Kansas aging programs must be understood in the context of the state's historical conditions and organizational constraints. Kansas has a history of minimal development and support of planning and programming in aging. No broad-based aging programs existed there until the mid-1950s when initial thrusts were generated by persons interested in the problem of nursing home licensing. These efforts were housed administratively in the state Social Welfare Department until later in the decade when health issues were emphasized rather exclusively, and nursing home licensing was shifted administratively to the Department of Public Health. This left Aging Services in the Department of Social Welfare with a small budget for social services.

In that period some Title XX programs were developed. For a brief time there was an intergovernment committee on aging appointed by the governor. The committee never functioned and for all intents and purposes was ineffective. In the late fifties the Kansas Citizens Council on Aging was formed. In its early stages that body was largely run by a single individual, a woman who became something of a power in advocating for aging in the state. Indeed, it was suggested that for a time she may have largely influenced aging programs in Kansas. The council continues to function as a strong advocate for the aged.

In Kansas the emphasis was on small, limited aging programs, focusing on special interests. No overall program or planning efforts existed. That condition changed somewhat, but not drastically, after 1965 with the OAA legislation. Significant programming efforts only commenced under the 1973 OAA amendments, which created the AAAS and provided funds for direct service programs.

Even with the 1973 amendments—and perhaps because of them— state-generated funding for comprehensive programs and social services for the aged has been minimal. The contribution of some $100,110 of state monies to the Title III program constitutes an administrative match, and these are the only state funds allocated to OAA aging programs. (See table 7.1 for the distribution of funds.) In Kansas, as in 53 percent of the states, OAA aging programming is essentially a federal program with local matching. The state contributes matching monies and some state-only funds to non-AOA programs. However, Kansas decided to focus the bulk of its support for aging on the Department of Social and Rehabilitative Services in the health services area. These services are largely concentrated in nursing homes—including comprehensive medical care support of a variety of types. State policy allows for only the most judicious allocation of state funds to social services for the aging. Of the nearly $15 million of state monies administered through social and rehabilitative services and allocated explicitly to aging, almost $13 million is committed to medical and other support related to nursing homes.

George R. Peters

Table 7.1. Funding for Aging Programs
under the OAA in Kansas

Year	Types of Funds	Title III	Title VII	Title IV	Title V
1973	Federal	971,533	1,215,912		
	Local match	89,825	47,226		
	State administration	160,000			
	State match	53,333			
1974	Federal	958,018	1,176,919	56,000	
	Local match	503,927	208,013		
	State administration	160,000			
	State match	53,333			
1975	Federal	958,018	1,474,110	41,114	
	Local match	310,350	324,234		
	State administration	160,000			
	State match	53,022			
1976[a]	Federal	1,450,501	1,817,352	69,473	
	Local match	288,923	244,090		
	State administration	256,443			
	State match	100,110			
1977	Federal	1,398,498	2,355,951	69,473	231,578
	Local match	278,493	316,045		
	State administration	200,000			
	State match	107,989			
1978[b]	Federal	1,749,601	2,858,825	69,305	462,032
	Local match	219,594	632,156		
	State administration	200,000			
	State match	127,895			

a. Includes funding for the transition to the federal fiscal year.
b. Projected funding.

The strategy in Kansas has produced programs but not without certain implications. As Hudson would predict, the aging network, by its dependence on federal funding, has also become dependent on the AOA vertical system to determine priorities for program funding. This has limited the flexibility of both the KSUA and the AAAS in their ability to respond to the special needs of some areas (e.g., the high cost of developing a transportation system in rural PSAS). Hughes and Gibbs (1977) indicated that the single variable accounting for most of the variance in the allocation of Title III funds to PSAS in 1975 was the state formula developed and used by the KSUA.[6] The AAAS, in turn, allocate funds to counties based on the aging composition formula, need, and readiness of the county to plan and administer services. Considerable variation exists among AAAS in regard to needs assessments establishing priorities for service development.

The outcome has been a high degree of variation in Title III monies allocated to counties. Dollar amounts ranged from a low of $222 in seven counties to a high of $65,492. Per capita fundings ranged from 12 cents to $18.06 with a mean allocation of $2.81. The allocation of these funds depends mainly upon numbers of people 60 years or older in a county and past activities to develop aging programs. Hughes and Gibbs (1977) suggest that additional variables might be employed in considering allocations. Of particular importance in a state like Kansas is the aged dependency ratio.[7] The higher the aged dependency ratio the greater the proportion of older people in the county who, potentially at least, will be in need of services. Hughes and Gibbs found no relationship between the allocation of Title III funds and the aged dependency ratio.

At issue here is not whether Kansas is receiving its fair share of Title III funds or whether KSUA staff are sufficiently diligent in obtaining these funds. Rather, of concern is the basis for allocating federal monies. Beyond that is the recognition of the need expressed by many in the network for state allocations to aging programs.

There are other forms of state support for aging persons. For example, homestead law provides varying levels of financial relief to the aged. Kansas recently submitted and received funding for a comprehensive social services plan under Title XX-SSA. Included in that plan are programs directly designating the aged as target populations. But broad-based programs as envisioned under the OAA simply have not received state financial support.

At the time of the study, the KSUA was housed administratively under the Social and Rehabilitative Services (SRS) department of state government.[8] SRS is charged with administrating human services throughout Kansas. It is, under the new title, the reorganized Social Welfare Department. Whether rightly or wrongly, familiar and frequently negative social welfare connotations still adhere to programs and units under its jurisdiction.

Administratively, the KSUA is in the Division of Social Services within SRS. The Social Services is one of five major administrative units in SRS. The KSUA is a third-tier office within the SRS bureaucracy. It shares that organizational position with eight other offices in the Social Services Division, ten other offices within other divisions of SRS, and ten institutions under the State Institutions unit. Although debatable, it appears that the KSUA is administratively located low in the SRS hierarchy. Many persons in the state aging network have questioned the ability and effec-

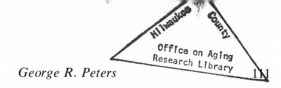
tiveness of the KSUA to generate support and resource allocations for aging at the state level.[9]

Given its location under the aegis of SRS, the KSUA must respond to and enforce the policies, rules, and regulations of the federal bureaucracy and those of a large state bureaucracy while simultaneously promoting the concept of local grass roots input and control. Thus, the agency is confronted with the dilemma of coordinating the activities of a bureaucratically structured organization, which by its very structure emphasizes centralized decision-making, with those of programs that by concept and intent are decentralized. There is little reason to expect that Kansas should be any more effective in solving this problem than are other similarly organized states. My impression was that the major SRS officials were not predisposed toward changing the system. I heard criticism of the inflexibility of federal guidelines and the "feds' " failure to assist in solving problems. The aging network was described as a "hybrid," impossible to administer and manage effectively.

Some officials suggested that AAA directors be State Civil Service employees—a concept obviously inconsistent with OAA guidelines. Others suggested that aging services, including AAAs, operate on a strictly contractual basis—which I understood was the present system. When I inquired as to the future of the network it was suggested that little would change.

The OAA specifically mandates local input into decision-making through area boards which are designated as advisory. In Kansas, area boards are, by state policy, policy units, and have been delegated considerable (potential) power and authority, subject to the constraints of federal and state guidelines. In Kansas, the AAA is the area board. The agency itself is the administrative and implementing arm of the board. This organizational model is consistent with the intent of the OAA, but it has not been easy to implement.

Without exception, the approach was first to establish an AAA, then hire a director who in turn hired a staff, then establish programs, and only finally develop county and area boards. The inevitable result has been that area boards are weak, frequently dictated to by AAA directors and state staff, and a rubber stamp for agency- and state-determined objectives and plans. Fundamentally, the Kansas concept is consistent with OAA intent, but it could not be realized given the lack of prior state planning in regard to board formation and function and the urgency with which the Kansas network was constructed.

Area boards are developing, if slowly, despite the lack of planning and training, and there was evidence of significant growth in some. A potentially positive development was the creation of a statewide association of board chairpersons. This association, if nurtured and promoted, could serve as an important catalyst for producing positive changes in the aging network.

Finally, the network reflects variations in AAA auspices and the delineation of geographical boundaries of PSAs. Of the ten AAAs two are under the auspices of city governments (a third had that auspice but following internal disputes has been dissolved, and the AAA and its nutrition project is now administered by the KSUA);[10] one is under the auspices of a regional planning commission; two are under the auspices of mental health centers; and four are private nonprofit corporations.

In a number of cases current auspices represent changes from an earlier form of organization. With some exceptions, and with KSUA and encouragement, there appears to be a trend away from the umbrella organization and toward incorporating AAAs into nonprofit organizations. That trend is a response to difficulties some AAAs have experienced with their sponsors. The AAAs vary in resources, support systems, influence in the area, and types of problems encountered because of variation in auspices. According to AAA and some state staff, the KSUA assumed a laissez-faire strategy in regard to the determination of auspices until, by necessity, they were called upon to negotiate jurisdictional disputes. That has eroded the level of trust AAAs have for the KSUA. The type of auspice, particularly for some AAAs, has produced organizational problems which impact on programming efforts. The most extreme example of this was the AAA that was dissolved following a dispute with its sponsor (a city government), involving a nutrition project in the PSA. Programs and projects were greatly hampered during and following the conflict. In other cases the necessity of having to meet the organizational guidelines of the sponsoring agency, in addition to those of the state and the federal government, introduced an additional decision-making level which reduced the effectiveness of AAAs. However, in some cases this sponsorship was a distinct advantage both in providing research resources and program support. This was particularly true for two AAAs sponsored by city governments.

The number of counties per PSA ranged from two to 28. That distribution reflected the geographical distribution and composition of the state's aging population and attempts to coordinate boundaries of PSAs and state regional planning commissions—even though the latter have been altered somewhat since PSA boundaries were drawn. Smaller PSAs in many counties were located in urban areas and larger PSAs in rural areas. Thus, even in a rural state such as Kansas it is meaningful to speak of rural-urban differences, at least as these relate to availability of and access to resources, existing service systems, and adequate measures of programming services needed and desired. The difficulties of coordinating and planning services differed among the PSAs if only by differences in geographical size and numbers of county governmental and other planning and service units which must be considered. Different, as well, were the types of populations to be served, their need levels, and the difficulty of delivering services. Interviews suggested that AAA directors have yet to develop an effective mechanism for collectively sharing their problems and a base for presenting their views regarding these problems.

The constraints were acutely felt and discussed by those involved in the state aging network. Unfortunately, frequently lost in the discussions was the fact that the KSUA and AAAS were in the early stages of what was a complex network of services and programs and that neither could be held accountable for constraints which they inherited and within which they worked. Thus, the KSUA was sometimes held responsible for actions or decisions over which it had little or no control. For example, the agency could hardly be held accountable for its administrative location in the state government, the boundaries of PSAs, or the state's fiscal policy on aging. By misplacing accountability, the KSUA and AAAS have been cast to some extent in the role of adversaries in a context where cooperation is mandatory if some of the constraints are to be overcome. For example, it was not fully clear to me that the SRS umbrella was an unworkable structure for delivering services to older people. To the extent that disagreements over this and related questions continue, however, concerted efforts toward making the structure workable and effective are unlikely.

STAFFING PATTERNS OF AAAS AND THE KSUA

Seven of the ten AAAS experienced a change in directors since their inception in 1973. Four agencies had at least one prior director, two had two previous directors, and one, three previous directors. In the last case one person served briefly as acting director. The current group of directors have served for periods ranging from one month to three years.[11] The director serving for a month was acting director of his current agency for three months and prior to that was assistant director for approximately one and one-half years. On the average, the directors served for about one and one-half years. One of the ten left during the course of the study when, because of severe difficulties between the AAA, its nutrition project, and its sponsoring agency, the KSUA intervened and ultimately terminated the AAA contract.

The AAA directors had diverse educational and professional backgrounds. Two had some college work, but no degree, one held a bachelor's degree, six held master's degrees, and one held a Doctor of Divinity degree. Their formal academic work included degrees in business administration, social work, sociology, education, history, physical education, and theology. None had any formal training in gerontology prior to joining the agency. Only four had prior professional experience in aging programs. Two of these had been employed at some time in the KSUA. The work histories of the directors was varied. Four had ministerial backgrounds, one had worked with VISTA programs and CAP agencies, two had research and planning experience, one had been an instructor in a small college, one had been a YMCA director, and one had been an office worker. The directors were youthful, both chronologically and professionally.

The number of staff employed by the AAAs ranged from two to 12. Several factors seemed to account for these differences. Some AAAs have implemented larger and more extensive service programs and have reaped the benefits that a larger funding base provides for staffing. Some have been more effective than others—often by virtue of ease of access rather than amount of effort expended—in tapping resource and support systems in their areas and accumulating support beyond the required project match. Thus, the agency with the largest staff included among its members persons supported by CETA funds, Neighborhood Youth Corporation Work Study funds, city funds and support resources, in addition to those supported by monies allocated by OAA. The agency with the smallest staff was hardly without support, however, since, by its affiliation with a large city government as its sponsoring agency, it drew support heavily from the city government and other community agencies.

Generally, AAAs in larger urban areas were more successful in developing non-OAA support, both in funding and indirect support services. Rural areas experienced problems of an order and magnitude different from urban areas, given their typically greater geographical size, the dispersal of target populations, and numbers of governmental units to be dealt with. Rural areas emphasized generating county monies either through direct allocations or passing mil levies, in part, because they lacked the greater pool of formal and community service and support systems typically available in urban settings. Thus, it is possible that rural areas may require a greater input of resources to accomplish programming levels comparable to those of urban areas.

Differences in staff size were also influenced by differing perspectives toward the organization and implementation of programs. One issue concerns whether project directors should be AAA staff members or whether the project should be subcontracted. The issue is one of control and who has it. In the former case, AAAs maintain control over the project director and thereby over the project. In the latter case, considerable control is lost. From the perspective of a number of AAA directors, the advantages of the first model in areas of decision-making accountability and effective management far outweigh possible advantages of the second model. These directors strongly believed that ultimately the KSUA would support the project and not the AAA. Having the project director on the staff lessens the presumed threat perceived by AAA directors. Indeed, nutrition projects, which by subcontract were removed from effective and immediate control by the AAA, have been the source of difficulties in a number of areas. The most serious and recent of these resulted in the termination of the state contract with an AAA, the assumption of that agency's activities by the KSUA, but the continuation of funding of the nutrition project. Six of the ten AAAs subcontracted their nutrition projects. Two of the six were experiencing serious problems with their projects, and two others reported problems which hindered effective programming. Significantly, eight of the ten new Information and Referral personnel were employed as AAA staff members. There was some evidence of KSUA support for the idea of bringing nutrition project directors on the AAA staff, where political and program conditions permitted or made it desirable.

The KSUA consisted of 15 professional staff persons, who were relatively young chronologically, professionally, and in terms of tenure in the office. Nine of the 15 were in their 20s or 30s. The current position was the first or second professional experience for eight of the 15. Length of time with the agency ranged from ten months to 20 years. Only six staff members had been employed in the agency for three years or more, two of the six were outstationed or Title III area supervisors, and one terminated employment during the course of this study.

The KSUA staff varied in educational background: three did not possess a college degree, five held bachelor's degrees, six held master's degrees, and one, the director, held the doctorate. Areas of formal training included social work, mathematics, nutrition, psychology, sociology, history, and theology. The most frequently mentioned academic training was social work, as might be expected, given the umbrella organization in which the KSUA is located. None reported any formal training in gerontology prior to joining the agency.

The KSUA has experienced phenomenal growth since 1973. Eleven staff persons have been added since that time. In 1970 the staff consisted of only two or three people. Obviously, the 1973 OAA amendments accounted for the accelerated growth. With growth came a series of staggering problems. In a short period the KSUA was simultaneously charged with the fiscal and administrative responsibility for millions of dollars, mandated to create a statewide aging network, insure that service programs were developed and delivering, and create a state plan for aging services. At the same time it was necessary to construct the organizational machinery requisite to accomplish these tasks. These duties were assumed by a staff, who, though competent, were lacking in experience, hindered by problems of continuity through turnover, confronted with overwhelming tasks, and seldom allowed to deliberate the long-range effects of their decisions and actions.

The relative newness of a greatly expanded and growing aging network undoubtedly accounted for staff diversity and variations among areas in staff size, resources, and organization. That newness coupled with the pressure to implement programs meant that persons were hired without adequate guidelines detailing a desirable fit between professional qualifications and experience and the job demands. Given the framework, it is hardly surprising that most people interviewed indicated that the bulk of their orientation and training occurred as on-the-job experience.

The staffs generally mirrored a common criticism of administrators of aging programs; namely, that they lack training in gerontology. Indeed, most of those interviewed reported attending training seminars, summer workshops, short courses, etc. as a means of upgrading their skills subsequent to their employment. Most frequently, these were training sessions related to particular programs or program skills—e.g., nutrition, transportation, grantsmanship, nursing homes, ombudsman services, legal services—which varied greatly in their emphasis on transmitting broader gerontological knowledge. Of necessity then, training related first to job skills, and focused mainly on concerns within the AOA network.

Most of the staff interviewed had no understanding of the broader theoretical research and public policy issues of gerontology, although the importance of both was recognized. Whether such a view is necessary to effective programming may be debated. However, given the multifaceted roles of SUAS and AAAS, and the increasingly complex nature of the AOA network, gerontological knowledge would also seem to be of increasing importance. An understanding of theories of aging and a working familiarity with current research in gerontology can provide a framework for planning, needs assessment, decision-making, and program development from the federal to the local levels. Without such a framework, activities may be responsive only to the most immediate and pressing issues.

Although it is unrealistic to expect all members of the network to become gerontologists, it is not unrealistic to build a provision into the ongoing training of agency personnel which periodically overviews the field of aging. Minimally, the theoretic and research bases of new and continuing program thrusts could be included as a normal part of training sessions. Further, it is not unreasonable to require training in gerontology as a job prerequisite, at least for agency directors.

Problems Generated by Staffing Patterns

Staffing patterns of the AAAS and the KSUA contributed to the agencies' problems. Turnover among AAA directors and their diverse backgrounds hampered the effective development of strong agencies. The AAAS had a continuity problem. As a director left, valuable time and resources had to be spent locating a new director. Once hired, time had to be allowed for the organization and its new director to adjust to one another. Only rarely did directors, AAA staff, or area board personnel have any formal background or experience in gerontology. In some cases the prior director left for reasons related to the inability of the KSUA and the AAA to agree on program or agency concerns.

By virtue of their diverse backgrounds and experience the directors brought to their jobs an array of interests, perspectives, and motivations. That diversity was expressed in their differing conceptions of their work and the function of AAAS. By temperament and style the majority of the directors were "action" or "program" oriented. However, the terms had differing meanings. For some, "action" meant being actively engaged in meeting the elderly, forming citizen groups, and building grass root programs; for others it meant generating mill levies and a solid direct and indirect support base; and for others it involved structuring and running a well-managed administrative operation. There is nothing inconsistent among these emphases; all are consistent with OAA legislation. Some difficulty occurred, however, when directors ordered these priorities differently, producing varying role conceptions. Thus, there was no common AAA consensus regarding the appropriate roles of directors; neither had the KSUA with the AAAS been able to clearly define the directors' role.

Directors varied in how they perceived AAAS. For some the agency was viewed ideally as a temporary one, whose function was to stimulate and facilitate locally based aging programs and then to "get out." Others saw AAAS as permanently established operations serving as the major—if not sole—clearinghouse for aging programs and monies in an area. Some directors viewed the AAAS in rather narrow terms as providers of fairly direct services. Others saw the scope as broader and spoke of the AAAS mission as an advocate for the aged, a clearinghouse for information, a producer of, and storage unit for, new information, a trainer and educator on behalf of the elderly. All directors indicated a desire for greater autonomy. Some, however, felt a need for stronger and more effective KSUA action in training, technical assistance, consistent overseeing programs, and planning. Only one of the ten directors felt the KSUA was providing useful assistance in these areas. Some directors accepted both the principle and the fact of the area board as a policy unit. Others expressed concern over the potential power a strong board could wield over the agency and preferred it to have a more subsidiary advisory role.

This diversity, along with the problem of continuity, has made it difficult for the directors to develop an organizational base for collectively sharing concerns and engaging in concerted action. While to some extent bound together by the similar demands of work and a genuine concern for aging people, their differences hindered the development of an effective means for representing their collective interests. Thus, aside from what they gleaned from the "grapevine," the directors were remarkably uninformed regarding issues of substance in other areas. Although the directors formed a state association, many felt their organization has not been encouraged by the KSUA; indeed, some believed the KSUA opposed its development, given its power potential and the possible inhibiting effects on the development of area boards.[12] The directors admitted to the potential value of the organization, but only several held hope for its development. Some anxiety was expressed over possible negative reactions from the KSUA were the organization to take strong stands. Most indicated that the time, program, and agency demands of their own areas made efforts toward building the organization of low priority. In at least two cases, directors stated bluntly that their power base lay in the area and with the AAA auspices, negating strong need for such an association.

Another source of staffing problems for the AAAs related to the structure developed to employ directors. Kansas state policy gives the area board the authority to hire and fire AAA directors; this is sometimes complicated by the desire of the AAA sponsoring agency to have a voice in such decisions as well. The state technically had no power to hire directors. That office provided advisory assistance but only when sought. Because it is administratively responsible for AOA funds allocated to it, the state requires that AAA directors and staff be hired under State Civil Service guidelines. Wage guidelines have been a constant source of complaint among AAA directors, even though their incomes may be supplemented by non-AOA funds. The job descriptions were, by the admission of state staff, sorely in need of redefinition.

From the state's perspective the system hindered state input into the hiring procedure. The KSUA may only resort to persuasion, it cannot take clear-cut administrative action in hiring procedures, since technically the area board decision is final. More critically, once hired, the KSUA's ability to maintain *legitimate* controls over directors is ambiguous. If the agency is displeased with a director it may plead, cajole, warn, and, as a last resort, threaten to withhold funds or terminate the AAA's contract. The KSUA's effectiveness is limited since, while the extent of its authority in these matters is unclear, the agency has been unwilling to either withhold funds or cancel an AAA contract unless political pressures necessitate. During the course of this study conditions in one AAA had reached the point where termination of its contract was imminent were the director retained. The state eventually retreated, given strong board support for the director.[13]

From the AAAs' perspectives, the directors faced the problem of not knowing who their bosses were. They were told that the area board is the boss, but they recognize who controls the pursestrings. They dealt daily with the demands of the KSUA in matters of interpreting and administering federal and state regulations and guidelines. The KSUA monitors, assesses, and evaluates their work, develops a state plan which provides the framework for AAA activities, and determines allocation of monies. A number of directors felt the KSUA lacked either the capacity or the will to act assertively on these issues. Thus, some of their anxieties were, perhaps, more apparent than real.

Similarly, these problems relate to the agency's staffing patterns. KSUA staff also said their jobs were complicated by the lack of clearly defined lines of authority. They were plagued by the problems of a rapidly assembled and growing organization, confronted with increasing responsibilities. Unfortunately, there were few experienced staff who are often capable of effectively easing an organization through growth and change. The KSUA staff were highly committed to their work; they desired an effective system and were as critical of themselves and the current network as were the AAA directors. As a group, however, they lacked the experience which might have allowed them to handle such problems more effectively. The staff, by necessity, spent a considerable amount of time and energy "getting themselves organized (and reorganized) and informed," time and energy taken from issues of substance.

Among the more disturbing comments of KSUA staff was the almost complete lack of a job introduction and orientation program. Frequently, I was told, "I was handed a state manual and told to read it—that was my job orientation." A number said they had not yet read the entire manual. On-the-job training characterized staff introduction to their positions. Yet, according to the staff, it was on-the-job training with minimal supervision. This procedure was understandable given the rapid growth of the KSUA. However, with other variables it produced a lack of confidence in capacity among some of the staff and is as yet unresolved. That was perceived by AAA staff who came to doubt the competence level of some of the state staff.

The rapid growth of the KSUA, the relative lack of staff experience, and the inadequate orientation contributed to philosophical differences in regard to conceptualizing KSUA and AAA roles and functions. Although complex, the differences from the KSUA point of view revolved around the dual issues of AAA autonomy and KSUA control. Some staff would allocate considerably more autonomy to AAAs in areas of program development and control, provided that the KSUA retained effective and clearly defined monitoring capacities. The state "would have teeth and teeth that bite," but the bite would have less to do with programming per se than with ensuring that programs are accountable. Others suggested lessening the autonomy of the AAAs, bringing them more closely under KSUA authority, and thereby assuring state control. A third concept, and the one which seemed to be operative, was to increase the illusion of AAA autonomy while at the same time maintaining lines of control at the level of proposal approval and fund allocation. Philosophical differences of this sort, while unresolved, perpetuated an atmosphere of dissension among staff and in the network itself.

Findings drawn from portions of interview materials which focused specifically on the problems of the aging network in Kansas are presented in the remainder of this section.

Problem areas and their frequency of mention were ascertained by means of a content analysis of interview schedules. Problem areas cited both by AAA and KSUA are summarized in table 7.2.[14] Problems areas were coded by whether they referred to KSUA/AAA interaction problems (s/a); KSUA/state system problems (s/s), or AAA system problems (a/s). This code is admittedly crude but does permit partitioning the data into categories reflecting focus of staff concern.

There are overlaps between problem area categories which must be eliminated by more refined analyses. That the referent of a problem area may be coded and discussed as a KSUA/state system problem or an AAA system problem does not mean it is unrelated to KSUA/AAA interactions. The complexity of interaction between different level problems will be determined in later analyses.

Two general comments seem justified. First, AAA staff more frequently cited and placed higher priority on KSUA/AAA problems while KSUA staff reported KSUA/state systems problems with greater frequency. That is hardly startling given the tendency for persons to focus on aspects of the environment most immediately affecting their well being, sense of identity, and importance. AAA staff recognized their dependence on the KSUA, knowing that nearly every agency activity was subject in principle, if not in fact, to KSUA scrutiny. Interaction with the KSUA became pivotal, since by its actions and reactions toward AAAs the KSUA legitimated AAA actions. The KSUA could cast doubt on the ability and effectiveness of the AAA and its staff and potentially held the power to act upon its doubts in ways threatening or at least demeaning to the AAA.

The KSUA staff, however frequently they interact with AAA staff, did not live in the world of the AAAs. Theirs was the world of the state bureaucracy. Within the context of that organization, activities were evaluated, legitimated, and rewarded. Its structure, policies, and procedures had the most immediate impact upon their working and professional lives. Thus, it was not surprising that the priorities and anxieties of KSUA staff focused on the problems of the agency and its broader superordinate system. Unfortunately the major reference group of KSUA was its umbrella agency, and the energies of KSUA staff were often given to the internal structuring and maintenance of the KSUA office. Less time and effort were available to oversee and assist in building AAAs, deliver services to the elderly, and insure the coordination of service systems.

Second, as table 7.2 shows, there was strong consensus among AAA and KSUA staff regarding what were the problem areas. The staffs differed as to the relative priority of any given problem, but 20 of the problem areas

Table 7.2. Summary of Problems Reported
by Both AAA Directors and KSUA Staff

Problem Area	AAA Rank (N)[a]		Referent[b]	KSUA Rank (N)	
1. Perceived support of KSUA for AAAS	1.5	(23)	S/A	16	(11)
2. Coordination between AAA and KSUA	1.5	(23)	S/A	18.5	(10)
3. Frequency of KSUA visits to AAAS	5.5	(19)	S/A	16	(11)
	tr. 5.5	(19)[c]			
4. Training and technical assistance provided by KSUA	ta. 16	(10)	S/A	12	(13)
5. Delegation of authority to KSUA staff	7	(16)	S/S	1	(24)
6. Competence of KSUA staff	8	(15)	S/S	20	(9)
7. Concept of the AAA	11	(12)	S/S	9.5	(15)
8. State aging policy	11	(12)	S/S	18.5	(10)
9. Lines of authority within the state aging network	11	(12)	S/S	2	(20)
10. Problems with the SRS umbrella	14	(11)	S/S	21.5	(8)
11. Planning by the KSUA	18.5	(9)	S/S	9.5	(15)
12. KSUA should enforce regulations more stringently	18.5	(9)	S/A	9.5	(15)
13. Reports	18.5	(9)	S/A	25	(7)
14. Political vulnerability of the KSUA	23	(8)	S/A	25	(7)
15. AAA problems with auspices and projects	aus/23	(8)[d]	A/S		
	pro/23	(8)	A/S	28.5	(5)
16. Competence AAA staff	23	(8)	A/S	28.5	(5)
17. Funding	26.6	(6)	S/A	21.5	(8)
18. Inconsistencies between federal/state/ local regulations	28	(4)	S/A	21.5	(8)
19. Role clarity regarding AAA and KSUA functioning	28	(4)	S/A	25	(7)
20. KSUA staff workload	30	(3)	S/S	3.5	(19)

a. A count was made of the number of times a problem was mentioned by staff. Thus, a staff member could cite a problem more than once. However, in no case is the number of mentions accounted for by a single staff member.

b. Problems were coded by the component of the aging network to which the problem referred. Thus, s/a = KSUA/AAA interaction; s/s = KSUA/state system; A/s = AAA system.

c. AAA staff distinguished between training and technical assistance provided by the KSUA, while KSUA staff cited them as synonymous.

d. AAA staff distinguished between AAA relations with auspices and projects, while KSUA staff combined the two.

were cited by both. Both agencies had perspectives on the focus and source of the problems.

The AAA Perspective

The AAA staff spoke freely and with excitement about their areas and programs and as freely about their problems. Interviews revealed that serious problems were perceived in relations between the AAA and KSUA. With a single exception, AAA directors expressed anxiety and concern over a perceived lack of KSUA support. One director's comments are characteristic: "The KSUA promise their support. But believe me if somebody's neck goes on the block it won't be the state's. As long as everything is going well the state is behind you, but if something goes wrong, suddenly it's a local problem. It's up to you to solve it. If they don't like your solution, well. . . ."

If frequency of mention indicates the severity of a problem, then AAA directors viewed various of their relations with the KSUA as problematic. Of the ten problem areas most frequently mentioned by AAA staff, eight were of this sort. The two state system problems mentioned in the ten most frequently cited problems—delegation of authority to and competence of KSUA staff—related significantly to s/a problems. The AAA directors perceived that the KSUA lacked confidence in them. From that they inferred that they could neither expect nor obtain support from those who did not trust them. They reasoned that they were trusted, their inputs would be sought, their judgments respected, and their actions supported. *From their* perspective these did not obtain. They felt that there were few areas in which their opinions mattered and that the KSUA was unwilling to release its control in areas of AAA decision-making. Their actions, they believed, were supported if and only if they were consistent with state preferences.

The foregoing was rather generally expressed by directors. Their comments were grounded in numerous examples and incidents which, in *the view of AAA directors,* supported their perceived lack of support. Most frequently cited was the instance in which the KSUA terminated the contract of an AAA and assumed its duties. That incident was complex, involving conflicts over expenditures, among the AAA, its director and board, a nutrition project, and the AAA's sponsoring agency (a city government). Objective data suggested elements of mismanagement on the parts of each of the principal groups. Given that, the decision to terminate the AAA contract but retain the subcontract with the nutrition project, around which much of the controversy revolved, elicited a negative response among AAAS statewide. The AAA directors did not question the state's right to take action even if that meant strong action. Indeed, a number of directors viewed as legitimate the state's obligation to "intervene in a preventative" manner early enough in conflict situations to halt potential damage to an agency and its programs. Rather, they expressed anxiety about why the procedures employed to arrive at final action and about why the KSUA allowed the situation to develop to its final, politically explosive proportions.

The directors found unacceptable the decision to terminate the agency but retain the nutrition project, if indeed both were at fault. Their response was characterized by an area board chairman who said, "It appears as if the bank robber has been promoted to the presidency of the bank." They were concerned by the manner in which they heard of the decision: many were never given formal notification, and most discovered what had transpired as much as a week after the event. This, despite the fact that the acting AAA association president had, with some difficulty, gained access to the meeting of the Governor's Advisory Committee on Aging to make an appeal in regard to the case. The decision was announced after this director and the principals in the case were dismissed from the meeting.

Directors did not question the state's right—and perhaps obligation—to act on such matters. Indeed, from table 7.2 it is clear that many directors felt one problem confronted by AAAS is the KSUA's lack of rigorous enforcement of regulations. But the type of action and enforcement viewed as prevailing was perceived as "wishy-washy," too late to be effective, and unilateral. A number of directors felt a sense of uneasiness and anxiety concerning the KSUA's willingness or ability to take a strong stand on issues. As one director put it, "If it could happen like in XAA, it could happen here."

A perceived lack of support was reflected in other concrete problems cited by AAA staff, such as a perceived lack of coordination between AAAS and the KSUA. Referents typically were in the area of planning. Although both the state and area are mandated to plan for aging programming, there seemed to be only minimal relationship between their plans. When asked about this relationship, a majority of the AAA directors and a number of KSUA staff stated, "there is none"; others indicated that it "is unclear what the relationship is." One KSUA administrator indicated that (s)he " is not convinced that a relationship is necessary."

Despite OAA language concerning coordinated state and area planning efforts the KSUA is principally charged with implementing mandated programs in priority areas. Mandated programs are operative in Kansas. However, according to AAA directors, these often entail little area input. From the directors' point of view this procedure limits planning which takes into account differences between areas, special needs and problems in an area, and local input into decision-making. They believe arguments about local decision-making and "grass roots" input cannot exist if the state is more responsive to federal determination of programming than to area needs. As one director said, "It questions the entire concept of the AAA."

Arriving at some consensual concept of the AAA and its functions was viewed as a source of problems. The directors felt that problems arise because the state planning is done by persons lacking first-hand awareness of the AAAS as separate areas with individual difficulties. They complained that KSUA staff visit the agencies infrequently and that some staff members have never visited them. Those perceived problems led a number of AAA directors to criticize KSUA planning efforts. Responses in this regard ranged from, "Well they try I'm sure, but they don't do a good job" to the seemingly facetious, but dead serious, "What planning!"

Problems of communication and consistent enforcement of regulations also were cited with relative frequency. Typically, communication problems referred to difficulties of obtaining straightforward answers to questions from KSUA staff. Directors often commented, "I will call the state office one day and get one answer, and the very next, get a different one, or later I find out in a meeting that something different is being said. Sometimes they even deny giving the first answer." Or, "They (KSUA staff) don't like to write things down because they might have to change their minds." Or, "If you talk to X you get one answer but if you talk to Y you get a different one." The directors expressed a need for clear responses to questions, since program decisions and allocations of money frequently were in the balance. Most stated that there were one or two KSUA staff upon whom they could depend when an accurate response was needed. For example, the KSUA financial officer was cited as a person "with his head on right," who was "sometimes hardnosed but could be depended upon to give straight answers." The AAA staff often selected certain KSUA staff "to call when I have a question because I know I can get my question answered." The KSUA discouraged this sort of "buddy" arrangement, although it continues.

Directors complained of the tendency of KSUA staff to inundate AAAS with memos, guidelines and their changes, and last-minute requests for information. From the AAA's point of view, the KSUA should sort through and selectively pass along only high priority or essential information, particularly in the areas of interpretation of federal and state guidelines. As the AAA staff saw it, "A myriad of communiques came down the line with only minimal deciphering." That produced two types of potentially dysfunctional responses from AAAs. I was told, "We pass the information and requests on down to the projects and try to get responses from them." Several directors stated, "We do a lot of creative writing here."

AAAs perceived that the KSUA enforced regulations inconsistently. In part the perception referred to problems of constant changes in guidelines and regulations. It also referred to what the AAAs called the "fence straddling" position assumed by the KSUA, i.e., a perceived inability to take strong stands on issues. They were perplexed by what they viewed as inconsistent policies of stated support for area boards and AAAs, a laissez-faire stance toward area boards and AAAs, and the apparent ease with which support was withdrawn under external political pressures. Some directors felt that projects and AAAs were differentially treated by the KSUA. In this regard, many directors felt the KSUA should enforce regulations more stringently.

The directors believed that effective training for AAA staff and area boards was lacking. To a lesser degree they reported problems in obtaining competent technical assistance from KSUA staff. They viewed the needed assistance as critical to staff and area development and as necessary and legitimate functions of the KSUA. All AAA staff commented on several positive training experiences, but most viewed the KSUA's efforts in this area as of questionable value. Several directors said, "While some activities are called training, the truth is the state doesn't do any training." In the area of technical assistance it was felt that the quality of assistance depended on who provided it. As a director put it, "Some are excellent, others don't know what they are doing."

Although the most frequently mentioned problems were in the area of relationships between AAAs and the KSUA, AAAs also viewed state system problems as contributing to difficulties in relating to the KSUA. Most frequently mentioned was a lack of delegated authority to KSUA staff within that office. It was widely felt that "every decision that gets made has to go across the KSUA director's desk."[15] That was viewed by AAA directors as unnecessary and damaging since it sometimes delayed decisions and produced conflicting statements from the KSUA. Most directors also felt it caused a loss of confidence among KSUA staff and hindered their ability to provide assistance.

The directors questioned the competence of KSUA staff, and their comments took several forms. In only a few cases was the staff person's ability to conduct his duties seriously questioned. More frequently questions of competence referred to the fit between a person's skills and the job he held, and the perceived lack of "in-house" orientation and training provided. AAA staff wondered about the wisdom of the State Civil Service System which placed great emphasis on social work training as a major selective device for employing KSUA staff. A number indicated that a reexamination of the KSUA job description and criterion system was in order. Most frequently was the sentiment that the competencies of KSUA staff were smothered by an unwillingness to delegate authority to them.

Whether rightly or wrongly, AAAs felt many of their problems emanated from the state bureaucracy structure. Eight of the ten directors cited problems with the SRS umbrella and said that the KSUA would be more effective if moved out of that setting. They felt that a separate aging department should be established, but few had given much thought to problems such action would create. In large measure the directors felt themselves subject to and constrained by the SRS bureaucracy. They believed that the lines of authority created by SRS structure pervaded the aging network and were hindering the development of effective programming.

Finally, the directors sensed a lack of, but a need for, conceptualizing aging at the state level. This was most clearly expressed in regard to state planning efforts and the creation of a state policy on aging. From the AAA's point of view state planning is to a large extent dictated by federal demands and policy. Planning, they said, when it occurs is frequently ad hoc, subject to extreme time pressure, lacking in an adequate understanding of area needs, and oriented toward meeting minimal standards. It is not undertaken with comprehensive concepts of aging needs. Most directors indicated that the state "has no aging policy" or, "If the state has a policy on aging, I haven't seen it."

The KSUA Perspective

Table 7.2 shows a fairly high level of problem agreement between AAAs and the KSUA, although the staffs did not always agree on problem priority, difficulty, and source. While KSUA staff cited many of the same s/a problems as AAA staff, they more frequently mentioned state system type problems (eight of the ten problems most frequently mentioned). That is understandable given their more immediate involvement in a dependence upon that system.

KSUA staff cited problems of authority as among the most important—

in their own office, in their relations with AAAs, and in the state network more generally. I am convinced that these are not independent but interrelated issues.

The staff reported that they frequently are not given authority to act. They found this distressing at two levels. First, they believed that by training and job requirements they were placed in responsible positions requiring decision-making powers. A number of staff said that incidents of "having one's decisions rescinded" had hindered their capacity to decide. A procedure of "checking it out," which reportedly prevailed among staff, provided a protective safety valve, but one hardly conducive to staff self-confidence and morale. Some reported an emphasis on building "an illusion of authority" when, in fact, they felt incapable of acting without direct assent "from the top." Second, the staff believed their lack of authority hampered relations with AAA and project personnel.

According to KSUA staff, internal problems of authority were mirrored in authority problems between the agencies and within the broader aging network. The difficulty was one of establishing clearly delineated lines of authority, understood and respected as legitimate by all segments of the aging network. These problems are the result, in part, of OAA legislation which mandates planning and decision-making at the area level but places major responsibility for accountability in the state unit.

In practice these problems have resulted in actions that erode bases of legitimate authority throughout the system. Thus, the KSUA promotes a concept of strong and autonomous areas which can expect state support in their actions, but, according to many KSUA staff, the promise of support is often kept only when AAA actions are consistent with state preferences. KSUA staff are concerned that when difficult problems arise within AAAs, KSUA support may be withdrawn, arguing that "yours is a local problem which must be solved at the local level." If accurate, that strategy can be costly, as the case of contract termination described earlier indicates. It is costly as well in hindering the concept of a coordinated team effort.

KSUA staff were concerned that AAA boards were promoted as primary policy- and decision-makers in an area when those groups were in no position to carry out that charge. They expressed concern that in some areas projects became more powerful than AAAs and that "running battles" occurred over time between the two. They were concerned that regulations were not enforced stringently, that the KSUA had developed a reputation for being "wishy washy," and that all too frequently commands from above in the state structure caused them to postpone work on important ongoing matters to respond. The KSUA staff were most concerned that they were seemingly ineffectual in influencing these matters. There appeared to be little effort at the state level to examine the present authority structure with a view toward eliminating conflict and delineating lines of authority in a functional manner. The staff desired a determination of appropriate and legitimate areas of authority for the KSUA and the AAAS, so that projects which were initiated would be followed. They believed that too many AAA concepts were "floating free" in their own office and across the state, and that for the sake of the aging network, the development of a consensual working concept of those agencies was necessary.

Shortly before the study, the KSUA staff had been reorganized in an attempt to implement a team concept around the major state program efforts developed under Title III and Title VII of the OAA. I was told that the KSUA had always supported the interaction of Title III and VII projects. Since the staff were adjusting to the reorganization it was difficult to know to what extent their concerns about staff organization, division of labor and communication among staff referred only to the difficulties of adjusting to a new system or to more basic problems. Work overload and clarity of KSUA staff job definitions were of a more fundamental nature.

KSUA staff indicated that already demanding work loads were increasing, despite the addition of personnel since 1973 and the reorganization to coordinate efforts. That created an attempt to produce more work but also increased frustration about the quality of output. The staff felt they were working under strong pressures to produce but with little time to reflect on their work or to determine the long-range implications of their decisions. This relates to staff frustration over the fact that they are expected to plan, but little time can be given to serious planning efforts. I was told, for example, that the preparation of the state plan is typically a frenzied effort designed to meet a deadline rather than to set up a long-term plan for aging programs. Staff time was often spent dealing with crises and last minute details rather than with the larger issues. Most KSUA staff stated that insofar as they could tell, the state has no policy on aging. Lacking a policy, it is difficult to define clearly and collectively a direction. As one staff member put it, "I thought I would be involved in planning, but I find myself nitpicking proposals to pieces and frequently rewriting parts of those proposals so they meet the guidelines. The AAAs know we will do that. That it's our style."

Many of the staff were not doing what they had expected to in their jobs.

Several commented on "the waste of talent." A number felt that the job descriptions neither fairly indicated the requirements of the work nor were appropriately defined within the state civil service system and were in need of redefinition. Most KSUA staff said they had received little or no job orientation. They wondered whether being "handed a state policy manual and told to read it" was adequate preparation.

KSUA staff stated that, with several important exceptions, the quality of training and technical assistance provided AAAs was low. They expressed concern about this since all considered it an important function of their office. They also felt it was important to visit AAAs and projects more frequently. They worried about their credibility with the AAAs, which they knew was not high. They were concerned that AAAs did not view the KSUA as a source of solid support and were frustrated because there existed a basis for that belief.

KSUA staff also cited problems in their relations with AAAs, in many cases the same problems cited by AAAs. They wanted the concept of the AAA to be more clearly defined throughout the aging network. There are multiple definitions which contain inherent contradictions and produce an atmosphere in which neither the KSUA nor AAAs function effectively. Both agencies have problems in coordinating efforts, and neither seeks needed inputs from the other very effectively.

Problems emanating from relations with AAAs were not solely the fault or responsibility of KSUA staff. Staff of both agencies were relatively inexperienced. The state staff too doubted, in some cases, the competence of area staff. On a number of occasions, I observed or was informed of the need to correct errors, revise documents and proposals, or clarify issues on matters that need not have required staff attention. Both AAA and KSUA staff indicated that the KSUA should act with greater authority on such issues. Nonetheless, KSUA staff were genuinely concerned about program survival and growth. With that as a priority they were willing to sacrifice some administrative efficiency, although in the process they often took undeserved "raps" and assumed responsibility for actions not fully of their own making. For example, they could not be held totally accountable for delays, late reports, or conflicts and problems in PSAs resulting from the action or inaction of AAA staff. Neither could they fully control the flow of funds when often new or unexpected allocations arrived late and with little time allowed for planning its uses. By virtue of their position in the network they were required to make decisions on such issues. Inevitably, they could not please everyone. In their administrative role they became easily tagged as the "bad guys," whether they deserved to be or not.

AAA staff understood, but did not always appreciate, that they were responsible for area activities, while the responsibility of the KSUA extended to the entire state. Although significant efforts were made to insure equity across areas, charges of "playing favorites" or "ignoring our area" were made, despite sound evidence to the contrary.

An example of how that process worked may be seen in the mandated process of assessment of area activities by the KSUA. Within the constraints of federal and state guidelines and available resources, it appeared that the staff worked diligently, with fairness, and allowed for considerable flexibility in their assessments. Often changes—either suggested or required—met with opposition from an AAA. Occasionally it became a question of the AAA and its board against the KSUA. In one case, the KSUA had proceeded with cause to require the resignation of an AAA director or terminate the AAA contract, but, because the area board took a strong stand in behalf of the director, and the KSUA feared that strong action would harm area programs, the state extended the AAA more time for corrective action. Unfortunately, the KSUA's action contributed to its perception as "wishy washy," despite the ameliorative nature of its decision. Some of the issues of concern remain unresolved in that area.

These comments highlight the KSUA's difficult position in the network. In some ways it is the "man in the middle." Despite the tendency to be self-critical, some of the problems experienced reflect that structural arrangement and the "normal" difficulties of administrating a program of the magnitude and complexity of a state like Kansas.

Interviews with the KSUA staff indicated the lack of a clear sense of direction, a feeling of movement toward a common goal in concert with their AAA colleagues. In the words of one KSUA staff person:

. . . maybe a lot of the problems or conflicts between our office and the AAAs is a lack of clear role definitions. When I started here, after reading the materials and everything, I had heard that the agencies really aren't sure of their roles. At the time I thought that was pretty dumb, because I had read the material and I thought I pretty well understood it. But, after you get into the program there are many areas that you're not really sure of—who can make decisions and that sort of thing. So now I've taken a different perspective on that statement. Now I believe that we have problems because the people involved—AAAs and us—are really not clear on what our roles and functions are.

Examining KSUA/AAA Interaction

The approach and emphasis of this chapter may leave the impression that Kansas has no viable programs in aging. That is untrue. An increasing number of programs are funded under various OAA titles across the state. With exceptions, however, AAAs and the KSUA generally agree that these programs are neither functioning to capacity nor with the effectiveness desired. Thus, for example, only about 4 percent of those eligible for Title VII meals are currently receiving them.[16] Moreover, it is not known what proportion of those not participating would do so if access to nutrition sites were more easily and readily available. This is a particular problem in rural areas and one not fully confronted at the federal level. Similarly, the earlier discussion of the uneven distribution of Title III monies to counties effectively means some areas will be handicapped in implementing, much less expanding, Title III programs. In part, at least the number and quality of programs depend on available funds. Does Kansas receive its fair share of OAA monies? If one applies the federal formula to this question the answer is yes. Further, there was no evidence that KSUA staff were lax in their attempts to obtain state federal funds due Kansas. If one recognizes some of the special problems of delivering services in rural areas which were alluded to earlier in the chapter, the answer to the question may well be no. It seems feasible to suggest that federal policy might be altered to recognize the special problems of the rural elderly, since so much has been done for minority and low-income older people.

An additional source of funding is, of course, the state. As pointed out earlier, the state contributes only matching funds to OAA programs. That has been a problem recognized both within the KSUA and AAA's, and across the state more generally. There is reason to believe that the elevation of the KSUA to a departmental level unit in state government places it in a stronger position to obtain state funding. Best present estimates are that such funding is unlikely to occur in the immediate future, neither are the amounts of money likely to be large for some time. Nonetheless, there is little doubt that the commitment of state funds to aging programs would greatly strengthen existing programs and would allow for confronting some of the special problems of delivering services in rural areas. At the least, such funds would provide both the KSUA and AAAs greater flexibility and latitude in their planning programming efforts.

I believe the problems in the aging network are less "people problems" than problems of structural arrangements. Staff at both the KSUA and AAA levels were genuinely committed to improving the life conditions of older Kansans. Aside from motives and intentions, however, are the real problems which affect programming efforts. Some of these are beyond the effective control of either the state or area. Thus, the newness of the AOA network and its mandates, pressures to implement programs under short time frames, the organizational constraints of the Kansas aging network, and funding issues comprised a framework within which the Kansas network had to operate. A case in point concerns the rules and regulations which govern OAA-funded programs. Despite the frequent complaints directed at the KSUA from AAA's that such guidelines are ambiguous, too constraining, unfair, or simply unrealistic, the fact is that the KSUA's task is to administer given guidelines. KSUA staff did not write the rules and regulations and whether they agreed or disagreed with the guidelines, they were held accountable for their enforcement. Indeed, it is possible to argue that many of the preceding sections reflect the frustration of having to deal daily with the implications of these broader problems.

Although Kansas has its problems, other research suggests that the state is not egregrious. That point is important, if only to highlight the need to examine more carefully the various aging networks and to act positively to assist the states in solving their problems.

Despite my argument that many of the structural problems in the Kansas system are beyond the immediate and effective control of the KSUA or the AAAS, there remain areas within the system which, if altered, could alleviate a considerable portion of the present tension. Earlier it was suggested that the KSUA and AAAS were in relatively high agreement as to what their problems are. Considerable disagreement existed over what, if anything, should be done to solve them.

One point of contention was the issue of "locus of control," that is, designating who has responsibility for what aspects of the aging network and *providing the authority and autonomy* to carry out those aspects. That issue crossed the entire system from the KSUA through projects area boards and county advisory councils. The unfortunate incident described above, involving the termination of an AAA contract, illustrated this problem in extreme form. There is a need to delineate carefully the span of control of the KSUA, the AAAS, area boards, county advisory council, and projects. Once such a delineation is made, it must be respected.

Similarly, the distribution of effort throughout the system must be reexamined and rationalized. That is implied by the idea of fixing responsibility. Presently, it is not always clear who has responsibility for what. For example, when KSUA staff rewrite proposals submitted by AAAS, they must take time from other important activities, and one can question whether that sort of task appropriately falls under the rubric of technical assistance. AAAS, on the other hand, should be able to obtain appropriate technical assistance when needed, without having to verify answers with other staff or being concerned that the assistance provided will be rescinded.

Although the KSUA and AAAS are mandated to coordinate their efforts, and must do so for effective programming, considerable concern was expressed over the extent to which coordination occurred and the form it took. Were a system of distribution of effort defined, progress could be made toward resolving problems of effort coordination. It is difficult to coordinate even under ideal situations; it is perhaps impossible to expect coordination in the present climate of distrust between the KSUA and AAA's. However, mistrust could be reduced by dealing with the particular issues that promote it. Thus, for example, the disjointed relationship between area plans and the state plan could provide an ideal arena for closer and productive coordination. It is necessary, however, to provide for cooperative efforts in which staff approach one another as equals in the planning venture. This would require KSUA staff—or at least some of them—to relinquish some areas of decision-making that they now define as clearly their own. Also, AAA staff must recognize and respect KSUA authority in specified areas. Such action should generate available resources so as to engage in long-range planning and ultimately the development of a state policy on aging. An important outcome of this strategy is that it would make feasible a coordinated assessment and implementation of federal, state, and area priorities. Such a coordinated system of priorities is currently lacking in the state.

Considerable concern is expressed in both agencies over the appropriate application of rules and regulations within the network. They could cooperatively resolve the problem of setting priorities on which guidelines and regulations require immediate action and which are second- and third-tier priorities. Granted, control over these matters is not fully at the discretion of the two agencies. Nonetheless, the apparent system of nonselectively passing the buck—i.e., rules and regulations—down the line for action and often interpretation has created problems. While control over guidelines is not always possible, discretion in the application of priorities of those guidelines frequently is.

The KSUA must work to create a sense of state support for AAAS. This is of utmost concern to AAAS since, whether rightly or wrongly, they perceive a lack of KSUA support. Some of these suggestions could also increase the confidence of AAAS in the KSUA. The KSUA must allow AAAS greater discretion and autonomy, *and then back them* in their actions. AAAS must respect and support the KSUA's legitimate actions.

Greater emphasis should be given to planning and implementation and to developing a system of training and technical assistance that responds to area needs. Training is properly a function and obligation of both AAA's and the KSUA. It is first the function of the KSUA to conceptualize a training and technical assistance program, drawing inputs from areas. Badly needed is a systematic assessment of resources available in the state and in surrounding states and the development of a rational scheme for matching resources with need. While funds are seldom available to purchase all the elements of a planned training program at one time, the creation of such a plan could be useful as a guide for allocating resources over a period of time.

These issues are of broad concern to the entire aging network. Their resolution cannot and must not occur unilaterally. The inputs of all relevant components of the network must be obtained. In some cases change would require rather substantial efforts and time. If change occurs it will cost some components more than others, but the outcome could be a stronger network working for the welfare of the aged.

POSTSCRIPT

Usually the final section of a research report consists of a summary of findings and a statement of research implications. In a sense, as a result of the fellowship experience, my work has just begun rather than ended. The data reported represent only a small portion of those which were gathered. Refinement and further analyses must yet be completed. I have established a continuing tie with the agencies which should allow for the translation of research results into action and to extend the research to other aspects of the network.

The fellowship experience was rich in many ways. Perhaps most rewarding was the knowledge I gained of the state's aging network—of the people who comprise it and of the structures within which they work. I have gained insights into aging programming that I am convinced only a "hands on" experience provides. I observed the impact of structures upon people and the struggle of those people to build programs. My ideas about the system have sharpened considerably, although I am less sure now than I was at the outset that I have answers for the problems.

In the course of the work several ideas to which I have been increasingly drawn were reinforced. I believe there is need in research, as in applied endeavors, to develop a sense of appreciation for the particular circumstances in which actors live and work and of the actors themselves. In its initial form, that sense of appreciation is nonjudgmental but is guided by attempts to understand the perspectives of actors within the contexts and constraints which influence their actions. I tried to understand the perspective of the AAA staff, the KSUA staff, and other components in the aging network. The world when viewed from any particular perspective made good sense. From that perspective judgments made on network problems, goals, or successes were perfectly correct. It was only when that perspective was examined within the framework of or in relation to another that problems arose, since the latter also made sense. Also, however, once the perspectives were placed in relation to one another a pattern emerged.

The pattern suggested that the difficulties of the aging network in Kansas are more legitimately viewed as structural problems than as people problems. I was sensitized to the need for rejecting *solely* psychologistic explanations and interpretations of organizational or system phenomena and the model of change underlying such explanations.[17] That approach characterizes the attitude taken toward many significant social problems in this society, including aging. Too often it has produced a process called "blaming the victim." I observed this all too often at various levels in the course of the study, whether the victim be KSUA staff, AAA staff, project staff, or aging people. Unfortunately, that has produced the too frequent reference to "unstable personalities" or "personality conflicts" offered and accepted as explanations for problems and legitimate bases for action. Such responses, however reasonable they seem to persons who must justify their acts, beg the question of the source of problems. Those who appreciate most strongly the structural nature of the network problems were not placed in the system strategically enough to have significant impact on resolving the problems.

My experience exposed me to the difficulty of effecting change. Like it or not, the network houses many vested interests and definitions of "what is right for the network and aging persons." I was struck by how little input aging people have to decision-making. I was struck by how frequently persons differentially located in the network talked about the need for change, but how little they talked with one another about it. I became aware of, but was not surprised at, the strongly political character of the network. Here I refer not only to the politics of state government, but also to the use of the term politics in a broader sense; namely the struggle for and exercise of power. Given such conditions, change in the network will not come quickly or easily. However, I am convinced that change is both necessary and possible.

The experience has sharpened my perceptions of my own role in promoting change. All levels expressed the need for data of the sort gathered in this study and the desire to bring about change. I believe that such statements were offered genuinely despite differences of opinion over an appropriate format for presenting results and some of the interpretations of the data. I will attempt to make my findings as broadly available as possible; whether or not they are accepted and used remains to be seen.

The fellowship experience was also frustrating in a number of ways. Particularly troublesome were the imposed time constraints. Indeed, parts of the study as originally conceived had to be deleted. I appreciate more fully the need for continuous feedback on the research efforts from both agency personnel and professional colleagues. More substantively, I was troubled by what I observed in the network. I puzzled over how the problems about which I was hearing might be resolved. In several cases my puzzlement remains.

The fellowship reinforced an already existing commitment to my professional interests in aging. My interests and skills remain oriented to research. However, I have gained a greater appreciation for the need and place of applied and policy research within the profession and in my own priorities.

In the two years since the completion of this study considerable change has occurred in the Kansas aging network. The KSUA has been elevated to a departmental status in the state government. Only three of the AAA directors who participated in the study remain in the system and one of these will have resigned his position by the time this paper is in print. Considerable change in AAA staff and project personnel has occurred. An additional AAA has been created. The AAA whose contract was terminated has been reconstituted and is again actively engaged in developing and delivering programs. One senses across the state and within the network an increasing concern with the issues of aging and the problems of older Kansans. That concern has been accompanied by positive action in the form of expanded and improved programs. Many of the constraints explored in this chapter remain and continue to create problems. But, the system has matured, the newness has worn off, and there seems to be a sense of direction that was lacking when the study was conducted. To be sure, Kansas still has problems. Many of these are the same or at least not greatly different from those discussed above. Yet, I believe that the network has achieved a vitality and viability which will allow it to respond effectively to the needs of older citizens.[18]

NOTES

1. An important paper by Robert Hudson (1973) details the history of the OAA through the 1973 amendments. That paper sets forth as well the conditions under which SUAs and AAAs developed and the programmatic outcomes mandated under the OAA. Additionally, a number of students have reported on the difficulties of implementing the "new" approach (e.g., Howenstein, Miller, and Tucker, 1975; Koeske, 1975; Steinberg, 1976; Tobin, 1976).

2. Hudson (1973) discusses in detail the role of the SUA as "a conduit for channeling federal moneys down to the local level" prior to the 1973 amendments. The Title III revisions presumably changed the SUA role from that of "pipeline" to one more akin to administrator, overseeing the activities of AAAs. The success of that strategy is yet unfolding and is addressed for the state of Kansas in this chapter. In 1973 federal monies allocated to Kansas under the OAA totaled $2,187,445; that figure increased to $3,337,326 in 1976 (the year of this study); and is projected at $4,939,763 in 1978.

3. Interviews with AAA staff normally took an entire day. On the average, three and one-half hours were spent with AAA directors (range—two to six hours) and an average of one and one-half hours were spent interviewing AAA staff. Interviews with state staff ranged from one to five hours, averaging about two hours. Formal interviews were supplemented by more informal contacts as well as other data-gathering procedures described below.

4. I later discovered that I was viewed by some AAA and state staff as an advocate of AAAs in the state, despite my efforts to discourage such perceptions.

5. State staff were aware that the movement for creating the department was in motion. They were unsure of what such action would mean and accordingly were sensitive to some of the more critical aspects of the report, despite the fact that it would not be released publicly for some time. I have maintained my contacts with the KSUA, AAAS, and other aging interest groups in the state and region since the completion of this study. It appears that the difficulties I experienced have now been largely resolved. Indeed, I received the support of the KSUA, AAA, and area board chairpersons to conduct a study of AAA boards and county advisory councils.

6. That formula consisted of the following components. (A) Aging composition formula developed by AOA (60+ population + 2 × 65 + low income population + 2 × 65 minority population). (B) Commitments to aging program grants from previous years. (C) Geographic factor—the population 60+ in the PSA and the number of counties served. (D) Performance of AAA personnel.

7. The aged dependency ratio assumes that certain age groups are economically

productive while others are dependent in large measure on the efforts of those who are productive. The Hughes and Gibbs aged dependency ratio is computed as follows: (persons 65+)/(persons 19–64) × 100.

8. In spring 1977, legislation was enacted creating a State Department of Aging. The secretary of the department is a cabinet level position in state government. However, presently only OAA programs are under the administration jurisdiction of the department.

9. This was a major argument employed by advocates of the Department of Aging.

10. That AAA was reestablished in the spring of 1977 as a private nonprofit corporation.

11. Since the completion of the study a change in directors has occurred in six of the ten AAAS.

12. State staff denied opposition; several indicated strong support.

13. The term "retreated" may be too strong. That was the view of AAA and some state staff. Clearly, the state position was influenced by the potential impact of termination on programming in the area.

14. AAA staff listed a total of 30 problem areas, KSUA staff cited 29 problem areas.

15. In part, that was due to a misunderstanding by AAA staff of state policy requiring the KSUA director's signature or initials on official documents leaving the office.

16. The 4 percent figure is an estimate which fluctuates over the course of a year but translates to roughly 23,000 meals served. Thus, for example, the KSUA estimates a target of 12 percent and has served as many as 10 percent.

17. This by no means denies the significance of incorporating psychological variables and explanations where appropriate.

18. I am grateful to those in the aging network in Kansas whose assistance made this study possible. They gave graciously of their time, were genuine in their interest, and spoke bluntly to the issues raised. In a significant way the work presented here is as much theirs as mine. I wish also to express my gratitude to the Gerontological Society under whose sponsorship the fellowship was awarded. The study, however, is dedicated to the development of a stronger and more viable aging network in Kansas—a desire shared by those of us interested in the welfare of aging persons in this state.

REFERENCES

Etzioni, A. 1960. Two approaches to organizational analysis: A critique and a suggestion. *Administrative Science Quarterly* 5:269–80.

Haas, J. E., and Drabek, T. E. 1973. *Complex Organizations: A Sociological Perspective*. New York: Macmillan.

Howenstein, R. A.; Miller, J.; and Tucker, R. C. 1975. Research on Social Systems and Interagency Relations: A Study of the Area Agencies on Aging. Gerontology Study Unit, Training and Consultation Division, Connecticut Mental Health Center, School of Medicine, Yale University: New Haven, Conn.

Hudson, R. B. 1973. "Client Politics and Federalism: The case of the Older Americans Act." Paper presented at the meetings of the American Political Science Association.

Hudson, R. B. 1974. Rational planning and organizational imperatives: prospects for area planning in aging. *Annals of the American Academy of Political and Social Sciences* 415:41–54.

Hughes, D., and Gibbs, J. 1977. "Structural Correlates of Aging Services in Kansas Counties." Paper presented at the Gerontological Society Meetings, San Francisco, Calif.

Koeske, R.; Feinberg, N.; Stromberg, A.; and Jameson, B. 1975. "The Impact of Implementing Federal and State Public Policy." Report submitted to the Pennsylvania State Office on Aging. Harrisburg, Pa.

Likert, R. 1967. *The Human Organization*. New York: McGraw-Hill.

Steinberg, R. M. 1976. A Study of Funding Regulations, Program Agreements and Monitoring Procedures Affecting the Implementation of the Older Americans Act. Social Policy Laboratory, Ethel Percy Andrus Gerontology Center, University of Southern California, Los Angeles.

Tobin, S. S.; Davidson, S. M.; and Sack, A. 1976. Models for Effective Service Delivery: Social Services for Older Americans. School of Social Service Administration. University of Chicago, Chicago, Ill.

Warren, R. L. 1971. *Truth, Love, and Social Change*. Chicago, Ill.: Rand McNally.

8. Case V. Energy and the Elderly: Developing a Telephone Survey for Quick Assessment

Charles B. White

EDITOR'S NOTE: One assumption in social science research is that reliable information and valid knowledge are better than guess work, hunches, or action based on isolated case studies. Another is that a state agency dealing with human services should not simply react or respond to past events and crises. A clever bureaucrat, alert to the political situation as it relates to the clientele he serves, can anticipate crises.

One contemporary problem is the threat of an energy shortage and the consequences for older persons without adequate sources of fuel for heating and cooking. The elderly are particularly vulnerable in such a crisis because of low income and lessened mobility.

With these concerns in mind, White reviewed telephone survey methods and wrote a succinct professional manual which a public or private agency could adapt to its purposes. This case illustrates clearly how certain unique and emerging problems demand the gathering of new information. Use of the telephone survey presupposes the availability of a WATS line and interviewers (probably volunteers). Since over 90 percent of the elderly have telephones, this is an effective mode of interviewing. Furthermore, in contrast to door-to-door interviews, this technique may increase both accessibility and participation: Security considerations may make some elderly reluctant to admit a stranger to their homes, but they would cooperate in a telephone survey.

IN the winter of 1976, in anticipation of a recurrence of the energy shortage of the winter of 1975, a major question was posed to a State Office on Aging (SOA): What will be the effect of various proposed solutions (e.g., rationing, redistribution, change in kind of fuel) on the aged residents of a northeastern state should such emergency steps become necessary? It became clear that the legislature would have to act should the anticipated energy shortage materialize. Hence there would be little time to determine impact. The State Office on Aging, in order to protect the interests of its constituents and carry out its mandated function, needed a way to rapidly assess potential impact of the various alternatives should such become necessary.

My assignment, as a State Office on Aging consultant, under the auspices of the Gerontological Society Fellowship Program, was to develop a technique which would provide rapid assessment of the energy needs of the older citizens of this state. It was necessary to design a rapid and inexpensive needs assessment methodology which could be implemented quickly yet provide reliable and valid information. Accurate, immediate, and inexpensive were the major criteria for determining the utility of any proposed solution. A door-to-door or mail survey, in addition to being too cumbersome and expensive, would take too long. Thus, a telephone survey methodology was pursued as being the potentially most effective. The SOA felt it could best represent its constituency to the legislature by means of respectable data, but the personnel initially expressed some skepticism at the idea of needs assessment via telephone. Was not the telephone forever discredited as a biased survey technique after the *Literary Digest* utilized telephone directories as a sampling frame to predict Roosevelt's defeat by Landon?

First it was necessary to develop a convincing argument for the validity of a telephone survey. Second, the methodology would be developed. Third, the technique would be tested. (The last step was not done for lack of adequate funding.)

In the course of developing and formulating the techniques, I also gained considerable insight into how a large social services bureaucracy operates, how it fits into the larger public services operations of state government, and how research is viewed by the state social services personnel.

THE CONSULTING EXPERIENCE

The consultantship was carried out in the Division of Research and Systems of the SOA. The division had no personnel with background or training in gerontology, aging services, or related fields. (All of the employees were young people.) The individuals could have worked in almost any state agency with equal ease; in fact many of them came to the SOA from other units of state government. In fairness, some of the staff acquired knowledge relevant to aging, and related areas, after spending some time in the agency, but they were still unfamiliar with the scientific literature on aging.

THE POLITICAL CONTEXT

A major impediment to the effective utilization of my services was the highly political nature of the SOA. This had two immediate implications:

first, nobody outside the division to which I was assigned had any conception of who I was or what I was doing there, and, second, there was a great deal of suspicion about my role. The state office divisions were extremely competitive for political advantage. I was often viewed as part of the division head's attempt to parlay additional advantage with the office director. My assignment to a particular division was thus a mistake in such a politicized situation, because it had the effect of attaching political significance to work which was basically apolitical. Such a circumstance meant that any utilization of the projects would take on political importance. One might call this the political context of the consulting task. The state office consisted of a large number of interdependent competing subsystems. Anyone who entered such a system risked being at least an unwitting party to the competition.

The implication of the political context for the telephone survey was that it was far from clear whether there was any real interest in the ostensible goals, i.e., to increase the adequacy of the advocacy role of the state office. Rather, the project was treated as just another political issue with potential kudos for, or advantage to, one group. The consultant should ascertain the political organizational climate, in order to see beyond the ostensible purpose to perhaps a hidden agenda in seeking his services. In this case it seemed to be to gain advantage over another subsystem within the larger office.

ATTITUDES TOWARD RESEARCH

Given the above competitive context, it is not surprising that attitudes toward research reflected the pragmatic political climate. Research conducted by the Research and Systems Division consisted mainly of gathering descriptive statistics and handling the computer operations of the SOA. Discussions with personnel indicated the division had no clear mandate and hence did little research, though it did let research subcontracts with other institutions. Staff consisted mainly of computer specialists and policy analysts with little knowledge about aging and even less understanding of research methodology. Although they were sensitive to the aged as people, they had little comprehension of the complexity of "research design." This was a belated discovery on my part as I had assumed that anyone working in a division called Research and Systems in a state office on aging would be knowledgeable about research and gerontology. But these were systems-computer people, not researchers.

In retrospect, I conclude that a consultant could have played an educative role to the advantage of the division in carrying out or clarifying its purposes and thus facilitating future research where appropriate. The staff were not hostile toward research or researchers. They were cooperative and supportive because they were mystified, because they had been ordered to be by the division head, who evidenced his support quite visibly, and because they were nice people.

Office personnel showed little appreciation of the time frame or the expense of the telephone survey. The last questions asked were about cost and time when they should have been the first questions. As no financial or temporal parameters were provided, it was never clear to what extent the SOA was committed to the survey. The project was never taken beyond the design and rationale (methodology) of the technical report, because there were no funds or personnel available to implement it. For a time it appeared external money would be available, but that money became a political issue and was lost to the division in which I was working. Thus, the first negotiation should have been the establishment of the SOA's commitment to the project via a preliminary indication of fiscal and personnel support.

As an individual coming to a consultantship from an academic environment, one must adapt from the goals of academic research (for example, to address a theoretical point, to answer a research question, to test a particular hypothesis) to those of research in a very applied setting. In the SOA the goals are to address more time-bound questions, e.g., needs assessment, service delivery, or what will happen if the legislature restricts the supply of oil? Clearly both academics and civil servants understand and share the political goals of research, or "good deeds."

My primary interest was in the methodology of the telephone survey; the agency wanted the data. These concerns were not conflicting, but rather complementary. However, at another level, the division wished to upstage a group in the state office that wanted to gather information on energy policy impact through field representatives. The mutual suspiciousness with which these divisions viewed each other's activities became known to me very late in the project. Clearly, other divisions should have been involved in planning the project. That they were not may have been a partial explanation of the failure to implement the testing phase.

THE CONSULTANT'S ROLES AND INTERPERSONAL RELATIONS

The political hazards acted more as limiting factors than as deterrents. In such a politicized climate it was important to carry out the task without making the regular staff feel threatened. It was necessary to explain how the telephone survey project was being carried out and to assure personnel that the consultant was not being paid out of state funds. The latter seemed to be of great concern to the staff. Funding was a major source of inter- and intradivisional friction. Furthermore, the staff needed to know I was not there to evaluate them, the office, or the division, but to perform a specific task. Although the task had potential benefits for other divisions, it did not involve troubleshooting or problem solving, which would have implications for the budgets of other divisions.

A second procedure that seemed quite effective was to attempt to interact regularly with staff and to seek their advice. From secretaries to policy analysts, all were helpful and pleased to be helpful. Interaction also diffused any anxiety they may have felt over my role; i.e., I wasn't there to evaluate them. It also allowed one to deal with a common reaction to academics in consulting roles, that is, a perception of arrogance. The staff often commented that their previous experiences had been with the "know-it-all" academician whose attitude and behavior were condescending toward the personnel. By involving them in the project whenever possible they felt more a part of it and less defensive about it.

Another important role was that of a politically disinterested party. I was often approached to reveal some information about some other person, group, or division in the office. Such individuals were often seeking support for their position or attempting to ingratiate themselves. If I did not reveal special interest, or seek additional information about their topic, they often seemed to feel less threatened themselves. ("At least this is one less person to worry about.") Whether it be over lunch, coffee, or beer, any indication of allegiance to one faction will impair one's credibility as a neutral person. The art here is to avoid taking sides without seeming aloof or arrogant. Of course, any information revealed to the consultant is considered confidential. Thus, trustworthiness does not become an issue. I frequently felt like a Rogerian counselor in my attempts to be disinterested without being rejective. Any of these are potential traps which can destroy effectiveness in carrying out a research project.

The political context is clearly related to the values of the agency. In this case, the political conflicts determined what was important. While the consultant may think the feedback to the agency was important in improving its advocacy function in behalf of the aged, the agency or, in this instance the division, may believe that the prime goal is to upstage someone else, either with the product or with the consultant. In such a case the consultant's view of what is important is unshared by the agency. The conflict, in this consultantship, contributed to the product being unutilized once it had served its agency defined function, irrespective of the ostensible function.

Outcomes I: The Telephone Survey

This survey became a potentially useful technique for a much wider variety of purposes than the one (i.e., energy policy impact) for which it was created. The telephone may provide a useful and relatively inexpensive (compared to door-to-door or mail techniques) means for many forms of needs assessment. The complete report is contained in the appendix, but briefly: the telephone allows a special anonymity, great speed of data collection, close supervision of the survey personnel, and monitoring of the individual surveys. However, it is limited in utility if observation of the respondent's environment is important, if a special person-to-person rapport is desired, if people feel you are conducting a sales campaign, and/or if you are interested in the very small percentage of individuals inaccessible by telephone (e.g., the institutionalized).

Basically, the telephone no longer introduces the extensive bias into surveys it once did, and it allows a good random sample through the use of random-digit dialing techniques. It provides a special non-face-to-face situation which may reduce social desirability as an influence in the survey. In addition, the telephone may be utilized as a supplement in facilitating face-to-face interviews by establishing a cooperative and pre-screened sample for interviewers.

Outcomes II: Summary

The following is a list of the most salient points, with implications, of my consultantship experience.

1. Many aspects of the situation described herein had counterparts in the academic experience. That is, the difference between the academic environment, and/or basic research, and the external (to the academy) environment, and/or applied research, is only a difference in content, not form. The important difference appears in terms of the context. Clearly, political issues are as real in the university as in a government agency. The point is that the structural aspects of conflict, goals, need for achievement, etc. exist in both situations. The competition of interdependent subsystems in a state office on aging is not unlike departmental conflicts in the

university. Such an awareness ought to provide a foundation for mutual understanding between both parties.

2. The notion of a discrepancy between research and action is only a difference in how one defines action. For the academic it may be publication, advancing knowledge, the resolution of a theoretical question, upstaging a competitive view, promotion and tenure, or self-satisfaction, to name but a few. Surely these all have counterparts in any work situation. The fact that as academics we are often insensitive to the goals or actions of nonacademics hardly removes any basis for mutual understanding. If I were writing about academic departments, department could be substituted for state office and probably be equally accurate. Perhaps that realization more than any other removes any abstract notions of claims to purity on the part of the academic.

3. Agency people often feel that academics are insensitive to their circumstances. The common emphasis on the distinction between "academics" and the "real world" obscures the overwhelming similarity of the respective situations and, indeed, the complementary nature of these two contexts. While there are differences in content (e.g., specific goals, specific roles, specific accountability), the realization of this essential similarity is an asset to the consultant in comprehending the context. There are important differences (e.g., the need to implement a program with less data than is necessary from a research perspective), and these have been articulated here, but the similarities are equally important. We know situations by relating them to previous experiences. There is danger in "over-fitting," or stretching to fit, but there is an asset in noting the commonalities. Thus, the major obstacles here were in the realm of failing to initially note the essential similarity of academic and agency circumstances. Once that was realized, communication was facilitated, and the task became easier.

4. The title of a division in large state or federal offices does not often describe its function at least as it would be interpreted by an academic. For example, the division I worked in was called Research and Systems. Basically, it set up the external contract-monitoring function and established the mailing system for publicity, but it did not do research in the sense that the term is used in university settings.

5. Persons coming from a university setting need to be sensitized to the product orientation toward research in these applied settings.

6. The academic is often criticized for lacking relevance. Relevance itself is not really the issue, but relevance to what, for whom and when? Most of us likely play to audiences. While the audience may be different in

the two contexts, the dynamics of that interaction are similar. Any claim of lack of relevance may simply be an indication that the actor is playing to a different audience. Perhaps that is the basis of many conflicts between the academic consultant and the agency. There was no conflict between myself and the agency. There was simply conflict within the agency, which interfered as much with the agency personnel as it did with the consultant's goal achievement. By opting for a specific task that could be accomplished without extensive cooperation between the competing subsystems, I was able to complete the task successfully though not implement it.

Appendix. The Telephone Survey as a Method of Needs Assessment

The telephone survey deserves increased recognition as a method for rapidly and inexpensively gathering information formerly collected via personal interview or mail. Herein the general literature on telephone surveys is reviewed, and the advantages and disadvantages of the telephone as a data collection device are discussed. As needs assessment procedures become increasingly expensive, inadequate, and time-consuming, the benefits of the telephone become increasingly attractive relative to its disadvantages. The telephone survey may be combined with other techniques or used exclusively, depending on the needs of the particular program.

Advantages of the telephone survey include the following: the cost of calling is minimal compared to a personal interview; information may be collected rapidly; information is likely to be current as time lags between survey initiation and tabulation of results is short relative to both the mail survey and the personal interview; data collection may be centralized and supervision is thus simplified; and as face-to-face contact is eliminated, the likelihood of responses influenced by social desirability is reduced.

Disadvantages include: omission from the survey of those without telephones, or inaccessible by telephone, may result in a sample bias. (This problem is not as serious today as it once was. The number of people without telephones has decreased from about 50 percent just 20 years ago to 10 percent today. In addition, a larger percentage of the elderly possess or have access to telephones than do younger age groups.) The telephone may reduce rapport between the interviewer and interviewee, and thus it may be more difficult to attain cooperation. Information regarding personal characteristics and the environment may be unavailable. The telephone may be a limiting factor in the length of the interview and the type of questions (nonconfidential) which may be asked. Individuals may be oversurveyed via the telephone by businesses and be suspect of the purposes of the survey. (Door-to-door and mail surveys may confront a similar problem.)

Influences of Social Desirability

The impersonal nature of the telephone appears to reduce the threat associated with socially undesirable responses. That is, the interviewer's opinion of the respondent is less important in a telephone situation. Hochstrum (in Uhl and Schoner, 1969) found that telephone interviews, as well as mailed questionnaires, are likely to yield more candid responses than are personal interviews.

Wiseman (1972) asked identical questions of three different groups; the first was interviewed by mail, the second by telephone, and the third in person. Surprisingly, the mail questionnaires yielded the most completions, followed by the telephone procedure, and the personal interview. (The high completion rate of the mail procedure is likely due to the fact that 25 percent of those surveyed received prior notification via telephone.) No statistically significant differences were found between the groups on sex, marital status, age, occupation, income, and religion.

A difference between groups was found on two questions, one dealing with birth control, the other with abortion. The largest percentage of socially undesirable responses on the two questions was obtained from the mail questionnaire and the personal interview. The smallest percentage of socially undesirable responses appeared in the telephone method. The author concluded that those methods which provide the greatest confidentiality are more likely to get honest responses. It is thus likely that the assurance of confidentiality in the telephone method would increase honesty in responding, though this remains to be investigated. Apparently contradictory results of Wiseman's (1972) investigation may have resulted from procedures for assuring confidentiality of responses.

Noncooperation and Refusal Rates

The telephone may be useful in facilitating personal face-to-face interviews. In 1962, for example, the National Opinion Research Council (NORC) conducted a survey of adult and adolescent education in the U.S. (Sudman, 1967). The adolescent sample was divided into two groups, one of which was interviewed in a face-to-face manner without a prior telephone appointment. The other group was similarly interviewed, but an appointment was established via telephone.

In both groups the cooperation rate was 81 percent, though the prior appointment by telephone reduced by 25 percent the average number of contacts made to complete an interview, an important cost consideration. Most of the noncooperation rate was due to unavailability rather than outright refusals.

Another NORC survey (Sudman, 1967) utilized as its sample source a street directory which also listed area telephone numbers. An advance appointment was made by telephone with each member of one group while a second group of respondents was not contacted in advance. Though the cooperation rate was equal in both groups there was a 15 percent reduction in the time involved contacting a respondent in the group in which the appointment was prearranged.

It might be suggested that one would encounter a greater refusal rate when utilizing the telephone for interviewing, as individuals would find it easier to refuse in a non-face-to-face situation. NORC conducted a telephone survey in which it persisted in the telephone situation until an interview was completed or a firm refusal was given (Sudman, 1967). A 79 percent cooperation rate was achieved, which compares favorably to other forms of survey.

Potential Sample Bias

The sample bias introduced into a survey via the telephone was addressed by Leuthold and Scheele (1971) in a study of households with and without telephones. They utilized the results of two separate studies which had included identical questions with regard to telephone ownership. The data from both surveys were very similar with approximately 10 percent of the respondents (929 and 1,927, respectively) indicating they did not have a telephone. The authors cite a steady decline in nontelephone households. The increased incidence of telephone households would serve to further reduce potential sample bias introduced by use of the telephone for interviews.

Leuthold and Scheele found that those who live in rural areas or have a low income level are less likely to possess telephones than those with higher incomes and those living in urban areas. Of 9 percent of their sample with unlisted telephone numbers, they surprisingly found that the unlisted phone was most frequently associated with an average income and a grade school education. Of those above 60 years of age only 10 percent had no phone, and only 4 percent in that age group had unlisted numbers, the lowest percentage of unlisted phones for any age group.

Leuthold and Scheele concluded that sampling based solely on telephone directories will disproportionately exclude blacks, the separated and divorced, service workers, and city dwellers. These individuals tend to be without phones or to have unlisted numbers at a higher rate than others. On the other hand, the telephone is most common in households with older individuals.

Random-Digit Dialing

Sampling exclusively from phone directories will systematically exclude those without listed numbers and those whose names do not appear in the directories for some other reason (e.g., new listings). An alternative to directory based sampling was suggested by Glasser and Metzger (1972), who utilized a random-digit dialing procedure in which at least some of the digits of each telephone number are generated randomly. (Random-digit dialing techniques based on a ten-digit number will not include numbers with less than ten digits. About 89 percent of U.S. households, as of March 1970, were on a ten-digit system. Telephone directories are usually seven or eight months out of date.)

Glasser and Metzger (1972) reported that 20 percent of the telephone households may not be listed in the telephone directory, with as many as 30 percent unlisted in large urban areas. They utilized random-digit dialing procedures to obtain a national probability sample. Every assigned ten-digit number in the country had an equal probability of inclusion. The interviewer asked whether or not the telephone number was listed in the area directory, the sex and age of the persons in the household, the number of telephones in the household, and the county of residence. A 93 percent response rate was achieved with the random-digit dialing techniques.

In the Glasser and Metzger study the random-digit dialing procedure involved preselection of area codes and central office numbers and generation of a four-digit random number for each call within the selected area code/central office combination. The procedure yielded one-in-five dialings that connected with a usable residential household. (The rate of usable numbers would have been one-in-two hundred were all ten digits generated randomly.)

Possible outcomes of the random-digit dialing procedure include: connection with a nonworking number, (73 percent); connection with a business or nonresidential telephone (5 percent); and connection with a working household number (21 percent) (percentages refer to the 1972 study).

If a working household number is connected, the telephone dialing will result in a completed call, no answer, a busy signal, or either a wrong number or malfunctioning equipment. Follow-up steps should be taken to complete the call and avoid the additional potential for bias introduced by noncompletion, e.g., no answer or a busy signal. Further, one should verify with each dialing that the correct telephone number has been reached. An incorrect number should never be included or later used as it violates the randomness of the sample procedure.

A further potential for bias with random-digit dialing is created by households with more than one phone number. However, this applies to only 2 percent of households, and these tend to be families with teenagers; therefore it is not likely to pose a problem in contacting the elderly citizen.

Hauk and Cox (1974) utilized random-digit dialing procedures as a preliminary screening device to select a particular sample. The purpose of the overall survey was to determine the relationships between face-to-face interviews, self-administered questionnaires, telephone interviews, and randomized response interviews. For screening, prior to the actual interview, phone numbers were randomly selected from a Chicago street address directory. The last two digits of the number were dropped and replaced by two random digits, thus insuring the possible inclusion of unlisted or unpublished telephone numbers. The screening interview consisted of questions regarding community services, information about each member of the household, and the respondent's address.

Twenty-seven percent of the telephone numbers were ineligible. (Forty to 50 percent ineligible is not unusual, but this depends on the stringency of the criterion for inclusion.) Most of the ineligibles were business, disconnected, and nonexistent numbers.

The completed response rate was 57 percent. Noncompletions included partial interviews and refusals; refusals constituted 35 percent of the noncompletions. The refusal rate is highest among unlisted numbers. Clearly, an attempt at rapport building, which was not made in the above research, would reduce the refusal rate. In most studies utilizing random-digit dialing an attempt is made to build rapport which lengthens the interview time. A short introduction may be substituted for rapport-building questions.

While random-digit dialing is more expensive than other telephone survey sampling techniques, Glasser and Metzger (1972) calculated the cost per completed interview to be $3.20. They estimated that gathering equivalent data door-to-door using a probability sample with clusters would have cost $10.00 to $15.00 per completed interview.

An important consideration in utilizing random-digit dialing is cost efficiency in relation to sampling error. The major advantage of the procedure is the inclusion of unlisted numbers (both unlisted by owner request and by delays in directory listing of new numbers). The major disadvantage is its added cost over directory sampling. Depending on the precision desired, the added cost of random-digit dialing may be a small gain in sampling precision per dollar of added cost.

Sudman (1973) suggested that a combination of random-digit dialing and directory sampling is more efficient and less expensive than random-digit dialing alone. One possible combination would be to select a random sample of telephone numbers from the phone directory and ignore the last three digits. The last three digits are then randomly generated. Such a procedure will increase the frequency of connection with a working number. Further, one can eliminate business exchanges and other non-household exchanges and thus increase the useful connection rate. There are variations on the combination, such as varying the number of digits to be randomly supplied. Any procedure which decreases the number of random digits would increase the sampling error and potential bias due to the increased probability of bypassing newly activated numbers.

Sampling based exclusively on telephone directories risks excluding up to one-third or more of black people, the separated and divorced, service workers, and urban residents, all of which are without phones or unlisted at much higher rates than other groups (Leuthold and Scheele, 1971). Residents of medium-sized towns, socially active people, professional and business people, and the aged are the most likely to be listed in a telephone directory (Leuthold and Scheele, 1971).

General Considerations

The degree of usefulness of a telephone interview depends on the purpose of the survey. The telephone is a useful screening device to establish a special sample which will then be interviewed face-to-face. For example, the American Foundation for the Blind wished to conduct a survey of blind persons (Sudman, 1967) and used a telephone screening procedure to establish its sample. Although there were problems with the datedness of the telephone directories, the subsequent face-to-face cooperation rate was 83 percent higher than in previous studies in the same urban locale in which face-to-face methods were used without prior telephone contact.

It has been suggested that a telephone interview must be shorter than other procedures. The National Opinion Research Council conducted a telephone interview survey dealing with physicians' attitudes (Sudman, 1967). The interviews averaged 90 minutes with an 80 percent completion rate.

How does the telephone affect response bias? Colombotos (1969) reported, in a comparison of telephone and face-to-face interviews, that the response differences were negligible: the telephone interviews were less distorted in the direction of social desirability than the face-to-face encounter. Thus, he supported the earlier suggestion that the more impersonal the method, the less distortion toward socially acceptable response patterns. Kegeles, Fink, and Kirscht (1969) compared the telephone survey to personal interviews in a national sample. They encountered only a 4 percent refusal rate utilizing long-distance telephoning. The information from the telephone interview was consistent with data gathered via personal interview.

Once the decision to utilize a telephone survey procedure (or any other method for that matter) is made, it is necessary to determine the best time to call to minimize noncompletions. Such a decision is partially dependent on the desired sample. One approach is to select a sample from a fixed-address source and call to determine the pattern of presence or absence during the last five days (Politz and Simmons, cited in Stephan and McCarthy, 1958). However, such a procedure would not likely elicit the cooperation currently that it did in 1958, due to concern over the legitimacy and intentions of the caller. It would be more useful simply to call at various times during the day to establish the times of highest success rate with that population. Clearly, failure to get an answer makes it necessary to call until response is received or a refusal given.

Falthzki (1972) attempted to determine the best time to telephone housewives and female heads of households. It was hypothesized that weekday morning calls would result in the most completions. He selected communities of approximately equal size, constituting a cross section of all income groups. He then divided the day from 9 A.M. to 10 P.M. into three time periods. An equal number of interviews were conducted for each time period over three weeks. Monday, Tuesday, Wednesday, and Thursday had the highest completion rates. Mornings had the highest completion rate followed by afternoons. Evenings had the highest noncompletion and refusal rates. It would seem necessary as part of a general pilot testing of the survey to include sampling different times of day and days of the week to optimize the completion rate.

The telephone interview is rather different from the face-to-face encounter or the mail questionnaire. Problems of rapport, possible inconvenience to the respondent, and lack of visual contact are all inherent in the telephone survey. Many of the difficulties in completing an interview relate to the personal nature of the questions. The interviewer cannot see the respondent's nonverbal reaction to the questions. The trade-off is that such impersonal contact may give a greater sense of privacy and anonymity and may reduce the distortion of social desirability. Party lines may inhibit honest responses, and this factor should be considered in telephone research.

The training and supervision of interviewers is an issue in any survey research. The interviewer's skill will affect the completion rate and quality of responses. Supervision in the telephone situation is easier than in the field. Extension lines may be connected to the interviewers' lines to enable a supervisor to periodically monitor interviewers and improve their ability to persuade reluctant respondents and to get honest responses. A daily checklist on each interviewer may be helpful in determining patterns of success and general productivity. Further, such a system would encourage interviewers to improve their performance and skills via supervisor feedback.

Kish (1965) has developed a system to evaluate, correct, and follow-up sources of nonresponse which may or may not be related to interviewer behavior. A series of notations may be recorded next to each noncompletion.

1. Not-at-Home (NAH). This may be related to the time of the call. Determination of a more appropriate time and the use of callbacks should be considered.

2. Temporarily Unavailable (TU). The respondent has deferred the interview, though not refused to participate. The individual may have been ill or too tired, or the phone line may have been busy. Setting up a time to call back is the appropriate response here.

3. Refusals (R). The course of action is dependent on the reason for the refusal which may be related to the type of questions in the interview, the technique of the interviewer, and the circumstances of the respondent. These should probably be classed as unobtainable interviews with no further attempt made. A high rate of refusals may suggest interviewer problems or the need to reconsider the survey procedures.

4. Incapacity or Inability (I). In this category are those respondents who, due to illness, are unable to be interviewed during the entire survey period. It is important to distinguish this group from

refusals in that refusals suggest procedural problems while incapacity is fixed and hence not ammendable to procedural variables.

Conclusion

This literature review supports the potential utility of the telephone as a survey tool, either alone or in combination with other techniques (e.g., as a screening device to preselect a particular sample). It is possible to minimize technique bias in ways that make the telephone a procedural competitor to more traditional techniques. Criticism of the telephone survey has traditionally focused on the selective characteristics associated with phone ownership. Such criticism is currently much less compelling than it once was due to the widespread increase in telephone households. Random-digit dialing provides a way of reducing bias due to delays in directory publication, unlisted numbers, and newly activated telephones. Additionally, the cost per interview is significantly lower with the telephone than with face-to-face interviews.

The telephone survey may offer a large advantage in survey work with the elderly. In New York State, for example, the (1 percent) Public Use Sample computer tapes of the 1970 Census indicated that 88 percent of all households headed by an older person have a telephone. By age groups, this number broke down into age 60–64, 90 percent; age 65–69, 89 percent; age 70–74, 88 percent; age 75+, 85 percent (total 60+, 88 percent).

The benefits of the telephone survey are relevant to survey work with the elderly. The rapidity of data gathering via telephone, relative to other techniques, is a major advantage in presenting the most current data. The use of older individuals as interviewers has multiple benefits: the availability of retired phone operators might present a training-technique advantage; the employment of older workers is a desirable goal in itself; the availability and flexibility of retired workers allow greater flexibility in working times; and the rapport advantage of the elderly interviewing the elderly is likely to increase the rate of completed interviews.

REFERENCES

Colombotos, J. 1969. Personal versus telephone interviews: effect on responses. *Public Health Reports* (September) 84:773–82.
Falthzki, A. M. 1972. When to make telephone interviews. *Journal of Marketing Research* 9:451–52.
Glasser, G. J., and Metzger, G. D. 1972. Random-digit dialing as a method of telephone sampling. *Journal of Marketing Research* 9:59–64.

Hauk, M., and Cox, M. 1974. Locating a sample by random-digit dialing. *Public Opinion Quarterly* (Summer):253–60.

Kegeles, S. S.; Fink, C. F.; and Kirscht, J. P. 1969. Interviewing a national sample by long distance telephone. *Public Opinion Quarterly* (Fall):412–19.

Kish, L. 1965. *Survey Sampling*. New York: John Wiley & Sons, Inc.

Leuthold, D. A., and Scheele, R. 1971. Patterns of bias in samples based on telephone directories. *Public Opinion Quarterly* (Summer):249–57.

Luck, D. J., and Wales, M. G. 1952. *Marketing Research*. New York: Prentice Hall, Inc.

Parten, M. 1950. *Surveys, Polls, and Samples: Practical Procedures*. New York: Harper & Brothers.

Stephan, F., and McCarthy, P. J. 1958. *Sampling Opinions—An Analysis of Survey Procedure*. New York: John Wiley & Sons, Inc.

Sudman, S. 1967. *Reducing the Cost of Surveys*. Chicago, Ill.: Adline Publishing Company.

Sudman, S. 1973. The uses of telephone directories for survey sampling. *Journal of Marketing Research* 10:204–7.

Uhl, K. P., and Schoner, B. 1969. *Marketing Research: Information Systems and Decision Making*. New York: John Wiley & Sons.

Wiseman, F. 1972. Methodologies bias in public opinion surveys. *Public Opinion Quarterly* (Spring):105–8.

9. Case VI. Developing a Regionwide Information System on Aging

Robert A. Solem

EDITOR'S NOTE: One of the hall-marks of a complex bureaucratic society is the use of factual information systematically gathered and assessed for lawmaking and administrative purposes. Solem shows clearly and in rich detail the problems confronted by state and regional agencies when they try to get their constituent units to gather data more systematically for planning purposes.

Solem's goal was to develop an instrument and a manual that would enable Area Agencies on Aging to obtain and coordinate available statistical data without using the complicated and expensive process of a household survey. However, it was difficult to persuade some of the offices to cooperate.

This case is particularly interesting because the author has described with sensitivity and clarity the issues and problems of negotiating the contract, entering the bureaucracy, and carrying out the work of the consultant.

AT a symposium held at the 27th annual meeting of the Gerontological Society, Spinetta and Hickey (1975) illuminated the problems of bridging research and application with metaphors from the computer and the kitchen. They compared the mind of the academic researcher to the digital computer and his approach to his profession to that of the gourmet cook, whereas the practitioner or program administrator was cast as the analog computer and the harried homemaker. The digital mode of processing translates its input into an arbitrary system of categories, and proceeds by abstract symbol manipulation. This mode is highly efficient and flexible but, unfortunately, tends to be increasingly removed from the continuous nature of the behavior or the conditions being studied. The analog computer, although considered less efficient and powerful for abstract problem solving, nonetheless preserves reality in its true continuity of time and space. The academic researcher as gourmet cook "does not enter the kitchen to cook unless he has previously worked out a meticulous menu, has searched in esoteric shops for ingredients, and has at least a full day to spend preparing the one meal"; the practitioner as harried homemaker has "little time for shopping, less time to plan a fine menu, and the least amount of time to spend in the kitchen actually cooking the meal."

These metaphors suggest two principal difficulties of the academic consultant. The consultant is both digital thinker and gourmet cook trying for a time to behave purposefully and usefully in the kitchen of the harried homemaker. As digital thinker, the consultant tries to communicate in a language and from an intellectual structure that the practitioner may not understand or may regard as irrelevant to the day-to-day demands of keeping the family fed. And, the practitioner does not have time to wait for the gastronomic masterpiece to emerge. Unless these incompatibilities are overcome, the consultantship may result in misunderstandings or frustrations for both parties.

OVERVIEW AND STATEMENT OF THE PROBLEM

My consultantship, undertaken in the summer of 1975, was with the Region X Office on Aging, Seattle, Washington. The major focus was on developing a regionwide information system that would contribute to the agency's capacity for comprehensive planning. The regional office perceived a need for such a data base that would provide for comprehensive planning for the region as a whole. Staff members were searching for a vehicle by means of which area agencies could supply them with sufficient area data to be translated into broader regional needs. The regional office, however, was not certain what data and what format would be useful and was therefore receptive to the possibility of outside consultation.

We will focus on those features of the consultantship that might be helpful to prospective consultants or, equally important, to agencies and administrators who use consultants. These kinds of analyses and introspections are timely, for consultants and consulting firms have been less effective than expected in solving the practical problems, improving the day-to-day operations, and insuring the long-term effectiveness of public service agencies. Indeed, it can be argued that their contributions are not nearly commensurate with their cost.

I have divided my consultantship into six phases, which reflect my own sense of movement through the experience, and, I believe, have application to many types of consultantships. These are negotiation, "immersion" and orientation, "pilot draft," field testing, revision, and preparation of the final instrument. Not all consultantships fc llow this pattern, but the format can serve as a model for those that are concerned with establishing or improving data systems. Recent themes of social program management have been evaluation and accountability. Thus, it is no accident that the objectives of many consultantships are the design and installation of data systems to document accountability and conduct evaluations.

Organizational Context

The organizational context of the consultantship was concerned with the roles, issues, and problems of the regional office and its relationship to the other administrative units of the Administration on Aging (AOA). The principal function of the regional office is to monitor its state offices, i.e., for Region X these are Washington, Oregon, Idaho, and Alaska. Monitoring consists of compiling a detailed assessment of the progress, during a given period, made by the state office in meeting the objectives contained in its state plan, as well as in performing functions mandated by federal regulations. Monitoring is a relatively formal process, utilizing an assessment instrument and well-defined procedures. The second major function of the regional office is to provide technical assistance in improving the operation of state offices, especially in areas of weakness uncovered by monitoring. In turn, the state offices are responsible for monitoring their respective area agencies.

Because of strong accountability overtones, relationships of region to state and state to area agencies are not always smooth. The Region X director has been vitally concerned with expanding the positive aspects of the regional role. He feels strongly that the region should be more than just a watchdog of the states. For example, the regional office wanted to increase the capacity for communicating the special and unique needs of Region X to the national office. It also wanted to identify and spearhead regionwide initiatives such as improving accessibility of services to isolated, rural elderly and improving coordination of Title III and Title VII social services. Another initiative was the analysis of "natural communities" and how they should be considered in developing service delivery networks.

A more general goal, as these examples suggest, was to establish a capability for comprehensive planning at the regional level. State and area offices are required to produce formal plans, the preparation of which is often an unnerving yearly ritual. The region serves its monitoring and technical assistance functions without a comparable plan. Comprehensive planning, while perhaps not formalized as a yearly plan, would be directed toward identifying and prioritizing regional needs. "Need" at the regional level may cut across service categories. By "need," the regional director meant something in addition to the direct provision of materials and specific services to older persons, such as meals, transportation, chore service, health screening, or inexpensive legal assistance. From a regional perspective, the needs of the elderly may be concerned with strategies of identifying and training providers, building relationships with and monitoring vendors, producing reliable estimates on the number of trained personnel required for a sound service delivery network, or promoting research in how to persuade proud, independent elderly persons to accept services without feeling stigmatized.

Personal Orientation of Consultant

When I learned about the Gerontological Society's summer consultantship program, I was in the second year of a lectureship with the School of Social Work, University of Washington. This was my first position after receiving the Ph.D. in psychology from the University of California, San Francisco, where I had been a trainee in the Human Development Program. My area of specialization was age-related changes in capacity for information processing. At the School of Social Work I taught courses in social research design and methodology, in basic research statistics, and in the processes of aging. Like many academic gerontologists who did their predoctoral research in a laboratory environment, my knowledge was long on theory and short on practice. I had little direct knowledge of the social program aspect of gerontology. In this respect, I am probably similar to the majority of students in human development programs associated with theoretical research on adult life and aging in the United States. Yet, social and health services, including income maintenance and retirement programs, vitally help shape the way of life of older citizens.

In recent years there has been more emphasis, even, grudgingly, in academia, on the application of social science knowledge to real-life problems. In gerontology in particular (and this is an aspect that makes it such a challenging field), there is a natural kinship between the applied and the theoretical. The study of gerontology is often the study of phenomena that translate directly into problems of living and adaptation, and, as a field of study or as an applied career, it puts one in contact with one of the profoundest areas of human experience. Every society has had to come to terms with the phenomenon of aging and with the role and status of the elderly in its social order. Indeed, one way of comparing cultures is to study their accommodation to the aging process and the elderly. Because of dramatic increases in the average life span and the percentage of elderly persons in Western industrial society, interest in the aging process and the needs of the old has greatly increased.

As a frame of reference, I support a developmental approach to the life span that acknowledges every part as being important and as possessing tasks and rewards appropriate to it. The overall objective of legislation and programs for the elderly should be the creation of an environment that insures the essentials for building and maintaining a productive later life. Old age should *not* be regarded as a wasteland! The often-overlooked definition of welfare is a state of being or doing well. A true welfare program, in spite of the bad connotation that word has assumed, is one which promotes this state in the people it serves.

The purpose, then, of the Older Americans Act (OAA) and the administrative and service structure that it has spawned ought to be the building of a foundation for well-being in our older population. A developmental approach makes one aware that a state of well-being is different for each phase of the life span: it is not the same for the child as it is for the young adult or for the adult in midcareer or in the phases of later life. Gerontological research should examine what constitutes the possibilities for well-being under the various conditions of later life. This understanding then must be translated into program planning and administration.

THE CONSULTANTSHIP EXPERIENCE

Negotiation Phase

Perhaps the most critical phase in the consultantship is the negotiation phase. In the well-executed negotiation phase, the consultant and the administrator work out carefully the mutual expectations for the consultantship. The negotiation period should yield a well-specified product and some assurance that the product will actually be usable and applicable to the problem.

A plan of work should be indicated. Both sides should be tough-minded at this point. The consultant must resist a product that he suspects is either unworkable or that he is not qualified to deliver. The administrator must insist on a product that will be applicable to his problem-solving and decision-making roles. The administrator should not bow to the "superiority of knowledge" of the consultant, saying, "Well, do what you can, or give it your best shot."

In spite of the best efforts of both parties, a workable product may not

be attainable within the given time frame. Compromise, of course, is necessary. The administrator's original product specification may have to be altered as a result of reworking the problem with the consultant. The consultant must be prepared to compromise some of the purity of his academic methodology and depart from his conception of an ideal product, or ideal plan, to one that is workable within the program environment. Above all else, the consultant must not impose on the administrator a product that will not be useful just because it reflects the consultant's own knowledge.

The context within which the consultantship will be conducted should be reviewed. The administrator begins with the idea that if he had "this" he could do "that." "This" may be a certain kind of management technique, a regular report containing certain information, or some other tool; "that" might be the revitalization of a program, better monitoring of progress, or better planning. The consultant's first task is to carefully review the product desired and its purpose, so that he can examine the administrator's motivation for a consultantship. A good consultant should convince the administrator to evaluate carefully his own thinking and perceptions about his organizational problems. It is unwise for the consultant to say, at the end of the project, "Well, what you wanted to do wasn't really possible anyway." Such a modus operandi will not build bridges between the academic and the applied world.

At the outset the consultant may state he is not certain of the outcome or suggest that the administrator think about another approach or product which he has more confidence will produce the desired results. More study may be required before a final product and plan can be specified. One of the consultant's principal contributions is critical thinking. If the administrator holds firm (or stubbornly clings) to his original view of the problems and the role of the consultant, then the consultant should seriously consider whether he should be there at all.

It is best if the consultant can create a climate of dialogue where the administrator independently realizes the need for a new course or a new product. In other words, diplomacy is preferred over the pronouncement of the expert. It is very dangerous for the consultant in this negotiation stage to assert, perhaps in frustration, his intellectual superiority—"I'm the expert here, and I'm the one who possesses the intellectual tool-kit with which to operate on your problems." Such an attitude is precisely the wrong stance, likely to turn the consultantship into a game of one-upmanship.

The consultant, to be effective, must have the cooperation of all the agency personnel from whom he must obtain material or information. Steps to secure this cooperation must be taken at the outset. The administrator should set up the appropriate introductions to protect the credibility of the consultantship; he should also promote the purpose of the consultantship to other levels of the organization.

The personnel who will be most affected by any changes in the organization brought about by the consultantship should be allowed to provide input. For example, a new data system may effect changes in the way staff workers do their jobs. Staff should feel they have some part in helping to formulate and approve such changes. There are bound to be misconceptions and apprehensions where change is involved. The consultant must be a diplomat, but the administrator must make every effort to smooth the way for the consultant. The success of a consultantship depends as much on the organization's response and cooperation as on the consultant's expertise and ability.

The negotiation phase of my consultantship began when, after receiving notification of the Gerontological Society's program, I met with the regional and deputy regional directors of the Region X Office on Aging for an interview. I proposed the consultantship as a no-lose proposition, as the Gerontological Society would be paying my stipend. The agency turned that into a possible no-win proposition; because I would be taking their time and occupying space, the directors wanted some assurance that whatever I undertook should yield for them a commensurate benefit. They wanted to know what I had to offer; by that they meant not an advanced degree or specialized knowledge in the abstract but something that would contribute to their effectiveness as a regional office. At question was my potential to contribute to a large-scale federal organization that had responsibility for managing public funds and overseeing programs.

They proposed that I develop an instrument to provide their office with baseline data for identifying in a systematic and reliable manner the real needs of the elderly of Region X. I responded that there already were a number of needs assessment instruments as well as an extensive literature on needs assessment methodology. In fact, the Administration on Aging (aoa) had funded several studies directed towards producing better needs assessment methodologies and monitoring techniques for area agencies. They replied that these instruments were too sophisticated and complicated for the kinds of largely rural, low-budget area agencies typical of Region X. The existing instruments simply were not suitable for their purposes.

They proceeded to elaborate on the desired product. The data would be gathered at the area agency level and transmitted via the state agencies to the regional office where they would be aggregated in some fashion and interpreted to supply the prioritized list of needs. The data sources would have to be available, then, to area agency personnel. These sources would have to be fairly reliable and efficient, straightforward and unsophisticated. The instrument should not require technical expertise to complete or statistical expertise to interpret. In order to assure the cooperation of area agency personnel, the benefit of the instrument would have to be obvious. There would have to be provisions for information feedback to the area agencies or they would regard it as a waste of time. Finally, they did not want me to create a totally new instrument but rather a hybrid developed from existing data collection instruments and routines already being used by one or more area agencies. They proposed I assemble the most useful items and features from local instruments and make this enterprise uniform and regionwide.

I do not believe I was firm enough during the negotiation period. Given the rather idealistic framework that I outlined previously, I had the desire to contribute where I could to make the operation of the regional office more effective. Thus, I was disposed to view their request without a lengthy critique, without exploring with them at length the relationship between a baseline data instrument and the prioritization of needs. I hoped that the designation of the product was sufficiently broad for some working room. I was uneasy with the idea of a modest instrument, hastily assembled from materials supposedly at hand, yielding the raw material for sound comprehensive planning at the regional level.

Orientation

Immersion consists of an intense but time-limited encounter with the corpus and spirit of an agency while retaining one's essential identity as the consultant. One needs to question sympathetically and listen to a number of staff persons, to take part in meetings if invited, to get a feel for the routines of the organization, and to understand the concerns of the staff. Immersion is not limited to encounters with staff. The consultant should also become familiar with all available written material such as legislation, regulations, and working papers relative to the establishment and purposes of the agency; recent papers or other work of staff members; and organizational charts, handbooks, manuals, and tools used by the staff in their day-to-day operations. Immersion is essential for gaining perspective and background, and it should help the consultant avoid the egregious errors of fact or interpretation that can mar or destroy the credibility of his product.

However, the term immersion suggests alternatives to becoming absorbed in the empathetic study of the agency, notably, "baptism" and "drowning." Ordinarily, neither is a desirable outcome of immersion. Baptism signifies a conversion in which the consultant adopts the values, approaches, concerns, and procedures of the agency as his own. A consultantship is not a traineeship; a critical stance must be maintained.

The activities of immersion, especially its social and participatory dimensions, can take over and dominate the consultantship. It is such a pleasant way to spend one's time. Staff enjoy discussing their work and taking slightly longer coffee breaks. Such interaction is also an opportunity for "defanging" the consultantship. Every day different points of view, new material, and fresh insights are revealed, until one figuratively drowns in a welter of conflicting ideas and incompatible proposals.

The best defense against the harmful aspects of immersion is to remember that this phase is not an end in itself. One should begin almost immediately spending some time each day making notes toward a first draft of the instrument. Also, the consultant should write a short critique of the day as a way of organizing and personalizing the information amassed. Immersion as an occasional activity will continue throughout the consultantship; immersion as a consuming activity must be time-limited by the task of drafting a test instrument. An initial testable draft of the product should be completed by the halfway mark (preferably earlier) of the consultantship.

At the beginning of the consultantship, the regional office staff were finalizing their work objectives for fiscal year 1976. I participated, by invitation, in staff meetings devoted to hammering out the final particulars of the plan and of individual responsibilities for these objectives. These meetings provided insight into the work styles of the regional staff. The environment was very different from academia. The vocabulary, the emphasis, the way of structuring work time, and the relationships among staff (both formal and informal) were all areas of difference. There are, of course, profound areas of similarity. Reading, digesting, writing, and attending conferences are basic to both domains. But, at the time, I was much more struck by the differences than the similarities.

All in all, I felt I handled immersion fairly well. I undertook a work schedule similar to that of the staff although, because of the short time frame of the consultantship, I usually arrived earlier and stayed considerably later. This schedule was necessary because I had to spend considerable time assimilating essential background material. For the first time, I encountered the annual report of the Special Senate Committee on Aging of the United States Senate and read the OAA in its entirety as a piece of legislation. These are documents with which every gerontologist should be familiar. They should be as much a part of his professional stock as the *Journal of Gerontology,* Eisdorfer and Lawton's *The Psychology of Adult Development and Aging,* or Baltes and Schaie's *Life Span Developmental Psychology,* the fare of the academic as gourmet. In other words, I had to put in extra time just to do homework I should have done as a graduate student.

During this phase, I reviewed all the material sent to the regional office from area agencies relevant to their data collection and information systems, both formal and informal. A letter, signed by the director, requesting such material had been mailed to the approximately 30 area agencies in May. Unfortunately, very few area agencies sent any material, and what was sent related chiefly to the collection of compliance data on the kinds and numbers of people being served by vendor agencies. Because the request for materials lay outside the reporting requirements of area agencies, the regional director could not (nor did he wish to) apply negative sanctions against nonresponsive agencies. One area agency reported on a needs assessment survey conducted through a local senior newsletter. Several others were also using limited surveys to obtain a more detailed assessment of the needs and problems of their elderly than was required for their annual area plan and compliance statistics.

Overall, these instruments did not contain the raw materials for a satisfactory regional instrument. The chief inadequacy was that they were not directed toward their target population as a whole. All elderly not in contact with the service delivery system did not contribute to the system's measures. Those not counted perhaps constitute a group more in need and more isolated than those from whom or about whom information had been obtained.

At this point, about two weeks into the consultantship, I suggested to the director that the basic issue of the consultantship was whether the average area agency possessed the sophistication to provide even rudimentary figures for any instrument that went beyond target population information available in the 1970 census or vendor reports. I further observed that many area agencies appeared to lack the capacity to assess the reliability of these reports. Much of the data in some area plans consisted of "guesstimates" (a phrase I heard around the regional office with some frequency). A guesstimate is a "seat-of-the-pants" estimate based on intuition, reading tea leaves, etc. An authentic statistic is a "best estimate" arrived at by following established principles of sampling, data collection, and analysis. But that is not its only virtue relative to the guesstimate. A proper statistic has a confidence interval associated with it that allows one to determine the magnitude of expected error of the statistic. It permits the planner to build in a rational degree of flexibility or margin of safety appropriate to the quality of the estimate.

It seemed that the most important data need of the area agencies was a profile of their target population as a whole. They had to find ways of learning about those persons who had "slipped through the cracks," and of measuring the extent and the characteristics of this population. By asserting that knowledge about the characteristics of the target population was a basic issue, I was redefining somewhat the regional director's original request for a needs assessment instrument. The deputy director was supportive of this change in emphasis, although the regional director showed some resistance. A tough negotiator, he was reluctant to back away from a product that he felt was essential to developing a forward-looking, responsive regional office.

During the third week of the consultantship, I visited three of the four State Offices on Aging (SOA) in the region to discuss the development of the instrument. In general, they agreed with my assessment of the limited data collection capacity of area agency personnel and their inadequate information about their target population. However, they were generally supportive of the area agency personnel, who had the difficult job of trying to coordinate and improve inadequate service delivery systems.

I asked state offices what kinds of information about the local elderly population would be the most useful for the day-to-day work of area agencies. Information on housing, living situations, transportation, access to medical services, and numbers of elderly with difficulty performing the activities of daily living, as well as an age-by-sex breakdown of the 60-plus population were cited. Also mentioned were the characteristics of those who were in their late fifties and their preparedness for aging.

After returning from my state visits, I decided to develop an instrument that dealt with assembling a target population profile at the area agency level. The unsolved problems were the data sources and the data collection method. Data sources are classified as primary or secondary. An example of a primary source is the older person himself. However, a methodologically rigorous survey employing primary sources is difficult to carry out. Most locally conducted "seat-of-the-pants" surveys have serious methodological flaws when used as estimates of an overall population. A comprehensive survey that reaches all members of the target population can be very expensive. For example, in Oregon's Lane County a systematic outreach program funded by ACTION had been contacting the hard-to-reach elderly for the previous two years. VISTA volunteers (who lived in the area and, therefore, knew both whom they were seeking—the old couple at the end of the dirt road—and who could establish sufficient credibility and rapport for effective information gathering) had, by their own estimates, reached 12 percent of the elderly over 65 in their district at a cost of nearly $100,000. Such an expensive method of gathering planning data is obviously not practical regionwide on an ongoing basis.

Secondary sources of data are tables and figures in already existing reports. These have already been collected from primary sources by other organizations for their own planning, monitoring, or evaluation. The best known and most used secondary source is the United States Census. However, as a basis for planning, these figures may be out of date, especially in the later years of the decade. The 1970 census established that persons 65 or older comprised 9.8 percent of the overall population. The national estimate for 1977 is 10.6 percent. If a planner uses the 1970 figures instead of the more recent percentage, he will underestimate the number of elderly in his area by almost 8 percent. For instance, in a population of 100,000 the difference between 9.8 percent (9,800) and 10.6 percent (10,600) is 800 persons.

The chief advantage of secondary sources is that the data do not have to be collected. It is far less expensive to transfer a figure from a report than it is to conduct a rigorous survey. A corresponding disadvantage is the lack of control over the methodology involved in the original data collection ("garbage in, garbage out," as the computer people say). The material in any given report was formulated for specific purposes and may not match the items and categories needed for another report. For example, 65 is the age for Social Security; for OAA benefits it is age 60.

Pilot Draft of the Instrument

In the fourth week, I prepared a brief interim report covering these issues. The regional director felt I was slipping further away from developing a technique for determining the "real prioritized needs" of the region, but he agreed that I continue in the current direction.

I began assembling a preliminary draft of the profile instrument and decided to utilize secondary data sources. The regional staff agreed that it would be constructive for area agencies to explore sources of data other than the United States Census and standard reports giving "national figures," based on studies conducted in other parts of the country. We wanted to determine which, if any, local sources (such as the community college, employment security office, local planning agencies, or local businesses) were routinely collecting information about the elderly. We also wanted to determine if area agency personnel had contacted these institutions and were using information from them. Or were area agency personnel sharing their own information about the elderly with these agencies? The instrument I was developing might answer these questions, and a draft emerged rather quickly after they had been considered.

It should be emphasized that constructing the instrument may be the least difficult part of the data system. An instrument is simply a guide to collecting information; it provides a format for putting down figures. Drafting an instrument may be the work of one afternoon; making it work—quite another matter—may take months or even years.

The instrument consists of a set of items, each pertaining to a distinct characteristic of the person over 60 in the geographical area served by the agency. Each item consists of a set of response categories that relate to the important differences among these persons, for instance, living arrangements. Responses might be: living alone, living with spouse, living with children as head of household, living with children where the child is head of the household, living with other relatives with no children or spouse present, living with unrelated others. I decided that the most useful responses would be the actual number of persons, rather than the percentage of persons, in the elderly population fitting each category. By knowing the number of persons who were affected rather than the percentage, the user of the instrument would have a better idea of the magnitude of the problem. The preliminary draft of the instrument completed the third phase of the consultantship.

Field Testing

Field testing occupied the next several weeks. Originally, we planned to send the instrument to a random sample of area agencies where personnel would complete it and return it with their comments. Instead, I decided to personally field-test the instrument in a sample of agencies. This was necessary because I would be asking area agency personnel to cultivate secondary sources of data in the community. I wanted to assess the availability of local sources in these communities and to ascertain whether the form of their data fitted the requirements and format of my draft instrument.

Field testing took approximately two days per site: approximately one-half day setting up contacts and the remainder in data gathering sessions. Included in the itinerary were local service agencies such as Community Action Programs, the Employment Security Office, the Public Assistance Office, the housing authorities for each county in the Planning and Service Area of the area agency, the Bureau of Motor Vehicles, community colleges, law-enforcement agencies, city and county planning offices, and the public health departments. A staff member of the area agency accompanied me.

Generally, I found people to be very receptive to my requests for information and to the general purpose of my inquiry. Most of these agencies already had data systems (ranging from rudimentary to fairly sophisticated) that monitored their clients and operations. Typically, they did not keep data on the elderly as a separate group; their information was independent of age categories. For example, a housing authority or city planner might know the percentage of substandard housing in a given area but not be able to tell how many of these units were inhabited by older persons. Even when they did collect information by age groups, their response categories were incomplete. For example, the Employment Security Office had data on the number of unemployed elderly still seeking work but not on the number of elderly (65 plus) employed full-time or part-time, as volunteers, or retired (i.e., not presently seeking work). Local law enforcement agencies had information on the crime rate categorized by type but no data on how many of the victims were elderly. Nonetheless, most of the items were filled out in part or in whole. This phase of the consultantship was certainly educational for me. As an experimental gerontologist trained to create his own data in the laboratory under controlled settings, I was gaining a perspective on the nature and role of data in the "real world."

I promoted the idea of sharing data among local agencies and organizations and viewed this as mutually beneficial for planning, advocacy, and avoiding duplication of errors. Incidentally, this exercise served as a way for the staff person who accompanied me to establish rapport with, and in some cases to be introduced to, other public service personnel in the community. Several years ago area agencies were much newer, much less known entities in the community than they are today. This data collection exercise was a way in which local personnel could become acquainted with other agencies and their missions, perhaps making these persons more sensitive to the elderly among their own client or target populations.

I returned to the regional office feeling better about the progress of the consultantship than in retrospect I probably should have. This was due in part to my own learning experience about the operation of small communities. However, the fundamental issue of the area agencies' capability to identify and use local secondary sources for baseline data was essentially unresolved. While local information systems did exist, and while local agencies were receptive, to a point, to sharing information, the data were not easily transferable. Information systems tend to be idiosyncratic and incomplete. Documentation and form completion are not the favorite pastimes of service providers. For the secondary sources to be truly useful to the regional office, these agencies would have to modify and augment their own data systems. I did not dare to risk their good will with this kind of a request during the pilot stage.

Revision and Preparation of Final Product

Based on the field experience, the instrument underwent further modification. Several items were deleted, others were simplified, and most cross tabulations (an item which asked for the number of individuals meeting all of several criteria, for example, over 75, female, living alone, and in substandard housing) were eliminated. Such information might be very desirable but simply unattainable from local secondary sources.

The problem with a structured instrument is that it predefines the areas of response. The regional office, however, was interested in determining an area agency's uniqueness as part of its attempt to understand how Region X was itself unique or different from other regions. To structure items in advance to include all characteristics of the target population that might be aspects of uniqueness would make the instrument unwieldy. Therefore, an open-ended question which asked an area agency to describe any special condition or situation of their elderly population was added to the instrument. Open-ended questions, however, require a response, and it is difficult to code this response without doing grave injustice to the content of the answer.

As part of the revision, I drafted a procedures manual based on my field experiences with secondary data sources. This manual gave examples of specific sources that might be contacted for information. It also provided some techniques by which seemingly incompatible information could be translated into the figures requested by the instrument. Information on some of the items was originally collected by local offices then transmitted to and maintained by the state administrative body. I felt that the soa could best negotiate with these other state administrative bodies for exchange of information. Therefore, the items on the instrument were explicitly divided into area and state office spheres of responsibility. This seemed a straightforward solution to some of the items, but at that time I had not tried to retrieve information from a state computer. The instrument, with these changes, was now in final form and titled a *Target Population Profile for Planning and Service Areas.*

OUTCOMES: SHORT–TERM FATE OF THE INSTRUMENT

The final report to the Gerontological Society contained a matter-of-fact account of the consultantship, focusing on the development, testing, and modification of the instrument. It ended with the optimistic note that plans were under way for a regionwide trial data collection with the revised version of the instrument. The instruments and procedures manual were sent to all area agencies under the director's signature. This mailing occurred several weeks after my departure, and I was unfortunately unable to advocate personally for area agency cooperation or to resolve difficulties. Furthermore, the regional office did not have the authority to compel area agencies to assume this data gathering role because it was not mandated as national AOA policy.

To be brief, the trial was not successful. Several area agencies submitted very incomplete documents and the rest, quite simply, ignored the instrument. Largely, this was their way of coping with what they regarded as one more unwelcome burden from "higher up." Informally, they acknowledged it might be helpful to know about items covered in the instrument, but they maintained they had insufficient staff resources to devote to it. Some area agencies also felt that too much effort and perhaps risk would be required to develop data exchange agreements with other local agencies. Thus, the only data on which to base a regional profile came from my personally conducted pilot test.

On balance, the consultantship demonstrated that the majority of area agencies at that time were unable or unwilling to engage in systematic data collection beyond the compiling of basic information required for their area plan and minimal vendor compliance monitoring. For the data to be genuinely useful to the regional office, the response from the areas and states to the instrument would have had to be virtually universal; otherwise, compiling the contributions into a unified profile would produce an unreliable, distorted picture of the region. It was not felt worth further investment of regional staff time to implement and manage a reporting system that would require considerable informal arm-twisting to produce even minimal response and that would still not serve to meet its purpose. Since at that time the regional office could not rely on periodic and consistent input from area agencies, comprehensive planning at the regional level would have to proceed by a different strategy.

OUTCOMES: PERSONAL AND GERONTOLOGICAL

In the spring of 1976, the Washington State Legislature enacted landmark legislation: Substitute House Bill 1316, the Senior Citizens Services Act (SCSA). This act established state policy on the development of programs to meet the support needs of vulnerable and frail elderly citizens through the creation and/or expansion of community-based services. The goal was to assure sufficient resources to restore or maintain elderly individuals at their highest level of independence. This act initially appropriated $1.9 million, matched by $3.8 million in federal funds, beyond the regular OAA appropriations to support a demonstration year (calendar year 1976). Authorized services included adult day care and treatment, night services, chores, home repair, health screening and evaluation, health education, and expansion of the Title VII nutrition program. This legislation designated area agencies, under the overall administration of the SOA, to manage SCSA funds at the local level, beginning with a sound local planning process. Each area agency was to determine the mix of services and level of support to best meet the objectives of the act in its own area. Then each agency was to identify, contract with, and monitor service providers and evaluate the usage, cost, and impact of the services delivered.

Legislative concern that their appropriations be efficiently and effectively spent led to an evaluation research project housed with the Office of Research of the Department of Social and Health Services. This is the umbrella agency that also contains the SOA. A hard-nosed, independent study of the area agencies' performance as local managers was conducted.

It is not within the scope of this chapter to present in detail the methodology and findings of the evaluation. However, it did uncover serious operational weaknesses in the majority of area agencies. They did not follow a systematic planning process leading to optimum program selection. Their method of vendor identification and selection was not rigorous. They did not set up adequate accountability and monitoring systems for vendors under contract. They did not monitor the per unit cost, quality, or coverage of services. Not all area agencies were deficient in these areas. To their credit, some began responding to the need for greater accountability in reporting systems by recruiting staff with basic research and statistical skills. These findings have begun to change the indifferent attitudes toward information systems at the local level. Funding for SCSA was renewed by the legislature for the 1977–79 biennium after assurances that progress toward greater accountability and cost-effectiveness of services was being made.

My role in these events has been as an interested observer and informal consultant. On completion of the Region X consultantship, I was employed as the research director of the Community-Based Care Project by the same Office of Research that later conducted the SCSA evaluation. This is a federally funded project addressing the organization and financing of long-term care for low-income, physically impaired adults (chiefly elderly) who require some degree of formal medical and nonmedical supportive services to maintain an independent living situation. This is one of several major research and development projects for which the bulk of funding supports geographically limited demonstration program. The budget also supports research which has the general objective of assessing the program's operation and accomplishments and of projecting its usefulness as a model of cost-effective, community-based supportive care.

As research director, I have supervised at various phases of the study a staff of data system developers, data collectors, coders, clerical workers, and data processing specialists. In designing and maintaining the several data systems, I have worked closely with state and local program personnel. I feel strongly that my role as research director and my contributions to the planning and interpretation of the SCSA evaluation have been positively influenced by the consultantship experience. Some of the contacts I made in the local aging network facilitated setting up data collection systems in the project communities. I also had a better idea of what would "sell" and what could not in terms of making reporting demands of local providers. The staff have been able to create workable and adequate (if not perfect) systems.

A multiyear project, the final round of data collection is (as I write this) about to be placed in the computer in preparation for creating the final report. The research staff have produced several in-house interim reports. It is gratifying that, increasingly, their findings are being used by task force and planning bodies of the department. These preliminary analyses have been increasingly identified and used by their staff as a principal and sometimes sole source of reliable and pertinent data on which to make projections and weigh alternatives in the planning and reform of adult and aging services.

My relationship with the regional office continues to be cordial. The director has followed with interest the response of the soa and the area agencies to the demands for accountability. Ironically, in view of the emphasis (in hindsight) I placed on the negotiation phase of the consultantship, it is apparent that in this particular case the "negotiated" product may have been the least important component. The lesson of subsequent events indicates that few consultantships are isolated occurrences—either for the agency, the larger environment of human services (within which the agency performs its roles), or the consultant.

REFERENCE

Spinetta, J., and Hickey, T. 1975. Aging and higher education: the institutional response. *The Gerontologist* 15:431–35.

10. Case VII. Research and Practice: Detroit

James O. Carpenter

EDITOR'S NOTE: The Older Americans Act requires that Area Agencies on Aging "tap and pool" resources of groups and organizations in their bailiwicks. Using available resources is an admirable goal often set forth by legislative and administrative bodies, but the implementation of law, regulation, and guidelines to reach this goal is a complicated process. Thus, a common theme of a number of the cases herein is the need for both agency personnel and social scientists to understand the interorganizational dynamics of social delivery systems.

Carpenter's experience as a research fellow in interorganizational relations entailed devising criteria to be used to evaluate service contracts and to develop standards for new contracts under consideration. The research instrument he developed could be used as an evaluative tool that would ensure the application of universal rather than idiosyncratic criteria.

Carpenter shows how the agency staff's day-to-day concerns about interorganizational networks can be translated into an approachable conceptual problem whose solution can be communicated to agency staff so that policy issues are concretely linked to service delivery. This case is a good example of how theoretical ideas can be usefully applied to agency problems.

THE need for a holistic approach to the development of gerontological knowledge, including a multidisciplinary view of aging as process and old age as status, is matched by the necessity for an integration of substantive and theoretical knowledge with programmatic concerns of providers involved in the planning, design, and provision of services for older persons. Such factors as the different orientations of service providers and social scientists serve at times to reduce the essential interplay between emerging empirical and theoretical advances in the field and applied and programmatic issues in the community. Moreover, the institutional locus of the investigator and that of the service provider, including norms governing professional behavior, may also influence the rate of dissemination of knowledge from the academic environment into service delivery systems and the movement of investigators into research within the community.

Nevertheless, there are some interesting trends, which, over the next few years, may be conducive to an increasingly viable interplay between the interests of the social scientist and those of service professionals. Such trends may lead to an increased role for the social gerontologist and other scientists in more applied research endeavors. Included are the following factors. (1) The shift from acute to chronic diseases in terms of the prevalence of health problems associated with the maturing demographic profile. These changes require the development and application of behavioral science techniques to the understanding of illness and health-related behavior in the older population. It is consistent with the continued development of such fields as social epidemiology, social gerontology, and medical sociology. (2) Requirements for what might be considered an analytic epidemiology of aging; that is, there is an increasing need for research which moves beyond descriptive studies to analytic approaches designed to define factors predicting need in the older population and then to develop programmatic approaches to impact upon such factors. (3) Changes in patterns of service delivery and associated interest in research into inter- and intraorganizational dynamics. These changing patterns of service delivery, together with concerns regarding organizational accountability, and increasing consumerism suggest a unique area for inquiry by social scientists—inquiry which will also be of importance to improved service delivery. (4) Increasing interest in adult socialization, including professional socialization and developmental issues in the later years of life. (5) Increasing visibility and numbers of older persons. This factor may stimulate the increasing application of scientific skills to areas of applied significance in gerontology. (6) Increasing emphasis in aging agencies and other groups, including the gerontological research community, on evaluative studies, including the development of quasi-experimental and experimental evaluative designs and their application. (7) The apparent reduction of career opportunities in traditional academic fields will result in an increasing demand for and challenge to persons with sound methodological and disciplinary training who can apply this expertise to the applied substantive issues within the field of gerontology. (8) The consumer thrust in the area of service delivery may also serve to increase the allocation of attention to understanding community dynamics, help-seeking behavior, and organizational relationships. The increasingly visible consumer role is also associated with organizational demands for accountability and the application of methodological skills to evaluative studies within the community. (9) Older persons will appear increasingly within the service delivery system, and providers will be called upon to use the best available gerontological knowledge. This should stimulate interest in the dissemination of new knowledge in the field of gerontology.

Although these and related factors would be expected to enhance the relationship between service providers and investigators, such an emergent synthesis is not, for the most part, readily apparent on an institutionalized basis. Nevertheless, there are emerging areas of applied disciplinary research reflective of the above trends. These include medical or health sociology, behavioral sciences in public health, health gerontology, thanatology, social gerontology, and other specialities each of which suggests the importance of the application of major disciplinary concepts, models, and theoretical perspectives and methodological skills to areas of applied significance, e.g., medicine, public health, death and dying, and aging. Moreover, although one may speak of the sociology *of* aging or sociology *in* aging, just as one may analytically distinguish the relationship between other disciplinary fields and their applied contexts, in reality, the relationship between the investigator and the applied area is more complex. More specifically, it is sometimes maintained that the contribution of the scholar to an applied area may be enhanced through the study *of* that particular area. Within this perspective the models and theories of the discipline may be extended into the applied sphere with some possible programmatic implications for the future. The major goal, however, is the development of an original contribution to knowledge. The potential difficulties held to be implicit in becoming a disciplinary specialist *within* an applied sphere, on the other hand, have been noted by a number of scholars. Some investigators suggest that such involvement may result in becoming disciplinarily estranged and removed from the development of knowledge by virtue of becoming heavily invested in the immediate front-line problem-solving context of the service agency. While this perspective relative to studies *in* or *of* an applied domain may be analytically helpful, in reality investigators involved in applied research may find that the distinction is not particularly meaningful. Moreover, distinctions relative to one's being *in* or *of* an applied substantive domain may serve to reduce the necessary interdisciplinary perspective required for the development of a holistic gerontology. The prospect that traditional academic opportunities within disciplinary fields may continue to be reduced by societal processes increases the prospect for the involvement of disciplinary scholars in applied research. Such a trend would also be consistent with an increase in the number and quality of applied investigators in gerontology.

Although general demographic and inter- and intradisciplinary trends appear to imply not only the need for the intersection of academic and programmatic concerns but also an increasing likelihood of such an emergent synthesis, there have been few operational efforts to link the perspective of the investigator with the more practical operational interests of service providers. The national gerontological fellowship program would appear to be one of the few endeavors designed to enhance this interaction. The program contributes to meeting the needs of the fellow by providing increased insight into the programmatic sphere, including potential areas for research in gerontology, while simultaneously providing the agency with the expertise of the gerontological fellow in meeting informational needs and emerging agency problems and in providing a broader knowledge framework within which to view gerontological dynamics. The fellowship program of the Gerontological Society, sponsored by the Administration on Aging (aoa) provided a unique prism within which to see the diverse reflections cast by the different worlds of the scholar and agency administrator.

The Setting

Fellowship activities were conducted in conjunction with the Detroit–Wayne County Area Agency on Aging. Detroit, the fifth largest city in the United States, provided a variety of options for fellowship involvement. The fact that the Area Agency on Aging (aaa) addressed both city and county service areas served to highlight the complex jurisdictional entities involved and suggested a useful environment within which to examine interorganizational relationships. The complexity of service need (frequently defined in terms of objectified need or demand) when related to jurisdictional levels and service functions raised additional issues of interest to both fellow and agency director. Involvement in these issues also resulted in a fairly rapid socialization into the "real world" of the local agency and surrounding community.

The population of Wayne County is 2,668,809 of which 360,000 are over 60 years of age. Thirty-one percent of the latter group are 60–64 years of age, 25 percent are 65–69, and 19 percent are 70–74. Persons over 75 years make up the remaining 25 percent. More significant, in terms of potential service demand, is the fact that 63,000 persons, or approximately 18 percent of those persons aged 60 years of age or above, have incomes below the poverty level.

In 1970, the population of Detroit was 1,511,482—a 10 percent decline from 1960. With respect to selected subcultural groups in the Detroit–

Wayne County service area, 18 percent of the population over 60 years of age are black, 7 percent are Spanish language, 2 percent are Oriental, 2 percent are American Indian, and the remainder are white. Finally, although Detroit's population declined by 10 percent between 1960 and 1970, a 12 percent increase was reported for the general standard metropolitan statistical area including suburban counties (Macomb, Oakland, and Wayne).

These figures suggest that Detroit may reflect complex needs patterns comparable to those of selected other industrial-urban areas. Emergent patterns of unmet need in such areas may also be expected to differ, somewhat, both in quality and magnitude, from those characterizing more rural sectors.

An analysis of need among older citizens in Michigan provides a better understanding of the dispersion of service need in the Detroit–Wayne County area as well as insight into selected urban-rural differences relative to perceived need. An indirect measure of need, i.e., the extent to which a random sample of older persons view selected areas as problemmatic for older Americans, indicated a number of needs areas of particular importance to city dwellers. While this measure poses problems, the data suggest potential areas of service demand for the Detroit–Wayne County AAA as well as some urban-rural differences in perceived need. Older urban respondents were more likely than their rural counterparts to view each suggested needs area as a problem for older Americans, e.g., income, housing, health, transportation. The primary concerns of rural elders were income, health, and transportation. The older city dweller was more likely to report crime and income as the most salient concerns of older Americans, with health and transportation sharing third place. Detroit's suburban areas appear to fall between the city and rural areas in terms of perceived importance of selected needs areas. For our purposes, such global observations may be useful in sketching the complex responsibilities of the Detroit–Wayne County AAA and for suggesting the organizational framework within which one of the designated Michigan AAAS functions. It is worth noting, for example, that the mandate of the Detroit–Wayne County AAA extends from the central city into the more suburban Wayne County areas, thus covering a varied service area.

As a major urban area, Detroit's needs differ from those of more rural or non-SMSA areas. These differences and, more specifically, the perceived uniqueness of each local community held by different AAA directors, became increasingly visible within a number of fellowship contexts. For example, the fellow was the AAA representative at a biregional conference of directors. At this meeting, which resulted in a number of insights into interorganizational relationships characterizing the network on aging, a number of local agency directors expressed concern with what they perceived as the rural/urban difference in service need and delivery approaches, holding that in some cases federal policy development was insufficiently attentive to community diversity. For example, some of the agency directors from the more rural areas suggested that policy specifications at the federal level appeared, at times, to be predicated upon assumptions more appropriate to the requirements of urban areas. They suggested that such directives might require modification when applied to the related, but in some ways different, concerns confronting rural elders. At a more general level, such agency director perspectives may be taken as symptomatic of a concern with the level of local agency involvement in policy formulation, i.e., a reflection of the centralization-decentralization issue. Many AAA directors felt that they were most knowledgeable of and sensitive to patterns of need in their communities and to the resultant service requirements. They stressed the necessity of a two-way flow of policy development from the federal to the local level and from the local back to the federal level.

FELLOWSHIP ACTIVITIES: YEAR ONE

Objectives

The Gerontological Fellowship entailed a series of activities directed toward the application of disciplinary skills to the concerns of the Detroit–Wayne County AAA. These activities were conducted in conjunction with the director of the AAA, agency staff, and the agency board. The overall objectives of the fellowship included:

1. Consultation relative to current gerontological knowledge and its application to specific agency concerns, including needs assessment, and the meeting of programmatic objectives of the AAA.

2. Consultation relative to the current research and knowledge base with respect to the development of improved service delivery systems for the older population, including an assessment of delivery patterns and service use.

3. Consultation with the AAA in its efforts to monitor the complex needs of the older population in the service area.

Specific Activities

The fellow was involved in a great number of activities, which ranged from the initiation of a consultation program with the director and staff of the AAA to a final review of evaluative needs and approaches for the agency, including the possible development of an evaluative workshop for directors of agency-sponsored programs. The first stages involved becoming familiar with the objectives of the Detroit–Wayne County AAA and the population structure of the service area. Then an approach to meeting specific objectives was designed in consultation with the agency director.

The planned program was submitted to the program steering committee of the Gerontological Society with further elaboration and discussion at the first meeting of fellows and agency directors. This initial conference was held prior to the initiation of fellowship activities. Formal and informal sessions were designed to familiarize fellows and agency directors with the program and, more generally, to enhance the mutual understanding of the perspectives of both. While formal presentations were helpful in setting the stage for fellowship activities, the work groups and other less structured opportunities for discussion served to highlight, in greater detail, major issues of importance with respect to the perspectives of agency directors and fellows. Although there were exceptions, the operational concerns of the agency directors were readily apparent as was the emphasis of the gerontological fellows upon seemingly more academic issues, including the need for the use of sound research approaches. Illustrative of the different orientations of providers and investigators was the response by an agency director to a question posed by a senior scientist. The question dealt with the reason for conducting needs surveys within AAA. The response was: "Because otherwise we don't get funded." This reflection of concern with the practical implications of research or its applied significance contrasted somewhat with the general views of fellows relative to rendering contributions to theoretical knowledge. Gerontological fellows, for example, emphasized the need for sound methodological approaches in assessing need and in evaluating program outcome. This stance was accepted in principle by most agency directors, but they expressed some concern with the practical implications. For example, one agency director stated: "That is all fine and good, but where do we get the money to do it?" The fellows were more likely to draw upon expertise in a disciplinary field as well as their methodological backgrounds in addressing research concerns in the discussions. This approach may have appeared to be rather abstracted from the more programmatic concerns of agency directors.

Two major positive outcomes of the fellowship experiences were an increased understanding and appreciation by the fellows of the needs and operational concerns of agency directors and an increased awareness by the agency directors of the value of involving investigators in the major problems of agency life. Although the perspectives of agency directors and fellows would not be expected to become isomorphic as the result of this experience, some increased compatibility accrued to those fortunate enough to participate. One very positive result of the gerontological fellowship was the agency director's increased interest in advanced study in gerontology. The fellow was also able to bring the agency into the classroom through discussions of agency activities and concerns as they affected the multidisciplinary field of gerontology. A more structured extension of such an approach would entail the utilization of an AAA as a laboratory which could be utilized by students in the development of theoretical, methodological, and programmatic/policy constructs in gerontology. This might provide an impetus to the desired intersection between sound disciplinary and research training and potential areas of research application in the community.

Further meetings were held with the agency director, staff, and the agency advisory board relative to review and approval of the working plan. The advisory board staff members were pleased with the fellowship protocol and indicated their support of the program. In order to become more familiar with the policy-relevant configurations within the agency, the fellow also attended a number of meetings of the advisory board. This contributed to a better understanding of ongoing program dynamics, organizational factors influencing service delivery, and various conceptions of community need. Extensive reading and review of existing policy statements, and the development of needs estimates and discussions with the agency director contributed to familiarizing the fellow with the role of the Detroit–Wayne County AAA.

Evaluative Study

Through the review and assessment of contracts and their relationship to agency objectives, a broader perspective of agency evaluation needs emerged. Two major areas of concern became apparent: the lack of sound programmatic evaluation of existing contracts and the lack of evaluative criteria for the technical review of contracts for funding.

The lack of sound evaluative information of an experimental or quasi-experimental nature in earlier contracts was emphasized by the fellow, as were the methodological problems associated with existing retrospective evaluative approaches. Strategies for prospective evaluative approaches were discussed and, in developing a device for the technical evaluation of proposals, an explicit plan for agency evaluation was requested. Evaluative approaches were discussed with the agency director and his staff, and these discussions resulted in a commitment to encourage an evaluation plan among all project applicants. A gradualistic educational approach to evaluation was suggested, moving from fairly general approaches among various agencies in the community to increasingly refined studies. These discussions led the AAA to propose workshops for project directors to encourage an emphasis on program evaluation as an essential component in addressing community need.

The agency director and advisory board were particularly concerned with the lack of objective criteria with which to evaluate new project proposals. Accordingly, the fellow was asked to develop an instrument which could be employed in evaluating agency proposals. Such a need to objectify organizational decision-making is a reflection of the heavy agency demand for existing funding, community service demand, and the simultaneous pressures for program accountability stemming in part from increasing consumer concerns. That organizational demand for funding far exceeded available AAA resources and also rendered it necessary to have objective criteria for proposal evaluation. The need to ensure the application of universalistic rather than idiosyncratic criteria to such evaluations was also conducive to the development of such an instrument. The instrument was developed in consultation with the agency director and advisory board and consisted of 25 items, each of which was rated on an scale of 0 to 4. Each item could, of course, be assigned a specific weighting, depending upon the priority configurations characterizing the community and the decision-making role of the advisory board. Five major areas were considered in the development of the instrument: proposal quality, personnel to be employed, and selected managerial issues; problem definition, target population for receipt of services, and documentation of client need; objectives of program and specification of activities designed to meet documented needs; specific implementation strategies and plans; and impact statement including plans for the evaluation of program activities. The resultant instrument was then presented to the agency director, staff, and advisory board and was approved and adopted.

Needs Assessment

In addition to consulting relative to the evaluative concerns, the fellow was involved in the delineation of needs of older persons within the service area. The resultant definition of need was helpful in discussions with agency staff and members of the board in terms of program development. A review of needs was also conducive to the refinement of the evaluative instrument to be used in assessing program applications. A number of approaches were utilized. First, the fellow was able to describe generic needs of the older population based upon reviews of existing gerontological investigations, some employing national data sets. Second, the fellow made an effort to become familiar with the major specifications, objectives, and requirements delineated at the national level as they related to specific need in the Detroit–Wayne County area. A review of demographic data on this area also provided a basis for conceptualizing need. Finally, state agency staff provided data from a representative sample of older persons in the state. Information bearing directly on the older population in the Detroit–Wayne County area was isolated from this data set. The director of the state agency on aging also conferred with the fellow relative to this needs survey and expressed interest in further analyses of these data. Findings relative to existing needs as defined in this manner were referred to the agency director.

Additional Activities

One of the more unique opportunities to contribute to the Detroit–Wayne County AAA and to obtain more extensive insight into the national and local aging network consisted of representing the agency in a meeting of Title III and Title VII directors. In order to prepare for this biregional policy meeting, the consultant reviewed all major policy documents relating to Title III and Title VII programs. The meeting permitted the development of additional insight into programmatic activities at a variety of jurisdictional and geographic levels. The Commissioner on Aging reviewed major issues involved in moving toward the development of a network on aging. In addition, there was further review and discussion of major policy and programmatic needs and prospects covering all jurisdictional levels. The roles of local and state agencies were reviewed as was the need to increase the impact of aging agencies at all levels upon aging policies and upon the development of a comprehensive network of services. A written report relative to this activity was prepared and submitted to the AAA director along with additional information relative to other policy configurations. This was particularly useful in enhancing the fellow's insight into organizational dynamics, operational concerns, and other complex issues associated with the development of comprehensive service programs for the elderly. Some general observations emanating from this and other meetings will be offered later.

Follow-up Fellowship Activities

A number of follow-up activities brought the fellowship program to a close. Toward the end of the fellowship period a site visit was conducted by a representative of the steering committee of the fellowship program. This was particularly helpful in bringing closure to selected fellowship activities and in analyzing the contributions made by the agency to the professional development of the fellow and of the fellow to the improvement of agency activities. An all-day conference was held in which fellowship activities were reviewed, agency considerations were analyzed, and implications of the fellowship for overall programmatic endeavors were highlighted. Both the agency director and the fellow felt the site visit was most beneficial and supportive. In addition to reviewing specific considerations with the Detroit–Wayne County fellowship experience, possible approaches to strengthening the fellowship program were offered at the request of the site visitor. The site visit also gave the fellow and agency director the opportunity to develop a holistic synthesis of overall fellowship accomplishments.

A follow-up meeting of persons involved in the fellowship program was held at the annual meeting of the Gerontological Society. This was helpful in providing a general overview of activities and an arena for the exchange of observations. The meeting also highlighted the fact that many seemingly unique and independent observations and experiences were actually being shared by fellows in many agencies. In short, a number of universal concerns which cross-cut the specific agency activities of the different fellows became readily apparent in this final session. Among the common observations were the different orientations of fellows and agency providers in terms of applied and basic research considerations, and the salience of needs surveys, the importance of evaluative studies, and an emergent awareness of factors influencing involvement in policy-relevant research. That the experience had been a valuable one for all was also generally acknowledged. This meeting also permitted individual fellows to again conceptualize their activities within the broader framework provided by the general fellowship program and assisted in bringing to closure, in a holistic manner, the fellowship experience.

FELLOWSHIP ACTIVITIES: YEAR TWO

The fellow was particularly fortunate in obtaining a fellowship for a second summer with the Detroit–Wayne County AAA. Areas of inquiry examined during the initial fellowship period were extended, and additional areas of importance to the agency were explored, i.e., specification of organizational and interorganizational factors influencing potential utilization of services within the Detroit–Wayne County area. During the first fellowship period a considerable amount of time was invested in becoming familiar with the AAA, its charge, the agency plan, objectives, and other agency concerns through extensive review of documents and discussions with agency director, staff, and board members. Although such activities continued during the second period, the earlier experience permitted the fellow and agency director to initiate the second summer with a better understanding of each other's professional orientation and a greater awareness on the part of the fellow of existing programmatic agency activities. The resultant continuity was clearly facilitating of fellowship activities. The benefits of such continuity both to the agency and to the fellow's development also suggested the importance of possibly extending the time frame of fellowship activities within the general fellowship program. This issue was raised with the site visitor on his trip to the Detroit–Wayne County AAA.

Objectives

Three major areas were outlined as worthy of further involvement: consultation and monitoring of the knowledge base required for the improvement of the service delivery system of the AAA; contributing further to the assessment of need of the older population within the service area; and assisting in the development of an approach which could be employed in examining the emergent service profile of the AAA in a manner consistent with improving agency decision-making.

While some attention was to be given to each of these concerns, more extensive discussions with the agency director and advisory board lent urgency to the issue of service delivery and utilization of services. Thus, considerable effort was allocated to a review and development of a conceptual framework relative to the service patterns in the community from an organizational standpoint and possible operational steps to improve the quality of agency decision-making. This involved assisting the agency by developing a conceptual understanding of interorganizational dynamics within the Detroit–Wayne County area and the national network on aging and in suggesting possible approaches within this model for generating elements of a service utilization profile.

Specific Fellowship Activities

A number of social scientists have called attention to the need to carefully examine the role of interorganizational dynamics in service delivery. This theoretical concern from the disciplinary perspective is matched by the concern of agency directors with day-to-day organizational considerations. Thus, the view held by some that the key to organizational survival is knowledge about the organizational environment is shared by AAA directors. In order to properly assess the role of the AAA and its relationships with other elements of the aging network, an attempt was made to conceptualize the distribution of service need or objectified demand on a horizontal plane, i.e., in terms of distribution of service need geographically within the Detroit–Wayne County area and the organizational structure designed to meet those needs which could be placed along a vertical axis reflecting different levels of jurisdictional abstraction. This conceptualization was presented to the agency director and staff, and its implications for agency functioning were outlined. The definable substantive areas for which each element of the interorganizational network was deemed responsible from an evaluative standpoint were also examined. This conceptualization was helpful to both the fellow and agency director in terms of defining analytic and programmatic issues posed by interorganizational dynamics operative in the service fields with particular attention to substantive policy issues in the service delivery area.

An attempt was then made to conceptualize service-relevant issues within the system and the service agencies as the provider elements supported by the AAA for which available resources could be specified. With the definition of resultant service elements provided by such service agencies, comparisons of organizational results could be made within and across service categories. There was also the possibility of generating a service utilization profile. Operationally, such a profile would entail an assessment of those persons utilizing services; e.g., by demographic and other variables, by objectified need (demand), and by other selected characteristics. Comparisons could then be made employing the information relative to characteristics and needs in the general population and of those entering the professional referral system to disclose existing gaps in service delivery and to suggest selected intervention and outreach modalities. Moreover, selected characteristics and features, including the needs of the target population, could then be prioritized, and, using a utilization profile developed from information collected from each agency, comparisons could be made on a system-wide basis, within and across service categories, in an effort to determine the extent to which prioritized objectives of the delivery system were being met. If successful, such an information system would result in a much desired improvement in the fit between geographically distributed need in the community and available resources.

Although there was considerable interest in these approaches, especially on the part of the agency director, the advisory board was more interested in elaborating the major programmatic aspects of the model. In an interesting comment on the role of research in the delivery system they indicated an interest in obtaining "more bang for the buck" in highlighting the centrality of programmatic concerns. Thus, it was felt that additional attention should be allocated to an attempt to conceptualize factors essential to generating a utilization profile for the Detroit–Wayne County AAA.

Discussions were held with the agency director, staff, and the advisory board relative to evaluating existing strategies employed by service agencies in defining the population served by them. Additional attention was given to policy discussions relative to defining and prioritizing target populations for the delivery of services and to available data sets which could be helpful in identifying community-based need. Some of these activities benefited from the needs survey activities of the previous summer. These discussions, needs survey activities, and other approaches resulted in the development of a set of variable categories which could be employed by the AAA in developing a service utilization profile. The categories included the following with a further specification of variables within each category: demographic variables; social support levels; health status, e.g., attention to disabled/poor health; source of information relative to AAA services; transportation of service location; reason for service utilization; need for other services; general attitudes and beliefs regarding services; other utilization variables; and services being requested (demand).

A list of potential variables which could also be addressed by service providers was also included. Data collected relative to these variables could then presumably be compared with those provided by consumers in order to assess the fit between client need and provider assessment. Included in this section were the following: major service category provided; specific service units provided; referral to other services; provision of information to client relative to other community services; staff perception of the extent to which service provided met need of client; and provision for client follow-up. This conceptualization was modified through discussion with the agency director and staff and was expected to provide the basis for an emergent service utilization profile. These and related efforts were well-received by the AAA, and the fellow profited greatly from relating academic and programmatic issues productively.

General Results One: A Look at Needs Surveys

With the consumer's increasing role in the development of service priorities and in response to demands for organizational accountability and cost-effectiveness, needs surveys have become of major importance for service agencies and in this particular case for AAA. Because the needs survey is seen as an increasingly central element in the evaluative structure of any service agency, it provides a unique opportunity for community-based research of applied significance. Therefore, it may be helpful to review some of the central considerations in this area.

Ideally, one would like to know the distribution of service need in a given geographic area (not only demand or objectified need). One could then attempt through the use of multivariate analytic tools to determine which factors contribute to such need. Then one could presumably develop innovative programs designed to impact upon risk factors predisposing individuals to the development of various problems. Evaluative studies employing experimental and quasi-experimental designs could then be conducted to assess the effectiveness of such programs. With notable exceptions, such a lofty script is not enacted in the "real world" of the frequently stressed community service agency. A number of factors may contribute to this situation. For example, sample surveys designed to assess need distribution cost money. Accordingly, although agency directors may agree that a methodologically sound survey would be highly appropriate, they might simultaneously inquire: "But where do we get the money to do it?" Moreover, from an interorganizational or a systems standpoint, needs surveys of a given community may be viewed by local agency directors as extrinsic or possibly irrelevant to meeting organizational goals essential to survival. For example, policy decisions made at higher jurisdictional levels—levels which provide support to the local agency on aging—are likely to suggest priority areas developed at the national level which are then employed in arriving at an assessment of the effectiveness of local agencies within the aging network. Since funding is directed to the local agency from higher levels the agency is likely to concentrate on meeting needs defined and prioritized at the federal level in its service activities. The AAA may thus see itself as basically incapable of responding in selected instances to unique or discrete areas of need identified through a community-specific needs survey by virtue of the fact that funding may be based to a considerable extent on the agency's success in meeting nationally defined policy and programmatic expectations, including prioritized needs areas. Moreover, to respond creatively to community-defined need within a given geographic area, an AAA must have considerable organizational autonomy from the vertical system and in effect reduced autonomy or increased accountability to the local service area. In short, the agency may be more likely to attempt to satisfy needs defined by higher levels, which provide funding to the local agency, than to meeting particular community-defined need unless this is specified in the AAA mandate. For these and related reasons, needs surveys tend to become bookkeeping activities rather than rendering meaningful contributions. In other instances the needs survey may be defined as something to be endured in order to obtain continued funding. In this case, the definition of need in the population or an accurate description of such need does not appear to be as important as submitting a device, which is simply called a needs survey, to the appropriate funding source.

An additional factor, an attitudinal variable, which may be antithetical to the development of competent needs surveys and evaluative approaches is the view held by some persons that conducting a survey of community need is equivalent to appointing a committee; i.e., it is an organizational "cop-out." Some providers may see this "cop-out syndrome" as a salient affliction of those who would prefer not to become entangled in direct service delivery issues. Such a reaction is synonymous with the resonant sigh which greets the appointment of a committee by city council to look into a selected urban problem. In other cases, it is argued that we know enough about the needs, now is the time for action. A discussion between the fellow and community representatives at a AAA advisory board meeting illustrates this situation. At the very mention of needs surveys, by the fellow, an individual responded: "We don't really need a needs survey or any other study. We already know what the

problems are!" This view, as expressed by this obviously dedicated community representative, was shared by a number of others. While it appeared that this person would have been agreeable to the need for improved data collection relative to unmet need in the community, he tended to perceive such research as peripheral to the agency's service responsibilities. Implicit in this orientation is the position that research detracts from the process of "getting on with the job"; that is, providing services to persons in need. Parenthetically, this view was not held solely by persons involved in service delivery.

Such orientations raise questions concerning the potential ease of entry into the community for the purpose of conducting research and concerning prospects for the rapid dissemination of new knowledge into the service delivery system. Finally, these and related views held by scientists and service providers raise the issue of the ways in which people are socialized into professional roles.

While it is reasonable to want to move ahead rapidly in terms of programmatic activities at the community level, negative results may accrue from the easy acceptance of the view that we already know what the needs are. Excluding the use of research literature, service providers may come to "know" the problems of a given community through familiarity with those persons entering their practice or service domain. However, one does not, through such a selective sample, know what the population of older persons looks like and what the overall needs are. Indeed, in some cases, such impressions gained from clinical practice have provided the basis for gerontological stereotypes. For example, a physician's general impression of the nature of the symptoms presented by older clients may result in the more general and erroneous impression that aging and ill health are synonymous, or at least go hand in hand. It takes a significant number of scientific studies and their broad dissemination to shed the negative effects of such stereotypes. One may also suggest that clinical views and impressions frequently emerge from that which already exists; that is, the problem as presented within the practice situation. The problem in effect presents itself within the practice situation as a fait accompli. However, it may be argued that in order to obtain the right answer about the distribution of need and its nature one must ask the right question, rather than having the question structured solely around individuals presenting in the clinical setting. For example, does dependency reside in the older person, or should dependency be increasingly conceptualized as a reflection of a shortfall in existing interdependency mechanisms? Should analyses be focused on assessing need at the individual level or on community and personal strengths and potentials for enhancing the quality of life of older persons? More refined research within the community is required in order to obtain meaningful answers to these questions.

Finally, traditional needs surveys, when done at all, have been basically descriptive. Although such descriptive analyses are an essential cornerstone of knowledge, providing a taxonomic base for the scholar and a community description of unmet need to the agency director, they appear to add little to the analytic knowledge in the field of gerontology. In this respect such surveys constitute a descriptive epidemiology of need within the community. Gerontology is now at a stage where it can begin to move more strongly into an analytic epidemiology of need in which potential etiological factors are more carefully explicated. Programmatic interventions may then be targeted upon such predictive factors in improving the quality of life in older persons within the community. Evaluative studies of program outcome can then be utilized in assessing program effectiveness.

General Results Two: Organizational Perspectives

A number of meetings and observations resulted in additional insight into selected interorganizational dynamics confronting the AAA. For example, discussions at the initial meeting of agency directors and fellows disclosed not only somewhat different views of research held by both, but also provided some interesting observations relative to organizational concerns. Although agency directors tended, in general, to share the praxis weltanschauung, interorganizational factors also entered into their presentation of self. For example, concern relative to issues of organizational turf had been internalized so that AAA directors appeared to share a given perspective, state directors were concerned about a different level of program development, and regional directors were further abstracted in perspective from that of the local agency director. This internalization of organizational norms was also visible in the operational sphere of organizational activities. Such a situation is of both theoretical and applied interest. It is of particular interest in the sense that the commissioner on aging was at that time engaged in the development of what he termed the "network on aging." Such a network would seem to imply a systems approach to service delivery. Moreover, just as a theory acquires its meaning from the systemic linkages of its laws and is, thus, greater than the sum of its parts, such an aging network would presumably entail linkages of service elements into a whole. This in turn would suggest that the subsidiary organizations such as the AAAs are open or that their walls are permeable. Thus, if selected subsidiary elements of the network or system come to be relatively autonomous or, in effect, tended to become closed subsystems, serious questions would be raised about the prospects for the development of a viable national network. Such a closed subsystem model would be inconsistent with the development of a national systems-based approach to service delivery.

The possible internalization of a closed-systems model by subsidiary agency and staff could contribute to a further lowering of interorganizational permeability requisite to the elaboration of a national network on aging. Internalization could also result in a "we"-"them" view of organizational goals, service provision, and other considerations. In short, organizational level phenomena are reflected in the reductionistic perspective of a social-psychological mirror. This orientation toward the organization within a local organizational unit may then conflict with the systemic open-systems requirements of the parent organization. The resultant dualistic demands may place the local agency director in a double bind. For example, the director of a local AAA may have purported responsibility to the community or task area within which the agency is located, while at the same time he is visualized as a basic constituent of a broader comprehensive national network. The systemic linkages carry connotations of response to the broader system and higher jurisdictional levels while, simultaneously, pressures occur at the local level for more direct response to uniquely defined local need.

The advocacy role is another example of the double bind complex. Consumerism and accountability issues have stimulated increased interest in the role of service agencies in advocacy. This concern has been reflected at the federal level. For example, the commissioner on aging informed a gathering of AAA directors that advocacy was the most important process in the field of aging. Although many would concur, agency directors at the local level who became too enamored of the advocacy role could find themselves engaged in attempted, if not successful, organizational suicide. An examination of Perrow's (1966) idea of intrinsic and extrinsic organizational referents may help clarify this situation. Intrinsic referents are the basic formal reasons for the existence of a particular organization; e.g., patient care, rehabilitation, etc. Extrinsic referents are those designed to "sell" the organization to the environment in which it is located. They are designed to generate support and resources for the organization. Extrinsic organizational referents generally receive a great deal of attention in order to insure continued agency survival within the interorganizational system. When pushed by the environment, organizations are likely to respond by emphasizing extrinsic organizational referents as proof of their value. Because, from an interorganizational standpoint, advocacy may be more directly related to the internal goal structure of the organization, i.e., meeting community need, and less to extrinsic referents, i.e., meeting the requirements of the funding source, local advocacy may fall between the organizational tracks with, perhaps, appropriate noises being made but with limited patterns of action resulting.

Some concern about policy development and the centralization-decentralization issue was also expressed by representatives of the local agencies. For example, local agency representatives would appear to have a superior body of knowledge about the community they serve and to visualize themselves as more "street wise" than agency executives at higher jurisdictional levels. Thus, if at times some agency directors view the scientist as a rather vague theoretician estranged from practical concerns, it may also be said that persons involved in policy formulation at the parent organizational level are viewed at times by local agency personnel as equally estranged from "what's really going on." The call on the part of some AAA directors for a "two-way flow of information, including from the bottom up" is illustrative.

These interesting questions relative to organizational or systems approaches to service delivery and the relationship between the organizational structure and unmet need offer important opportunities for future community-based research.

CONCLUSIONS

We have been happily borne—or perhaps have unhappily dragged our weary way—down the long and crooked streets of our lives, past all kinds of walls and fences made of rotting wood, rammed earth, brick, concrete, iron railings. We have never thought of what lies behind them. . . . In addition, we have failed to notice an enormous number of closely fitted, well-disguised doors and gates in these fences. All these gates were prepared for us, every last one!

. . . They are invisible, but they exist. And the invisible slaves of the archipelago, who have substance, weight and volume, have to be transported from island to island just as invisibly and uninterruptedly.

—Solzhenitsyn

Aging and old age, process and status, do not occur in a vacuum; they are woven into the social cloth, the "gerontopelago" of modern society. This environment may be colored by agist stereotypes or may embody the final islands of the older person's gerontopelago, be it a nursing home, a hospital, or one's own home. Who charts these islands? What winds serve to move the older person along through the age structure of modern society to a possibly increasingly uninhabited plane? What features characterize the terrain of the final island? The answers to such questions may depend, in part, on the extent to which links are forged between the scientist and the community. The gerontological fellowship provided the opportunity to explore this nexus in detail. Through the fellowship program the AAA obtained support in terms of the fellow's knowledge and capabilities as they related to the applied domain. The Fellow acquired a broader view of research avenues and potential areas of study within the community. The AAA was given the opportunity for a renewed examination of broader issues and concepts in the field; gerontological concepts and concerns which cross-cut and extend beyond the day-to-day operation of the agency, with the prospect of developing an increasingly holistic view of gerontology. Accordingly, an increased awareness of and sensitivity to the concerns, perspectives, and potential contributions of fellow, agency director, and staff emerged. That such perceptions or role identities were expanded during the course of fellowship activities is a tribute to the program, reflecting, as it does, the expanding horizons essential to an evolving field of gerontology.

REFERENCE

Perrow, C. 1966. Organizational prestige: Some functions and dysfunctions. In *Medical Care: Readings in the Sociology of Medical Institutions,* ed. W. Richard Scott and Edmund H. Volkart. New York: John Wiley and Sons, Inc.

11. Case VIII. The AAA and Public Management of Human Resources in Aging

Charles E. McConnel

EDITOR'S NOTE: Employment and manpower problems are traditionally studied by economists. McConnel discusses some issues in the development of public employment and service programs for older workers. He shows that rational utilization of funds is often not possible because day-to-day operational concerns take priority over systematic management of labor market information. For example, CETA funds are intended to apply to the elderly as well as the young, but several factors interact that more or less eliminate the elderly from such programs.

A recurring theme in this book is found in this selection—an emphasis on the importance of political issues concerned with power and decision-making, which tend to dominate operation of service programs and the allocation of resources.

ONE of the primary objectives of the Older Americans Acts of 1965 and the Older American Comprehensive Service Amendments of 1973 and 1975, is to facilitate the employment and employability of the involuntarily unemployed low-income, minority and discouraged elderly worker by creating and furnishing "meaningful employment opportunities" and "counseling" through the agency service structure. Thus, it is not unusual for Area Agency on Aging (AAA) objectives to include promotion of a broader range of employment opportunities through the elimination or reduction of social and bureaucratic barriers in local labor markets and public manpower programs. Such employment related concerns, however, have been typically considered subsidiary to a predominating and pervasive strategy toward implementation of the "custodial" objectives of the seminal legislation.

Because of the range, intensity, and high visibility of the elderlys' need for housing, transportation, nutrition, information and referral, and homemaker services and the relative ease by which staff recruitment and training requirements for the relevant agency functions can be met, the present service emphasis of the typical AAA can easily be construed and justified as a rational compromise in the utilization of scarce resources relative to competing objectives. At the same time, there is sufficient evidence to suggest that because of the diversity and legislative fragmentation of employment and manpower programs and the relatively specialized staff required for their coordination, such programs are not easily integrated into the AAA's administrative/service structure.

While it is generally true that the AAAS have, in accordance with federal regulations, relegated elderly employment needs to "gap-filling" status at both the planning and operational levels, there is considerable variation in the degree to which the area agencies have been willing to initiate community awareness of the vulnerability and wasted productivity of unemployed persons 55 years of age and over. But, more important, there is an apparent disregard for the potential effect the area agency could have on the operations of federally funded local manpower programs. These programs, often conveniently located within the same governmental jurisdiction as the area agency, are mandated to serve individuals from all age groups who are experiencing income and employment problems. Yet, it is well known that the older worker has been systematically discriminated against by local manpower "prime sponsors": funds have not been allocated to help the older worker, and this group is yet to be effectively integrated into the nation's training and public service employment network. While failure of manpower policy in administering to the needs of the older worker is most notably registered in the national statistics of declining labor force participation rates, high unemployment and unemployment duration rates, widespread discouraged worker effects, and an increased volume of age-discrimination cases, the present system of decentralized and decategorized planning, programming, and administration requires an organized intervention effort at the local level.

As a Gerontological Society Summer Fellow in 1976, I had the opportunity of providing academic support for older worker manpower concerns in the Los Angeles County Department of Senior Citizen Affairs. Under the direction of Leon Harper, the director of the AAA, my responsibilities included developing a research, coordination, and planning strategy for more effective intervention in the local manpower system and establishing a basis for negotiating interagency implementation agreements.

THE CONSULTING EXPERIENCE

After several weeks of administrative orientation and familiarization with the structure and operations of the AAA, the director and I tentatively identified several areas of research and action which would most effectively promote the agency's concern for the community's older workers. We agreed that the principal objective would be the coordination and systematic development of public employment and service programs which were most likely to have some impact on the broad array of employment problems of the elderly. The project thus entailed two parallel activities—research on the relevance of manpower programs to older worker labor market problems and an attempt to interact with managers of local manpower programs.

The research component commenced with a review of the Comprehensive Employment and Training Act of 1973, the Senior Community Service Employment Program authorized by Title IX of the OAA and amendments, Job Opportunity Programs (Title X of the Public Works and Economic Development Act), programs established under the Emergency Jobs and Unemployment Assistance Act of 1974, Community Services Act of 1974, various state and county programs, and finally, the Age Discrimination in Employment Act of 1967.

In the course of a preliminary review I gathered substantial evidence on age discrimination in the management of local and national manpower programs. This material made it clear that an effective research program should focus on the relationship of a variety of manpower agencies and programs and the network's effectiveness in meeting the demonstrated needs of an age-specific "significant population segment" the relevant legislation had targeted. The goals, I thought, would be to present (1) a relatively convincing demonstration of the existence of age-discrimination in federally funded manpower programs and services, and (2) an objective basis for ascertaining the degree to which such discrimination exists. Although my analysis was to be used on labor information obtained for both the national and county levels, I felt confident that at the end of the study I could make recommendations to the Los Angeles AAA on how best to protect the interests of older workers and enable them to become an integral part of the local manpower network.

My attempt to interact with the local manpower community began with discussions and review of L.A. County agencies (e.g., Human Development) believed to be coordinating or managing manpower and training programs, national contractors such as the National Council on Aging and Green Thumb in the area, the State Employment Security Agency, and the county agency designated as a "prime sponsor," i.e., responsible for Comprehensive Employment and Training Act programs. The purpose of this exploratory work was to inventory and assess current county manpower program efforts and express to local manpower planners the AAA's concern with an equitable allocation of funds to older workers.

After several uninformative meetings with county manpower officials, it was clear that interest in the elderly worker was limited to making a token allocation of public service employment slots to eligible workers age 55 and over. As with decentralized Comprehensive Employment and Training Act programs across the nation, a systematic approach to planning and labor market information management, which would provide a basis for a rational utilization of funds, appeared to be a concept completely subordinate to piecemeal day-to-day operational concerns. At the county level, municipal politics and civil service bureaucratic haggling completely dominated the procedures required for an efficient and equitable implementation of the legislated decategorization of manpower programs. It was quite obvious that little attention was being given to the requirement that all age segments of the labor force (as well as discouraged workers) be systematically integrated into the various federally funded programs as the diverse fragments of the former categorical system were phased out.

After amassing a considerable file of background materials on federally funded local programs and establishing contacts with virtually all manpower agencies in the community, I found that as was the case with the several federal programs "earmarked" for older workers (e.g., Title III of CETA), the extent of employment program allocations directed toward the special needs of the older worker was primarily a function of the sophistication and intensity of interest group advocacy. Specialized knowledge of local elderly employment and income needs along with a working knowledge of available programs were obvious requisites for effectively promoting increased attention to the rather unique employment and training problems of the older worker. It seemed reasonable to conclude, tentatively, that the lack of agency staff with an economics orientation and the lack of an aging manpower plan for local manpower authorities to consider, simply perpetuated underrepresentation of older worker participation in federal noncategorical manpower programs. An effective course would be to provide the necessary manpower orientation.

BARRIERS TO ACTION

To establish a basis for evaluating my experience as an academic consultant to a public agency it is necessary to present some rough theoretical notions that seem to bear on the problem to which I was assigned—the negotiation and consumation of agreements between one public agency and another. I do this for two reasons. First, because I found the perceptual, contextual, and procedural barriers to effecting change so inextricably fused and deflective (in sum, the academic consultant as an intruding foreign agent in the bureaucratic organism), it occurred to me that any attempt to relate my experiences within these traditional categories would undoubtedly end in a muddle. Second, as I began a retrospective examination of my AAA work, it became all too apparent that I lacked the necessary understanding of municipal politics to generalize from an experience of such short duration and tenuous administrative context. At the least, I felt this shortcoming would be excusable if I were able to demonstrate that I gave the matter the proper amount of attention.

Theoretical Considerations on Interagency Agreements

Economic theory states that a plausible explanation of the manner in which public services are produced and allocated requires an understanding of political and economic self-interest of those individuals who make public policy *as well as* those who administer it. Certainly, anyone familiar with the operations of municipal government—or for that matter any collection of public agencies—could not be so naïve as to believe that the underlying motivation of individual agents is predicated on collectively securing the common good. (Even when observing the results of the actions of a single agency which produces a single service, it is frequently difficult to identify motivations, which are most often veiled in the working out of a problematic set of individual actions.) The more complex the agency's output and the looser the confederation of individuals and agencies involved in its production, the greater the difficulty in understanding the relationship between the public's needs and the mechanisms by which they may be met.

The problem of understanding the process and outcome of collective action is further compounded when the agency is one whose legislated goals require some degree of interagency coordination. By using interagency agreements, i.e., instruments that commit independent agencies to some form of cooperation, the coordinating agency attempts to secure a place in the public service environment which will ensure its political/ bureaucratic survival and generate an acceptable level of services for its legislated clients/constituents. The difficulties in securing such interagency agreements seem obvious: the agency enters an environment of politically diverse interests with dissimilar public goals and attempts, without statutory authority, to mediate the scarcity of public resources.

It seems reasonable to assume that municipal agencies compete for public resources not on the strict basis of rationalization of needs of legislated goals, but primarily on the basis of power. Thus, public resources do not necessarily flow to those areas or activities that have collectively been demonstrated to be most beneficial; instead, they are mediated by a complex of political and bureaucratic factors, which are involved in setting the "budget," and the network of political linkages that have historically evolved. Thus, unless interagency interests happen to coincide, the coordinating agency, if it is to be effective, must have sufficient political power to secure indirect control over the budget of another agency. The problem is much more acute for organizations such as the AAA, whose functions in many cases have been defined as subordinate to the major and much broader focus of other agencies and which must, for political survival, obtain from those agencies concessions to service a particular population segment. Here, an understanding of interagency agreements requires a firm understanding of the difference between an agency's actions predicated on a budgetary process and extrabudgetary actions (e.g., actions based on political or bureaucratic alliances, contrivances and disputes) that are only coincidentally related to "budgeting" by virtue of the fact that a budget establishes the financial basis for the agency's day-to-day operations. An agency does not "pay" for cooperation or coordination to indirectly meet its legislated objectives, but is awarded, granted or, in one manner or another, is able to coerce concessions from agencies directly responsible and accountable for the desired services.

The aged require a broad range of specialized services, e.g., health, welfare, employment, security, transportation, legal aid, education, and physical environment, which are most often beyond the direct control of the AAA. Furthermore, the agency itself may require support services, e.g., informational, which will improve the service delivery system over which it has direct control. Where it is generally understood that these services are best supplied through joint production by independent agencies, the process of coordinating activities, while admittedly political, will at least be anchored in what is jointly perceived as a rational reallocation and recombination of an original allocation of public resources to the independent agencies. Each agency specializes in a task which is coordinated into a program. But it would appear that the majority of programs which are funded for a specific function (i.e., transportation) with obvious implications for servicing a special need of the aged, will, unless categorically designated by statute, provide little basis in initiating a secure component in a comprehensive aging service network. Notable are the low priorities assigned the aged in transportation programs, community mental health programs, Title XX (ssa) social service programs, and health service programs under Title III of the Public Health Service Act. But even where the aged are provided a categorical assignment (e.g., Title III of ceta) under a program funded for a specific function, the designation of the aaa as a coordinating agency rather than a service agency reduces its capacity for interagency reciprocity and weakens the prospect for a successful service union. It is simply a matter of *quid* lacking a *quo*.

There is, no doubt, within the theory of competitive and cooperative games, an articulated account of the mechanism through which interagency agreements are reached, where potential parity and symmetry in exchange of resources provide for a range of feasible solutions. Yet, I doubt that this theory can accommodate a third consideration, an attitude of neutrality or indifference—the administrative environment to which the typical aaa and its client population is generally subject. Hence, given the legislated functions of tapping, pooling, and coordinating social services for the elderly and the obvious asymmetry in its relationship to the local interagency network, it is not surprising that the successful area agency is typically characterized by a highly aggressive advocacy effort, a costly preoccupation with visibility, and an inordinate degree of politicization.

Some of the Experience under the Theory

How does this theorizing relate to the academic who is temporarily placed in an aaa and who is expected to be something more than an observer? First, the agency, as an ongoing political entity, will rationally view the temporary alien as an intruder and as one who should not be allowed to bring about any internal or external political realignments. Anything that depends even remotely on the academic person's future interest in the agency's operations will be held suspect. This is not to say that the agency will be unwilling to exploit the academic's technical expertise or be unappreciative of the consultant's presence (evidently a minor political coup in itself). But in spite of the generous provision of resources which the agency is willing to commit to the academic, the willingness of officers and staff to share insights on the internal and external political environment, and the status accorded the consultant, it is difficult to envision how any of this could be parlayed over the consultant's three-month tenure into a change in the agency's behaviors.

Second, individual actions that would result in a predictable and desirable impact on the agency's behavior most likely would require a rather astute understanding of internal agency politics and an understanding of the historical development of the agency's external relationships with other political/bureaucratic entities. This seems especially true of the AAA, whose effectiveness partially depends on the continued development of a political network that increases its capacity to tap, pool, and coordinate resources beyond its direct budgetary control. Can the summer fellow be expected to master such an understanding? Of what value would it be to expend the time and effort to do so given the short duration of the fellowship?

Third, there is the unavoidable conflict between professionals from different milieus. Undoubtedly, mutual condescension, while more comfortable, will be considerably less rewarding than a willingness to clash on substantive gerontological issues that most likely will arise.

It is important to realize that the principal actors in the area agency are not professional social workers, but a curious blend of seasoned managers and politicians—bureaucratic entrepreneurs. Shop talk does not center around gerontology, but bureaucratic mechanics and political alliances.

Another slightly irritating aspect of agency attitudes is what might appear to be shared bureaucratic indifference to the range and intensity of client problems. This is especially apparent in the typical agency's insensitivity to the professional concern of the social workers who must interact with agency staff. However, as social researchers need not be intimately concerned with their subject matter to be ultimately effective and insightful into the complex of social problems, it is also true that public agencies need not internalize client group problems in order to administer effectively and efficiently toward their solution. While this attitude is manifested in an unseemly insensitivity to the plight of those in need of the agency's services, this possible deficiency need not, and probably will not, translate into a diminished supply of services or less responsive service structure.

The agency is an administrative unit, not one of primary contact, care, and service. The agency is management intensive and as such its managers, the public entrepreneurs, are constrained by a complex interaction among the need for high municipal visibility, departmental longevity, and career development. They operate intuitively in an attempt to maximize the correlation between given public allocations and the hierarchy of client needs. The academic, who is convinced that a systematic effort at estimating relative client needs through data analytic procedures is the most defensible way to proceed in rational public management may, therefore, be disillusioned to find that it is hardly a sufficient condition of successful agency management. The academic should have known this all along.

As an economist, my predilection is toward a fairly general acceptance of the concept of specialization and division of labor in most areas of organized human activity. That I desire this principle to carry over into research and social action activities should not be surprising. My experience in the area agency reinforced my prior belief in the segregation of purposes and activities—the pursuit of research and the effective communication and advocacy of method to those in the field of implementation. The opportunity costs associated with the academics' direct involvement in the social agency's daily operations quite possibly will be too high a price to pay for the returns from such familiarization with agency behavior.

THE RESEARCH

The methodology employed in relating manpower system outcomes to older worker labor market characteristics is relatively simple. By utilizing national and local labor market data, along with other socioeconomic data, a number of older worker labor market risk factors are systematically examined and an index of age-related vulnerability established. Age-segment risk differentials and age-segment differentials in manpower program allocations and manpower services rendered are compared. Finally, the efficiency and equitability of program outcomes are judged by evaluating the constructed comparisons on the basis of a reasoned interpretation of legislative and regulatory intent and expected (normative) agency behavior.

Relevant Manpower System Components

The distinguishing characteristics of current national manpower policy and planning efforts are the decentralization of decision-making and operations to the local level, allocational decategorization, and process integration of a number of disparate service components into a comprehensive coordinated national manpower system. As a major facet of the "New Federalism" in the early 1970s, enactment of the Comprehensive Employment and Training Act of 1973 (CETA), and creation of an administrative structure in the Department of Labor, the Employment and Training Administration provided for umbrella funding and organizational entities which facilitate a more viable network of employment, training, and service opportunities for the nation's low-income, unemployed, underemployed, disadvantaged, and minority workers. The major thrust of CETA laws and regulations was toward the systematic coordination of its programs with other established manpower programs such as the Wagner-Peyser Act programs (Employment Service), Vocational Education, and Vocational Rehabilitation.

As the national program took shape, a number of serious policy and administrative inadequacies became apparent. Local planners and politicians were unprepared to assume the administrative role of "prime sponsors," and severe inequities in interunit fund allocations were created by blatant political manipulation.[1] Most serious, however, were the inequities which evolved in program coverage and allocation of funds and services between specific demographic and socioeconomic groups. This was especially true for low-income, unemployed, and underemployed workers 55 years old and older.

Expert opinion on the dismal failure of the public management of aging human resources is almost universally shared by those involved in industrial gerontology and economic problems of the aged. Congressional testimony of John B. Martin, former commissioner on aging, and Michael D. Batten, director of Industrial Gerontology, Kirschner Associates, give some indication of present professional dissatisfaction with the national manpower program impact on older worker problems. First, Mr. Martin testifying before a House Committee on age discrimination in employment: "Past manpower programs have shown a consistent lack of interest in the older worker and, based on general revenue sharing's practically total disregard for the needs of the elderly, it would appear that there is little hope of having older workers share in CETA programs in any real relation to their needs. . . . CETA which has several titles that might be a basis for the older worker employment, has been of very little use to the older worker" (U.S. House, 1976, pp. 35, 40).

Batten, in noting the integral role the Employment Service (ES) plays in serving the employment related needs of all those in need of assistance, observes that the older job applicants are generally ignored. (Hearings, 1975, p. 47). Further: "In a nutshell, the Employment Service data indicates that the older one is, the less likely he or she is to receive support from the United States Employment Service. This is regrettable, especially when the White House Conference on Aging recommendation called for special manpower and employment services for older persons in search of work. . . . The committee will want to find out more in this regard'' (U.S. House, 1975, p. 48).

More recently, the United States Commission on Civil Rights, in its investigation of age discrimination in federally funded service programs, found "unreasonable age discrimination" in public manpower programs at virtually every level of government (U.S. Commission on Civil Rights, 1977).

The present study is intended to serve as a quantitative supplement to the many charges of age discrimination by examining the relationship of a number of mature labor market risk factors to two interrelated components of the nation's manpower system—CETA and the ES. A brief description of the relevant programs follows.

CETA:
Title I. Comprehensive manpower service development emphasizing training, manpower, or supportive services leading to employment not subsidized by the act. Intended to replace prior categorical manpower programs.

Title II. Creation of public employment programs in areas of high unemployment. Funds transitional subsidized positions in public sector leading to permanent unsubsidized employment.

Title VI. Emergency jobs program which establishes temporary public service jobs for the unemployed.

These three items are primarily administered by local officials of cities and counties with populations over 100,000 upon attaining eligibility as a prime sponsor. Es activities as mandated under the Wagner-Peyser Act of 1933 authorizing the establishment of a national system of employment offices to provide placement and counseling services to all persons in need of employment related assistance. CETA Prime Sponsor and Employment Service coordination is mandated in CETA, Section 106(b) (4).

LEGISLATED TARGET GROUPS AND DETERMINATION INEQUITIES

While considerable flexibility has been written into the acts under examination and respective federal regulations, the general demographic and socioeconomic characteristics which define the risk groups are quite specific. CETA Titles II and VI give special consideration to persons who have been *unemployed the longest time*. Specifically, Title II gives service priority to those who have been out of work the longest and who are experiencing the greatest difficulty in finding jobs, while Title VI targets those unemployed *for 15 weeks or longer*. Those who are expected to benefit from the job training and the economic opportunities under all titles of CETA are the "economically disadvantaged, the unemployed and the underemployed," which would of course include the discouraged—an especially acute problem of the older worker.

Title I of CETA is the most flexible. It requires that, to the extent feasible, programs be targeted to "those most in need" within the three broad categories of eligible persons; economically disadvantaged, unemployed, and underemployed (Comprehensive Employment and Training Act, 1973; Federal Regulations, 1974).

All CETA titles require that the "significant segments" of an eligible applicant's (prime sponsor) populations *be served on an equitable basis,* (Federal Regulations, 1975) and, most importantly, an age-discrimination umbrella provides that ". . . No persons shall on the ground of . . . age . . . be excluded from participation in, be denied the benefits of, or be subjected to discrimination under any program or activity funded in whole or in part with funds made available under the Act" (Federal Register, 1974).

There are admittedly some provisions in the cited regulations noting exceptions on the basis of age, but they appear to be considerably weaker than the age-discrimination proscription. Programs under Titles II and VI are unambiguously public employment programs, and, as such, they are subject to the provisions of the Age Discrimination in Employment Act of 1967, covering prospective participants up to the age of 65.

The ES plays an integral role in the overall manpower system, including several functions which bear heavily on the final outcome of older worker placements and manpower fund allocations to this age segment. By providing direct placement services through referrals, the ES is responsible to a client population defined on the basis of employment service needs. An ES coordinate activity with CETA is the timely provision of labor market information to prime sponsors. Indeed, a number of ES positions are funded through CETA appropriations for the purpose of collection, analysis, and dissemination of labor market data through the State Employment Security Agencies. Es offices ostensibly train senior worker specialists who deal with all facets of older worker employment needs. However, this function, as well as the overall integration of the ES into the operations of CETA, is riddled with administrative, regulatory, and operational problems.[2]

While there are legislative and regulatory pressures and encouragements for prime sponsor utilization of ES capabilities for data collection and analysis, as well as Department of Labor (DOL) guidelines indicating that labor market information should be made available through the ES, there are no specific directives as to age-specific disaggregation which would allow for an assessment of the older workers labor market situation. Nor are there directives on how such information, if available, could be used in ascertaining *relative* "significant segment" needs. The DOL, with full knowledge of the inexperience of the typical prime sponsor in allocating manpower funds, has refused to indicate what a desirable method might be for age-specific designations of a "significant segment."

Serving the Elderly, one of the DOL's guides to prime sponsors, suggests that all the elderly poor be considered potential CETA participants, as opposed to just those elderly in the labor force, but fails to develop an underlying strategy through which the demographic and socioeconomic information characterizing this group could best be used in establishing priorities. After stating that the procedures in the guide will in most cases "point to a need to increase income of the elderly," the guide addresses the question of establishing priorities, i.e., how the funds should be apportioned across the identified risk groups in the community, and the quality and intensity of services to be applied. In order to appreciate the extent to which the CETA philosophy of flexibility can be conveniently used as a screen and rationale for inequitable and inefficient allocations, the DOL's perceived responsibility in assisting in the setting of priorities must be quoted in its entirety: "This technical assistance guide does not instruct CETA prime sponsors as to the specific priorities which should be established for allocating limited resources among the many employment and training needs found within the community. However, where the prime sponsor follows the data gathering, analysis and evaluation procedures outlined previously, the question of establishing the elderly as a CETA target group can be dealt with knowledgeably and objectively. This will also be true with regard to establishing CETA priorities among community service needs" (U.S. Department of Labor, 1976, p. 19).

Contrary to the DOL's apparent position, the prime sponsor does not operate in a legislative and regulatory vacuum. At the very least a guideline should set forth procedures and methods by which the legislated intentions can be reasonably implemented. There is a substantial difference between instructing prime sponsors in the setting of specific priorities and instructing them in the use of defensible techniques.

The guide's procedures for gathering, analyzing, and evaluating data are also questionable. It states that "it is more than likely that any data needed by the prime sponsor" can be readily obtained from the state and area agencies on aging, which thus should be utilized as a primary source. Yet, it is well known that the federal regulations applying to the AAAs have relegated "employment related services" to "gap-filling" status and that any meaningful resource commitment by AAAs to this activity is nonexistent. It would indeed be a welcome integration of the AAAs into the manpower planning system if the DOL or the ES were to finance the necessary expertise, or, alternatively, the AOA were to reexamine the efficacy of its present "custodial" orientation.

Age-Specific Manpower Allocations and Services and the Universe of Need

Establishing a set of socioeconomic, demographic, and labor market characteristics which provide an optimal basis for determining the relative size and individuated composition of the "risk group" to which manpower funds and services will be applied "has been one of the long-standing conceptual dilemmas of the manpower planning profession (Magnum and Snedeker, 1974, p. 115). Certainly this is true of the appropriate age-segment representation, where variations in life-cycle situations and needs are not that well understood and where normative judgments of relative age-segment needs are virtually unavoidable. There is little doubt that an arbitrary specification of an age segment and the measurement of its size as a proportion of the total population is wholly inadequate. Yet, analysis and criticisms of public allocations decisions are often based on comparisons using such a crude measurement. To suppose, for instance, that the efficacy and equitability of ES decisions should be judged on the basis of relative age-segment size or relative age-segment unemployment rates, clearly misses the methodological requirements under specificity of the assessment of need—in particular, individual intensity and duration of income-employment inadequacy (Levitan and Taggert, 1974). Or, to arbitrarily specify the "older worker" as an individual 45 years and older for reporting purposes, as the DOL does, and then rationalize program policy and outcomes with the blurred distinction, again can hardly be methodologically justified. But to suggest that a set of clear methodological principles is obvious, would also be unwise.

Perhaps this is all mere quibbling, however, it is doubtful that an explanation of age discrimination in manpower allocations and services can rest very securely on such simplistic assumptions as stereotyping and misinformation about individual characteristics of the older worker. The system of discrimination is so administratively and politically complex that attributions to individual perceptions and behavior should not be allowed to dominate the discussion.

The manpower programs under scrutiny broadly designate the major potential beneficiaries of services to be individuals who are low-skilled, disadvantaged, or from minority groups, or who have low incomes and little prospect of productive employment. In some cases the specific designation of "those most in need" comprises that group in the labor force (as well as discouraged workers), who have been unemployed the longest and whose prospects of obtaining employment in the private sector are poor. Thus, background characteristics such as education; skill accumulation, along with obsolescence and skill depreciation, innate abilities; self-confidence; ability to perform on employment screening tests, etc.; and the group's labor market characteristics as well as its measurable economic status, all should be included in an employment-income risk function. Quantification, however, is not possible, in each case and even where it is possible, costs of individual assessment and data collection would be prohibitive.

It might be valuable to construct a set of age-segment unemployment probability functions, utilizing such characteristics as race, sex, education, and liquid assets as independent variables, a similar set for duration of unemployment, and functions for the proportion of discouraged workers. Subjective weights could then be applied to the three risks to form an estimator of probability of need, and a comparison with program outcomes could be made on this basis. Unfortunately, the degree of disaggregation required for a surrogate probability function of relevant risk factors is virtually impossible to obtain, both for the population and program outcomes.

A reasonable, but not wholly satisfactory, alternative to the construction of a set of age-segment probability to exposure functions is the use of arbitrarily selected age segments (based primarily on reporting categories) which could be partitioned and weighted according to a number of risk characteristics for final computation of relative incidence for each age segment. Ad hoc adjustments would then be made for characteristics which do not fit neatly into the scheme. Age-segment vulnerability to a particular labor market risk factor, adjusted by selected weights, would thus define the proportionate representation of the risk group for some risks, while for other risks which do not form well-defined quantitative supports in the determination of risk group aggregate exposure to employment-income inadequacy would be used (Levitan and Taggart, 1974).[3]

ALLOCATIVE INEQUITY INDICES

A number of labor market risk factors, background characteristics, and temporal economic relationships have provided the focus around which tables 11.1 and 11.2 have been constructed for comparison with man-power program allocations.

CETA *Allocations and Older Worker Labor Market Risk Factors*

Tables 11.1 and 11.2 represent the percent distributions across age-segments for the major titles of CETA, by nation, state, and county in 1975. While reported periods are not coterminous, the durations appear to be sufficient for a meaningful comparison between reporting agencies as well as with labor market risk factors for various age-segments.

In order to compare CETA outcomes (table 11.1) with labor-market and socioeconomic risk factors, indices must be constructed which will expli-cate the relationship of legislatively intended ''significant segments'' and final allocations under the various titles of the act. Contrast indices are thus formed by simply forcing the across age-segment index to unity, facilitating direct comparisons between age-segment exposure to the risk factor and age-segment allocation.

Undoubtedly, the most relevant indicator of labor market is an age-segment index combining the effects of unemployment incidence and unemployment duration. Equivalent indices can be derived by several methods. The interesting feature of the derivation presented here, is that the commonly employed age-segment unemployment rate, which has the property of screening relative age-segment vulnerability, is modified by a consideration for the length of a spell of unemployment. The derivation is:

$$A_j = \frac{\text{No. age-segment unemployed}}{\text{total unemployed}} \times \begin{array}{c} \%\text{of age-segment} \\ \text{unemployed} \\ \text{15 weeks or more} \end{array}$$

INDEX of proportionate exposure of the age-segment to unemployment duration risk $\quad = \dfrac{A_j}{\displaystyle\sum_{i=1}^{n} A_i} = (\%)_j$

Table 11.1. Percentage Distributions across Age-Segments for Major Titles of CETA, by Nation, State, and County, 1975

	Nation				
	Under 22(%)	22–44(%)	45–54(%)	55+(%)	Enrollment
Title I	56.5	36.5	4.1	2.9	1,425,700
Title II	22.2	63.9	8.8	5.0	197,500
Title VI	21.4	64.7	8.8	5.0	431,600

	California						
	Under 18(%)	19–21(%)	22–44(%)	45–54(%)	55–64(%)	65+(%)	Enroll-ment
Title I	30.0	19.4	42.8	4.4	2.3	1.1	140,908
Title II	3.3	14.6	71.9	7.3	2.6	0.3	26,955
Title VI	3.6	16.0	70.2	7.4	2.5	0.3	41,972

	Los Angeles County						
	Under 18(%)	19–21(%)	22–44(%)	45–54(%)	55–64(%)	65+(%)	Enroll-ment
Title I	55.0	14.9	26.3	2.6	0.5	0.2	7,218
Title II	NA						
Title VI	7.0	21.0	63.0	6.3	2.5	0.18	1,688

Sources: nation, computer run, June 5, 1976, DOL, Office of Administration and Management; California, computer run, June 5, 1976, DOL, E and T Administration, Reg. IX; Los Angeles, Los Angeles County, CETA Quarterly Progress Report, June 30, 1975.

Table 11.2 presents the index using national data for 1975.

It is now possible to make direct comparisons of demonstrated needs and allocation outcomes at the national level. The severe under-allocations to the 55–64-year-old segment and 65-plus segment are most apparent. The CETA Title II percentage allocation of 5 percent and Title VI (table 11.1 rows 2, 3) allocation of 5 percent compares poorly with the proportionate demonstrated needs of 9 percent and 3.5 percent (= 12.5 percent) for the 55–64 and 65 and over age segments, respectively (table 11.2). A Title I allocation of 2.9 percent fares even worse with respect to the two segments. Discrepancies in the risk (needs)/allocation relationship for the age-segment 45–54 should also be noted. Clearly, the aging worker has been poorly represented in the present manpower planning process.

Although national labor market data could be used for rough approximations in evaluating assessment and allocation processes of individual

Table 11.2. Labor Market Risk Factor Index for U.S., 1975, by Age-Segments (in percentages)

	21 and under	22-44	45-54	55-64	65+
Age-segment labor force as % of civilian labor force	15.3	50.9	18.5	12	3.3
Age-segment unemployed as % of total unemployed	33	47	11.4	6.6	2
Age-segment unemployed for 15 weeks or more as % of age-segment unemployed	21.5	33.5	36.4	41.9	51
Age-segment unemployed for 15 weeks or more as % of total unemployed	7	15.7	4	2.7	1.1
INDEX—proportionate age-segment exposure to combined unemployment/duration of un-employment risk factor	23	51	13.5	9	3.5
					12.5

Source: DOL, Employment and Earnings, January 1976. Household Data, Annual Averages.

prime sponsors, some modifications in the evaluation procedures are necessary. Because of the paucity of timely local market data, possible comparisons are, of course, limited and less accurate.

One data set that can be used as a rough approximation of local labor market conditions, and, hence, a reasonable estimator of age-segment proportionality, is the Weekly Average Unemployment Insurance Claims Compensated issued by the state for each county. Claims for Los Angeles County are presented in table 11.3. There is considerable correspondence between the age-segment claims percentages for Los Angeles and the national labor market risk index. The Los Angeles manpower allocations are considerably more skewed against the worker 45 years and older than are the national allocations (table 11.4). Interestingly enough, according to Los Angeles County's CETA Quarterly Progress Report (1/1/75), Title VI allocations to "older workers" had exceeded planned allocations by 2 percent.

Presumably, planners base allocation decisions on predicted as opposed to demonstrated needs; hence, lagged comparisons would undoubtedly provide a superior basis for evaluating efficiency and equitability of the planning process and plan execution. While comparisons on the basis of 1974 data would no doubt be instructive, it would be shown that relative risk remained fairly stable over the period. An examination of 1974 unemployment insurance claims relative to allocations is in itself enough to expose the gross inequitability of the county's allocation of manpower funds.

The index derived above could be further bolstered by any number of social indicators, such as, incidence of poverty, median years of education, mobility, etc., all of which would signify a decided disadvantage for the older worker. Each indicator would provide a tool for sharpening the perspective on the older workers' deteriorating labor market position, especially in periods of recession. A substantial number of elderly workers who have past attachments to the labor force find themselves victims of age discrimination and immobilized in the search when unemployed. This "discouraged worker" effect is extraordinarily difficult to estimate, yet it should be of prime importance to manpower planners. Some indication of the dimensions of this problem could be derived from the Bureau of Labor Statistics measurement on attitudes toward labor force participation by those outside the labor force and an index of proportionate exposure to the discouraged worker effect constructed similarly to that for unemployment duration. Such an index would provide an appropriate

Table 11.3. Weekly Average Number of Unemployment
Insurance Claims Compensated by Age for Los Angeles, 1975
(in percentages)

Age	Over 16	Under 22	22–44	45–64	65+	INA
% of total claim	100	8.5	51.9	24.4	3.1	12.1

Source: State of California, Health and Welfare Agency, EDD.

Table 11.4. Summary of Los Angeles County Older Worker
Manpower Policy, 1975

	45–54	55–64	65+
Percent of 1975 CETA allocations to older workers			
Title I	2.6%	0.5%	0.2%
Title VI	6.3	2.5	0.18
National unemployment/ duration risk index, 1975	13.5	9.0	3.5
Percent of Los Angeles area unemployment insurance claims for			
1975	24.4		3.1
1974	27.0		4.0

manpower accounting for the severity of older worker exposure to this
labor force participation problem.

Age Discrimination in the U.S. Employment Service

While the tenuousness of the relationship of CETA to the ES has implications with regard to an equitable CETA allocation, it is the direct effect of
age discrimination by the ES that is to be addressed here.

Unemployed older workers, as a group, invariably experience longer
periods of unemployment than younger workers, and the ES could be a
vital resource in the search for employment. More than one-quarter of
older job seekers attempt to use ES services, but the agency's overall

response to older workers' needs has been disappointing (McConnel, 1977). Only a small proportion receive attention beyond the filing of a standard application.

Labor market analysts familiar with the special problems of the unemployed older worker have expended considerable effort in examining inequities in ES delivery of services, especially those resulting in limited access to jobs for middle-aged and older applicants. The most important issue appears to be the inverse relationship that exists between the applicant's age and services received. Yet it has also been established that when older workers are referred to a job, their prospects for successful employment are at least equal to those of younger workers (Heidbreder and Batten, 1974; Sheppard and Belitsky, 1966). So it is not surprising that most analysts support the proposition that a more equitable allocation of services in terms of older worker job referrals could be accomplished without a loss in the agency's overall efficiency (Heidbreder and Batten, 1974; Sheppard and Belitsky, 1966). Unfortunately, this proposition emerges from studies whose methodologies are too restricted to support the conclusions.

In a more recent study of ES service structure, McConnel (1977) examined the efficacy of an increase in resource commitments to older worker job referrals. A "rational use of resources" model was constructed and linear regression techniques were utilized to relate agency services to placement outcomes for the various age segments. It was concluded that the ES, in attempting to optimize service outcomes under complex administrative constraints, discriminated on the basis of characteristics related to "skill" and employability rather than on the basis of age, per se. But at the same time, no justification could be found for the blatant discrimination against the older worker in the allocation of over-all services, especially counseling and training.

Concluding Comments

During my tenure as a summer Fellow in the Los Angeles County Department of Senior Citizens Affairs, I had the unique opportunity to observe firsthand the implementation of a significant body of recent aging legislation. Under the privileged position afforded me through the negotiations between the Gerontological Society and agency, I was able to explore the rather exclusive domains of a county bureaucracy, inquiring over the range of agency concerns and operations but without the constraints generally imposed by permanent attachment to an organization.

Responses to my questions were quite candid and in considerable contrast to my preconceived notions of an ideal implementation and advocacy of aging programs. Yet, it soon became clear that there was logic behind the politicking and subtle manipulation within the agency and that the process I was observing would ultimately benefit the local community of elderly. After the experience I am simply unable to identify with that group which generally views the area agency system as one infused with incompetence and unresponsive to the needs of the elderly. A more accurate portrayal may be one in which agency officers and staff expend considerable effort and ingenuity in contending with bureaucratic entanglements to put aging programs in operation.

I hope that my work on age-discrimination in manpower programs reflects the amount of available research time and the resources that the agency were willing to commit to my consulting experience. I was able to show, with somewhat greater precision than is generally attempted, that older workers have been discriminated against in public manpower programs. Further, my research confirmed, at an aggregate level, those attitudes and bureaucratic manipulations which are characteristics of the nation's manpower programs I suspected but was unable to substantiate in my field work at the local level.

In retrospect, the pleasant working environment led to far too much time spent in the office and too little time in the field. Because of this, I am less able to assess the problems the area agencies are likely to encounter in interacting with those groups whose support they must secure to be successful. Considering that my original intention was to become involved in negotiating interagency agreements, I find that spell of inertia a bit regrettable.

It is premature to evaluate the degree to which the fellowship experience was beneficial to my academic interests in gerontology. But surely it will be reflected in any future research I attempt in the aging area.

Notes

1. The Government Accounting Office has pointed up severe inequities in fund allocations through blatant political manipulation by local political officials (Government Accounting Office, 1976).
2. Cf. Manpower Program Coordination, 1975, pp. 79, 139, 211; Heidbreder and Batten, 1974.
3. The proposed measure, while not an index in the technical sense of Levitan and Taggart, is conceptually similar.

REFERENCES

Comprehensive Employment and Training Act of 1973. Sec. 105(a) (1) (D).

Federal Register. 1974. Vol. 40, no. 101, sec. 98.21, a and b (1,2).

Federal Regulations. 1974. 29 CFR 95. 14(b) (3) (ii) (A).

Federal Regulations. 1975. CFR 96.29.

Government Accounting Office. 1976. Progress and Problems in Allocating Funds under Titles I and II—Comprehensive Employment and Training Act. Report to the Congress by the Comptroller General of the United States, January 2.

Heidbreder, E., and Batten, M. 1974. *ESARS II: A Comparative View of Services to Age Groups*. Washington: National Council on Aging, Inc.

Levitan, S., and Taggart, R. 1974. *Employment and Earnings Adequacy*. Baltimore, Md.: Johns Hopkins University Press.

McConnel, C. E. 1977. Age discrimination and the employment service—another look. *Industrial Gerontology* 4:167–72.

Magnum, G., and Snedeker, D. 1974. *Manpower Planning for Local Labor Markets*. Salt Lake City, Utah: Olympus Publishing Co.

National Commission for Manpower Policy. 1975. *Manpower Program Coordination, A Special Report*. October, pp. 79, 139, 211.

Sheppard, H. L., and Belitsky, H. 1966. *The Job Hunt*. Baltimore, Md.: Johns Hopkins University Press.

U.S. Commission on Civil Rights. 1977. *The Age Discrimination Study*. December, pp. 10–77.

U.S. House of Representatives. Committee on Education and Labor. Subcommittee on Equal Opportunities. 1976. Hearings on Age Discrimination in Employment. 94th Cong., February, pt. I.

U.S. House of Representatives. Select Committee on Aging. Subcommittee on Retirement Income and Employment. 1975. Hearings. 94th Cong., December 10, p. 47.

U.S. Department of Labor. Employment and Training Administration. 1976. *Serving the Elderly, A Guide for Prime Sponsors under the Comprehensive Employment and Training Act of 1973*. February.

12. Case IX. Gerontological Training: View from a Regional Office

Jack E. Sigler

EDITOR'S NOTE: Most organizations, private and governmental, must train their staffs to carry out specific jobs. Indeed, many large private organizations, such as insurance companies, devote a considerable amount of time and effort to train their personnel to serve the public more effectively. Government organizations, particularly in the field of aging, are aware of the need for training, but often these needs have been slighted in favor of more urgent demands.

Sigler shows how training needs are involved in the struggle for resources which constitutes the daily life of complex organizations. He offers a realistic description of training in relation to aging services and illustrates the importance of clearly separating the resources from the actual training process. Sigler also shows that target groups must be specified if training is to be carried out effectively. He has devised a simple and clever model, the "hatrack," which sorts out functions, resources, and programs and specifies target groups.

ONLY a few years ago the elderly were not readily recognized by the average person as being a separate population group. Knowledge of their characteristics or needs was largely limited to information about the elderly in one's own family. But things changed. Older people were "suddenly" recognized. Their numbers had reached that "critical mass" whereby it was now economically and politically feasible to provide specially designed services. While this relatively sudden awareness of aging services needs was beneficial in obtaining federal financial support, it did impose certain problems for the service delivery system.

In the traditional service delivery system new services were introduced by adding them to the already existing system. Personnel were frequently reassigned to the new service, or it was added to their current assignment. The initiative for the new service, in all probability, originally derived from these same grass roots workers. This was not the case for aging services. With the exception of certain types of income maintenance, there was no comparable service delivery system to which these new services could be attached. For most communities, providing special services for the aging was a new idea, federally instigated and financed. Whole new delivery systems had to be organized.

This rapid expansion of new specialized services resulted in a demand for trained personnel which frequently exceeded the supply. In addition, many of these early workers adhered to the stereotypes and misconceptions about the elderly that were held by the population in general. The demand for staff from the limited trained personnel pool meant that many were hired with limited or inadequate job training. A concomitant effect was the proliferation of "crash" training courses. The universities, traditional providers of trainers, were not well-prepared to meet this greatly increased demand for practical, aging-oriented training programs. This created an open market situation which stimulated many nontraditional educational institutions, as well as many colleges and universities without previous interest in aging, to enter the training field. The predictable result was a confusion of competitive and overlapping offerings— many taught by instructors with questionable credentials.

Various educational institutions in the Midwest, as well as in other parts of the country, were stimulated to "think aging" by the availability of money for this purpose. However, there was, in this region, a pool of professionals who had been actively involved in gerontological research and education for a number of years prior to the "aging boom." These gerontologists, mostly sociologists, were uniquely organized into a confederation bound by their interest in aging. The main purpose of the Midwest Council for Social Research in Aging (MCSRA) was to promote collaborative gerontological research and the training of gerontologists. As such, MCSRA did not build up a single large gerontological center, but opted instead to encourage the involvement of Midwestern universities. By the time the aging boom came along, MCSRA had succeeded in encouraging the development of "mini centers" throughout much of the central Midwest. But this body of gerontological expertise was focused almost exclusively on traditional educational approaches and research. Only occasionally had it been tapped for the training of those involved in service delivery or planning.

The problem resolved into a series of questions: Who is to be trained? For what purpose? How should it be organized—taught? How do the different types of providers relate to the whole for planning purposes? Is there any way to reduce problems of "turf"? How can coordination-cooperation be effected across state and other political boundaries? How does the aging network function—what are its training needs? The last question is of particular importance since so few of the trainer's have had experience in the operation of the administrative network—and little experience in service delivery. It may be difficult to prove, but it is not hard to imagine, that many of the problems of poor service, misuse of

Jack E. Sigler

funds, etc. that characterized some of the early programs can be traced to the lack of proper and thorough job training.

It was with this in mind that I applied for a fellowship from the Gerontological Society for the summer of 1975. I contacted both the director of the Missouri Office of Aging and the regional Administration on Aging (AOA) director for HEW Region VII. Fortunately, both were interested in and concerned about this problem and agreed to serve as hosts should I receive the fellowship. I was eventually assigned to Region VII AOA office in Kansas City.

THE SETTING

HEW Region V II is comprised of Iowa, Missouri, Nebraska, and Kansas, with the regional office located in Kansas City, Missouri, the geographical center of the region. Awareness of aging problems in this region is heightened by the fact that these four states rank third, fourth, fifth, and sixth nationally in the proportion of their population over the age of 65 (Facts about Older Americans, 1977). Unlike areas with high in-migration of older people, the relatively high proportion of elderly in the Midwest is largely due to the fact that many of the younger people have moved out of the area, leaving the senior family behind—often on the farm. Agribusiness is a main economic force, with farming communities having disproportionately large proportions of elderly. Missouri and Kansas each have 20 counties where the elderly constitute more than 20 percent of the total population. In spite of the aging nature of the rural areas, very few specialized services have been available. A significant proportion of the rural elderly, especially those residing in the western third of the region, had held rather tenaciously to their "independence" and "pioneer spirit." As a result, the rural areas tended to respond rather more slowly to opportunities offered by the Older Americans Act (OAA) and other service programs. Needless to say, there was a shortage of trained personnel available for proposal writing and service delivery.

The organization of the AOA network is quite diverse in this region. Area Agencies on Aging (AAAs) vary in both geographical area and in organizational structure. These agencies may have the responsibility for only one urban county, a few urban counties, or for many rural counties. One of the problems in the western third of the region is the low population density. In order for a western AAA to serve a similar number of people to the other AAAS in the state, the former must serve a huge area. This not only creates transportation and service delivery problems, but makes it difficult for residents of one county to feel they have much in common with the residents of another "local" county, which may be nearly 100 miles away.

Administratively, AAAs may be assigned to a branch of city government, semiofficial agencies such as a Council of Government (COG), or a part of a community college; or, they may be located in a separate organization formed for the specific purpose. Citizens may become involved through the city council, a county council, specially constituted advisory boards, or through one of many citizen advisory committees. The AAA's function is to plan for and administer OAA monies that are passed through a state designated agency. AAAs are administratively independent of the state agency but are coordinated and regulated by the state, mostly through its control of the federal monies. The state contracts with the AAAs for the distribution of the money and services.

THE CONSULTING EXPERIENCE

The consultantship had three primary objectives: to develop an instrument or model that would be a useful guide in bringing about increased understanding of training efforts as they relate to aging; to develop a regionwide concern for and/or approach to training needs and activities; and for the consultant to better understand the complex interactions that take place in a HEW regional office. All three objectives were achieved, albeit not necessarily in the form and time originally envisioned. As a consultant, I spent three months in the regional office; however, to some extent, I am still working on the first two objectives nearly three years later.

The development of some method of viewing the overall gerontological education scene seemed to be of greatest concern. Generally there is very little communication, cooperation, or coordination in the development or execution of training packages. This situation prevails in almost all geographical areas and can be frequently observed in some of our larger educational institutions. Many opportunities for mutual support and assistance are lost. Both state and AAA planners and funders work very hard trying to keep up with paperwork and "putting out fires." These activities often take so much of the staff's time that they are unable to achieve a comprehensive picture of the situation.

In almost all cases, those involved in one type of training program have little interest and appreciation for the goals and methods of another type of program. Thus, it is common to hear academically oriented persons speaking critically of short-term training ("They don't teach the right things, the important things"), and to hear short-term trainers down-grade academics ("They don't understand the real world, they're a bunch of eggheads"). Still others think that only the education of service delivery staff is worthy of support, while their opposites wish to focus on education of the elderly themselves.

It was with this orientation that I attempted to construct some form of perceptual model that would address itself to some of the issues raised above. Such an instrument must have several characteristics: it must be simple to understand with a minimum of time and effort; it must be able to communicate the basic idea to an audience with a wide range of backgrounds; it must be comprehensive; it must be practical; it should be useful in a number of circumstances; it should be grounded in the actual experiences of those for whom it is intended.

The first draft of what was to become known as the "hatrack" (fig. 12.1) was developed to assist a community college in the Kansas City metropolitan area which was having trouble learning who was doing what in aging. This draft was taken to various state and area agencies on aging in the region for their reaction. After a discussion of activities and attitudes on training in general, I introduced the most recent draft. The model was revised after every interview in an attempt to make it more responsive to the expressed needs. To a considerable extent then, the hatrack represents the input of those for whom it meant to serve. The final version of the hatrack consists of a very brief statement of purposes and directions for use followed by several examples illustrating the mechanics of use.

The hatrack is intended to be a form of logic. In no way should the various levels of the charts be considered as representing a hierarchy. The point is to illustrate the various branches of a total system; each branch is equally important in establishing a complete system. Limited availability of resources, special problems, or personnel with special interests and skills may give one branch a higher priority at a particular point in time, but eventually the whole system must be completed.

The hatrack is a series of charts. Actually it is one big chart that was divided into several smaller, simpler charts to facilitate assimilation by potential users. The first part of figure 12.1, the overview, is an index to figures 12.1A–12.1E. At the left are listed the five levels of the hatrack. Levels one through three assist in determining a logical procedure for classifying available programs or pinpointing the type of program and target population for proposed training programs. Levels four and five are blank, to be filled in by the user and to include all programs in the geographical area of concern. The end box on each branch displays the

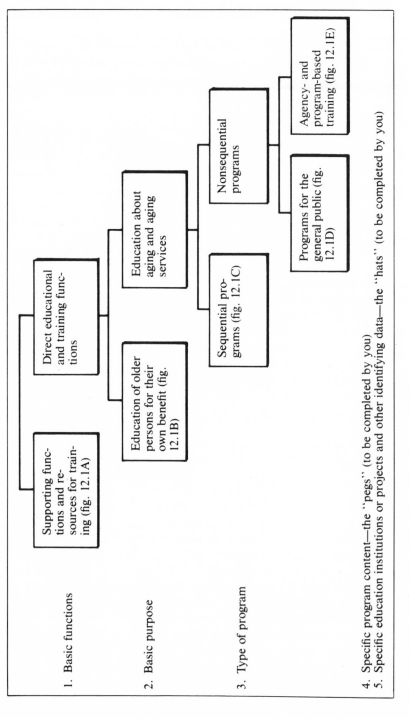

1. Basic functions

2. Basic purpose

3. Type of program

4. Specific program content—the "pegs" (to be completed by you)
5. Specific education institutions or projects and other identifying data—the "hats" (to be completed by you)

Fig. 12.1. Hatrack for Aging Education: Overview and Index

226

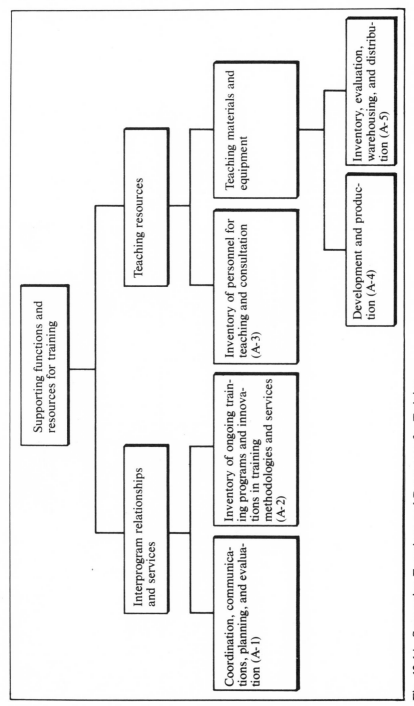

Fig. 12.1A. Supporting Functions and Resources for Training

227

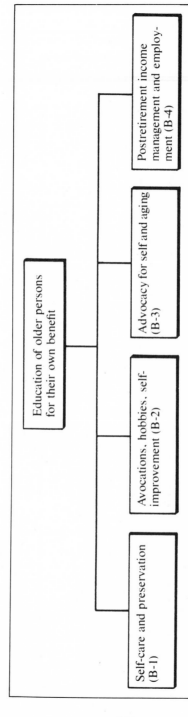

Fig. 12.1B. Education for Older Persons

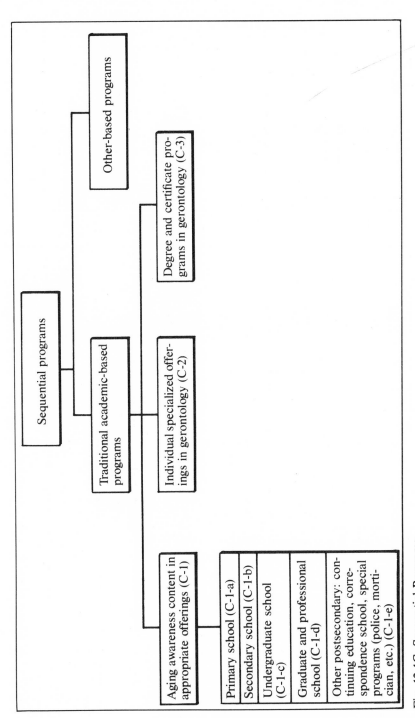

Fig. 12.1C. Sequential Programs

The diagram shows the following hierarchy:

Sequential programs
- Traditional academic-based programs
  - Aging awareness content in appropriate offerings (C-1)
    - Primary school (C-1-a)
    - Secondary school (C-1-b)
    - Undergraduate school (C-1-c)
    - Graduate and professional school (C-1-d)
    - Other postsecondary: continuing education, correspondence school, special programs (police, mortician, etc.) (C-1-e)
  - Individual specialized offerings in gerontology (C-2)
  - Degree and certificate programs in gerontology (C-3)
- Other-based programs

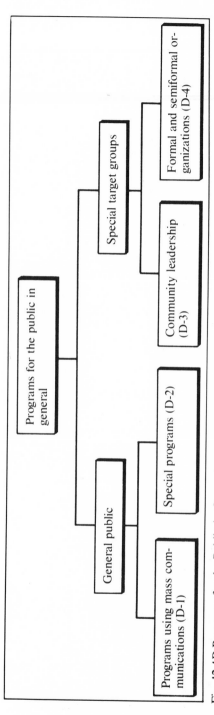

Fig. 12.1D Programs for the Public in General

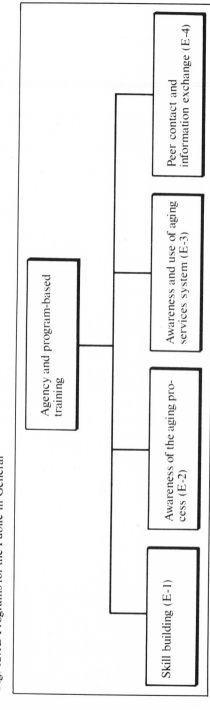

Fig. 12.1E. Agency and Program-Based Training

letters of the subchart, containing a more detailed breakdown. Since the first three steps are quite general it might be assumed that "everyone" knows that much about what they want to do. However, experience has shown that many new-to-the-field providers who want to "do something" in aging have not even made these rudimentary decisions. By following the chart, personnel will avoid fragmentation of purpose and be forced to determine where their strengths lie.

The end box on each branch of figures 12.1A–12.1E also contains a reference number. In geographical areas with very few training resources, available programs and resources can be listed directly on the charts. In most areas, however, it would be more expedient to list the resources on separate pages or file cards which have been keyed to the hatrack (A-1, C-1). In this way the "device" can be used as a coding mechanism by which a large number of resources can be listed.

The hatrack was originally conceived as a tool to increase understanding of how various training programs interrelate and as a guide to constructing an inventory of available training resources. However, a number of additional uses were suggested by the early respondents, and others have appeared since. In fact, the name hatrack was given to the tool by one of the AAA directors in Missouri during a heated discussion of what he considered to be the most important area of training. He was vehemently defending his position that educational services for the elderly were of the highest priority. After seeing the layout for the whole model he somewhat reluctantly admitted that it all was important and then said, "Okay, I can see that the rest of the training is equally important, but this area (pointing to the education for the elderly box) is what I'm best qualified to do. This is where I intend to hang my hat." In other words, the hatrack is a tool that helps people arrive at an "I'm OK, you're OK" attitude. Use of the hatrack outline has greatly reduced once common name-calling rivalry.

In another instance, a person employed by a community college to coordinate activities in aging saw the hatrack as a useful tool in setting priorities for her institution. Her administrator had been urging her to begin several projects simultaneously. She took the hatrack to the administrator so that he could better understand the different target populations and the methodologies needed to address them. She reported that the instrument had helped organize her efforts and made their aging program more effective.

One of the more effective uses of the hatrack is as leverage in that big poker game called planning and coordination. The stakes can be rather high—thousands of dollars for projects. Planning/coordinating/funding agencies are frequently approached by individuals or organizations who want to "get a piece of the action." Some of these people know exactly what is needed, or at least what they want to do; however, quite a few are flexible or unsure. Particularly those new to the aging services field approach the potential funder with ideas that tend to overlap already existing programs. The agency then has the unpleasant task of rejecting the applicant or of spending considerable time in educating and reorienting him to another topic. The process of telling a person that he cannot do project A but can do project B creates the impression of heavy-handed coordination. A properly completed hatrack can be an important tool in effecting the same results without appearing dictatorial. By talking the applicant through the hatrack and pointing out that the particular "peg" is already occupied (maybe by several programs), the applicant will be more likely to shift his attention to another "peg," which is currently unoccupied—it being obvious that the possibilities for funding would be greater for the new program. Thus, coordination occurs in a more "voluntary" manner.

Referring to planning, coordination, and project funding as a high-stakes poker game is a fairly accurate way to describe the activities that I observed within the AOA network. Getting a particular project funded is, to a considerable extent, a game of chance. However, like poker, the skillful players tend to be the more consistent winners. There are players that can manipulate "the cards" as well as any card shark, and there are plenty of novices around to feed the sharks. There were both sharks and novices among the AOA bureaucracy as well as among service providers seeking grants.

The most interesting part of the game was the bluffing. This takes many forms, but essentially the player wants to accomplish something for which there is no specific mandate or authorization. A memorandum is developed explaining the new request and is sent to the other players. If they like the memo they either act on it or pass it down the chain of command for action. Should any of the players not like the memo, they have two options—do it anyway, or make a fuss and send it back to the original player saying it cannot (or will not) be done. The frequency with which his bluff is called depends upon the bluffing skill of the original player (the implied power or assuming authorization). The receiving players also have the opportunity to bluff. Not only can they pass the memo down the line (usually knowing it is a bluff), they can use their bluff to "reject" it. The original player then has to decide whether to accept the rejection or to try again—only harder. In order to avoid a direct showdown the second bluff attempt is usually reworded or modified in such a way as to still accomplish some or most of the original intent while answering some of the objections of the players who rejected the first attempt. This process continues until some action is, in effect, negotiated. Should the original bluff attempt succeed with the majority of the other players, the memo then becomes working policy with almost as much authority as if it had been mandated by law.

Like poker, there are rules to this game. To violate the rules brings penalties or rejection. One must go through channels, grant applicants must not apply inappropriate political pressure, must follow rules and instructions, and must know grantsmanship procedures. Funds must be accounted for in certain ways and not spent for red flag items. But rules are made to be broken, and at times one or more of the players is playing the game with a stacked deck. Fortunately, both rule bending and deck stacking are usually employed only in order to make the system more workable. At no time did I observe anyone trying to "rip off the system" for personal gain. In fact, while many of the people enjoyed playing the game, all were really dedicated to the essential task of bringing service to the elderly in the best and most efficient manner. Like a friendly game of poker, should anyone become too aggressive the other players take considerable pains to isolate that person and bring him back into line—or throw him out of the game.

It is very difficult to compartmentalize my experiences—so many of the "in-office" events related to the major objectives in training. For instance, the director of a regional resource and training agency visited the regional office and explained the "regional" aspect of his agency was based more on the title than on the services delivered. Also, only one state had provided any substantial financial support for its operation. The project director was trying to get the regional office to either provide funds or to urge the other three states in the region to provide them. At the same time the regional director was trying to shift the responsibility for obtaining regional support back to the project director. Various strategies were discussed, advocated, rejected, etc.

A few days later I was at the office of the state director who was providing the major share of the resource center's funds. Discussions were underway as to how the burden of supporting this agency could be shifted to other resources.

The next day I was in an out-state AAA as a part of my regular interviewing. The director asked me to stay for a planning meeting with his staff and others (on nutrition). At the meeting, the discussion turned to the need for a permanent training site (to be located in their area). I pointed out that there was already such a site (the regional resource and training center) and that the AAA should develop their program to be compatible with the ongoing one. I suggested means by which the group's program could gain visibility and exert leadership without duplication and in a manner that the regional resource and training center would also benefit.

Around the same time I had the opportunity to discuss with the AAA agency, in whose area the center was located, the future roles and relationships of the AAA and the resource center. I attempted to show (via the hatrack) the relationship of the center to the whole training picture and encouraged the AAA to make appropriate use of the center.

About a week later I was asked to attend a meeting of representatives from the regional office, state office, local AAA, and the project. (I was asked to attend by each of them individually.) This meeting (at which the hatrack was referred to repeatedly) was the culmination of all the above individual discussions. It was indeed a miniature study of complex organizations. The finding, as mentioned above: it's all one big poker game.

While visiting the various planning agencies and projects in the region I also gathered some data on attitudes and perceived needs for training programs. I was not surprised that perceptions differed, but I was surprised at how they differed. In all cases, the need for training was recognized. What varied was their definition of the purpose, content, and amount of training needed, as well as differences as to who should do or support the training.

At the risk of oversimplification, the differences in perception were related to the level of concern: the farther down (closer to the grass roots) the AOA network one went, the more practical the orientation—the focus tended to be for solution of everyday, existing problems. The farther up (closer to the rule-makers and funders) one went, the more theoretical the orientation—concern for the definition of generalized problems and anticipation of new problems. While these two statements convey roughly the same idea, the rhetoric which supports them is quite different.

I have no doubt that most of the people I talked with would agree with the above observation if it was called to their attention. However, very few voluntarily indicated that they had any special awareness of this difference in perception. Area agency staff would say, "The only training we need is help in solving (X) problem," or, "They make us go to that training by those college professors who don't know anything about our special problems," or, "When we have a problem we don't know how to

Jack E. Sigler

handle, we get in an expert to train us so that we can solve the problem—and teach others if necessary."

State and AAA directors tended to make similar remarks concerning problem solving. However, there is increasing awareness of the need to anticipate trouble before it happens. There is much more awareness of "capacity building"—both as their responsibility to "their" AAAS and as a thrust of the regional office as it concerns the state staff. It is somewhat easier to accept the role of the dispenser of capacity building efforts than it is to be the recipient of these efforts. This is not to say that the state staff acted as "know-it-alls." They did recognize at least some of their limitations as capacity builders for the AAAS. To that extent they welcomed many of the training programs and much of the technical assistance (which is a form of training, of course) offered. Although somewhat skeptical of the value of "most" of the university training programs, they were willing to make use of much more of this resource than were the AAAS.

Regional office staff, while still focusing on practical applications and still questioning the value of some university programs (for regional staff use), were much more general in their views of training needs and much more aware of how an understanding of basic principles and theories could be of use to "their" states and AAAS. Selected university-based personnel were often utilized in problem solving and training efforts.

Perceptions of who should organize the training sessions differed widely, both between and within the three levels of agencies. In general, AAAS did not see themselves as being involved in the organization or financing of training programs, other than paying tuition or enrollment fees. This differed somewhat by size. AAAS serving the larger population centers were more interested in making training one of their direct responsibilities.

There is a certain amount of training mandated, or at least strongly encouraged, at the state level. In Region VII these state-funded programs varied from rather perfunctory, one-shot, short-term conferences or workshops, to the operation of an ongoing agency. While accepting the responsibility of financing at least some training, the states tend to want the AAAS and the region to provide more support than they have in the past. Agencies at all three levels are caught in the tight money situation and are looking for ways to stretch the little money they have. Therefore, part of the big poker game is to see how much they can "rip-off" from some other sources, both inside and outside the AOA network.

The second major objective of my consultation involved working on the development of regionwide concern for training needs and services. The original approach was to form a committee of representatives from the four state offices. However, as I traveled around it became clear that the subject was too extensive and the number of interested people too great to approach the topic with a narrow definition of education. The more the idea was discussed, the wider became the thrust. Training broadened into staff development which broadened into community education. As a result, the original training committee was never convened. Instead, those who had expressed interest were invited to meet and discuss what action to take. The actual meeting took place that fall (after the formal consultantship had ended).

After considerable discussion it was decided to create a regional society devoted to the betterment of aging through staff and public development. A subcommittee was formed to draft by-laws and to report to the group the following February, at which time the by-laws were accepted, and the Mid-America Congress on Aging (MACA) was born. After another year of planning, the new association assumed the task of organizing the Regional Conference on Aging. This young organization is still rapidly developing, and since I served as its first president and still serve on the board of directors, it might be said that the original consultation to the Regional Office never ceased. In any case, MACA has succeeded in getting professional workers, advisory council members, and others from all four states to meet and pursue common goals. It has also been able to involve professionals from other disciplines not usually connected with the AOA network. MACA is far from what we were planning when the consultantship started, but I believe that it answers the need more effectively.

The third major consultation objective was to learn something of how the various offices of the AOA network operated. In effect, my entire experience there (and this report) reflects the fulfillment of that objective. The poker game style of operation was a revelation to me. It was something of a surprise to learn that just because something looked like a regulation it was not necessarily so. But perhaps the greatest shock was the discovery of how seldom knowledge of gerontology was used or needed in the day-to-day operation of all the AOA agencies. Having spent many years in gerontological research and training, I "knew" that this knowledge was of primary importance to these agencies. With the rapid expansion of service programs for the aged has come a rapid and sizable demand for people to staff these programs and agencies. We "old timers" often speak of the "instant gerontologists," shake our heads, and wonder how these programs can operate. While my attitudes toward the need for gerontological expertise have not changed, I can see that much of the operation of these planning and monitoring agencies is purely bureaucratic office management.

I hope the above statement is not misunderstood. AoA agencies do need and use gerontological knowledge frequently, especially in the planning process. There is never a time when knowledge of the population they serve can be forgotten. Because of the complex nature of life in a bureaucratic agency it is not possible to determine meaningfully when gerontological knowledge is necessary and when it is superfluous. However, the fact remains. The particular instances when specific knowledge of aging is needed are rather few when compared to other knowledge areas. A knowledge of gerontology is useful when trying to solve certain problems in service delivery (making nutrition sites attractive to the target population, arranging better transportation schedules, planning for new housing), but it is little used or needed when monitoring specific projects, filling out forms, and interpreting regulations. In the regional office most of the direct use of gerontological knowledge was made by staff serving as resource persons.

There are times when a knowledge of older people would be helpful—and essential, especially when developing the year's plan—but generally such information is not pertinent. Lack of understanding of this point is one of the major reasons why many university-based training programs miss the target. It has nothing to do with the quality of the instruction, only misconceptions as to the job descriptions and requirements of agency staff. There is an obvious need for "practical" training programs. Academic types are fond of saying that nothing is more practical than a good theory. I believe this. I also now believe that the operating staff does not accept this point of view at least partly because they are being given theories on the wrong subjects.

Gerontologists must seriously rethink the problem of how to apply gerontological knowledge. They need a better working knowledge of how to operate an agency, the type of problems faced by that agency, the time frame in which the agency must operate, and when a knowledge of gerontology is useful and/or essential. In short, the university-based gerontologists need to be more closely "plugged into" the AOA network. The research problems could then be stated in a manner that would make them more easily identified with the problems and questions being raised by those in the direct planning and service phases of the system.

With this in mind, I talked at great length with several of my colleagues in sociology. I had the opportunity to introduce another sociologist to the Kansas Office of Aging and had some success in getting this faculty member to want to understand the aging network, and in getting the state director to welcome the sociologist to his office. Another colleague was sufficiently interested to apply for (and receive) a consultantship the following year.

I have become increasingly interested in the special problems of the application of gerontological knowledge to the service delivery system. I do not wish to downgrade in any way the work of those sociologists who are concerned with finding answers to other types of questions, but I found an increased awareness of, and appreciation for, the day-to-day problems. It is indeed intriguing how the same overall problem can be addressed by different questions. The service providers ask questions different from those that are often asked by academic gerontologists. Both types of questions need to be addressed.

A few years ago it was not considered professional for academic gerontologists to be interested in practical solutions to specific service delivery problems. I am pleased to report that this is no longer the case. As more gerontologists have the opportunity to engage in these consultantships and to discuss these experiences with each other and with their colleagues, there is a growing recognition that all questions are valuable.

CONCLUSIONS

The consultantship experience was rewarding beyond all expectations. It enabled me to do a project because *I* wanted it done, and my placement was ideal for my purpose. The staff personnel were accepting, understanding, and helpful; a pleasure to be with professionally and personally. The project was instrumental in helping to reach some of the goals set by my placement agency and was meaningful (not just an exercise) and of such a nature that some closure could be achieved. The project was worthy of further effort by myself and the agency. I expect that I will be "playing" with the topic for many years. My peers have been supportive in recognizing that the experience was more than a change of pace for the summer and that the "product" has some possibility of achieving its intended goal. This is particularly rewarding because the hatrack was especially designed to communicate with nonacademically oriented people.[1]

The consultantship has been a rewarding experience; I feel that I have a new understanding of the AOA network, and I wish that many more of my colleagues could have a similar experience.

A FUNCTIONAL MODEL OF EDUCATION AND TRAINING IN AGING: A HATRACK FOR PLANNING AND COOPERATION

Purposes

•To provide a schematic way of organizing education and training functions both for and about the aged, which will provide a Gestalt or overview of current activities and future possibilities.

•To provide the basic structure of an instrument that, when completed for a specific planning area, will provide the basis for logical planning and a tool for "coordination through logic."

•To provide a tool which will assist planners and program developers in clarifying program objectives.

•To provide, as a part of the overall Gestalt, a mechanism whereby providers of educational services can recognize the value of various educational functions in the total system, while at the same time identifying the specific functions to which they want to relate (where they want to hang their hat).

Uses

The planner of a given area is often faced with one of two extremes: a multiplicity of education and training programs in the area or very few, if any, such programs. The hatrack is designed to assist with the first situation by providing a framework by which educational agencies can be identified as to their major strong points, their various programs can be categorized, and the relationships between all these understood in terms of a total system. The hatrack can also be of use in the last situation by suggesting where to search for actual or potential programs.

Completion of the hatrack will be of special use in deciding future directions and goals by pointing out program overlaps and gaps. The process of locating a specific (or proposed) program on the hatrack will assist the planner in arriving at a clearer statement of program objectives and structure.

The hatrack is meant to be shared. Copies, at least partly complete for the planning area, should be circulated to as many of the local education and training programs as possible, asking their assistance in identifying aging programs not yet included. If a local planning committee is available, the hatrack could be used by them in establishing goals and recommendations.

The hatrack is also meant to be a dynamic tool which will need constant revision and updating as new programs are developed and old programs cease. It is hoped that the hatrack can assist in determining the direction of change.

How to Complete

The different charts of the hatrack are part of one large diagram. The basic structure of this large display is shown on the chart marked "Overview and Index" which can assist in locating the appropriate chart for any specific program.

On the left-hand margin of the Overview and Index are designations as to the type of information given at each horizontal level. Level one describes basic functions; level two, basic purposes; level three, general types of programs; level four, the specific program content/title (the "pegs" of the hatrack); and level five, the specific educational institution providing the training (the "hats"). *Levels four and five must be completed* for each planning area using the hatrack.

Example A

In a given AAA's community, teaching materials, primarily books and films, are available to (not necessarily *in*) the area. To put these resources on the chart, you go to fig. 12.1A, "Supporting Functions and Resources for Training"; to "Teaching Resources"; to "Teaching Materials and Equipment"; and then to "Inventory, Evaluation, Warehousing & Distribution" (Box A5). Under Box A5, you would then add a box (referred to as level four on "Overview and Index")—i.e. "Books and Films" (A5-a). Under "Books and Films" (A5-a), referred to as level five on "Overview & Index," you might list: Public Library, University Library, and Mid-America Resource and Training Center.

Example B

In the AAA community, the following educational programs are available: (1) Training for AAA board members under a statewide program; (2) a ceramic class for the elderly at the local community college; and (3) a regular course in social gerontology at a local college. These would be recorded by following the boxes on the "Overview and Index" to locate the appropriate chart.

Board member training.—Proceed through the different levels starting with: "Direct Educational and Training Functions"; to "Education About Aging and Aging Services"; to "Non-Sequential Programs'; to "Agency and Program-Based Training" (fig. 12.1E). You would then go to Box El "Skill Building" and add (as level four) Box El-a "Board Member Training." Under this Box, you would add (as level five) the organization actually providing the training.

Ceramic class.—"Direct Education and Training Functions"; to "Education of Older Persons for their Own Benefit" (fig. 12.1B). You would then go to Box B2, "Advocations, Hobbies, and Self-Improvement." The program content would then be added, "Ceramics" (B2-a) and the training organization (the community college) listed under "Ceramics."

Social gerontology.—"Direct Education and Training Functions"; to "Education About Aging and Aging Services"; to "Sequential Programs" (fig. 12.1C) and on fig. 12.1C to the "Traditional Academic Based Programs" box. You would list the course under Box C2, "Specialized Offerings in Gerontology" and list the college's name under the course listing (C2-a).

NOTE

1. For more information, write Jack E. Sigler, Co-Director, Center for Aging Studies, Institute for Community Studies, University of Missouri–Kansas City, 1020 East 63d St., Kansas City, MO 64110.

13. Bridging the Gap: Academics in the Real World

Gordon F. Streib

IN evaluating the Gerontology Fellowship Program, we will first analyze the results in terms of the target groups (the Administration on Aging [AOA], the state and area agencies, and the gerontological community) and then consider the findings from the nine cases presented here.

One of the primary goals was to sensitize academic gerontologists to the "real world" of service delivery to America's aging population, and this aim was generally attained. When we speak of the "real world," we are not referring to the world of individual American older people. Instead, we are referring to the gigantic system by which services are delivered to the individual—that maze of laws, directives, guidelines, bureaucracies, levels of government, channels of communication, evaluation analyses, eligibility requirements, chains of command and reports, reports, reports—all of which are involved in effecting the seemingly simple goals of helping needy older people.

Of the fifty gerontologists who took part in this program in the first three years, most were surprised by the diversity and complexity of the "real world" in delivery of services to the aged. Some had the idealized notion that knowledge and good will combined with appropriations of public funds would effect an orderly and automatic flow of services. Some of the gerontologists did not have a realistic picture of the sociopsychological factors that operate in a bureaucracy. They were not aware of the structure and complexity of the delivery systems or of the political nature of formal organizations.

In order to describe and assess the outcomes systematically, let us briefly outline the results in relation to the goals and objectives of the major organizations and individuals involved: (1) AOA and HEW regional offices; (2) state offices on aging and their area agencies; and (3) the gerontological "community," consisting of the Gerontological Society, university centers and programs, private agencies, and individual gerontologists.

OUTCOMES: ADMINISTRATION ON AGING

The AOA must operate within the legal framework set forth in the Older

Americans Act (OAA) of 1965 and amended eight times. The law provides a broad set of objectives for developing new and improved programs for providing services for older persons. Because of the multiple clients and interest groups seeking resources, the AOA operates in a demanding political context. Like most other government agencies, it has a fundamental responsibility to make reasonable and politically acceptable decisions on the allocation of the limited resources provided by Congress. With a legislative mandate requiring equal opportunity for all older Americans, there is a continuing necessity to determine how the allocation process should be implemented.

The Gerontological Society, as the leading professional multidisciplinary organization concerned with research on the elderly, was assigned to organize and monitor this Fellowship Program in the hope that it would contribute to the broad objectives of the AOA. Because of the overwhelmingly favorable response in the first year by both the state agencies and the gerontologists, the program continued to receive support in the suceeding five years.

OUTCOMES: STATE AND AREA AGENCIES ON AGING

In the evaluative surveys that concluded each internship, the state directors on aging and the academic gerontologists affirmed the usefulness of the program. Moreover, beyond the positive attitudinal response, the state and area agencies have continued to request placements in their offices. There have always been more requests for placements than resources available.

In evaluating the program, one state director said: "The interaction and exchange of information between the consultant and the Area Agency has been of the highest professional caliber. The resulting outcome of culling through Federal regulations, needs survey data on senior citizens, and demographic informational material on service-provider agencies within Detroit–Wayne County produced an evaluation instrument to assess Title III grant application funding proposals. We are most pleased that the Gerontological Society chose the Area Agency as a site for a consultantship and followed by a selection of a most distinguished and eminently qualified individual. We believe that this experience has been both mutually beneficial and rewarding." Another observed, "May I tell you how delighted I am, now that the summer is over, with the consultation provided to our Department by the Society. . . . (the consultant) stimulated us with her technical expertise that was instrumental in bringing together many ideas culminating in a workshop on future plans for home care in the State. She played a forceful role with staff and our Area Agencies on Aging and was effective in helping us achieve the goals for her consultantship.''

The gerontologists brought a broad range of skills and professional expertise to the state offices. Many performed specialized tasks for which the regular staff did not have time or resources, such as developing a managerial system to solve administrative difficulties, evaluating day care centers for the elderly, evaluating the linkage between state and local programs, and devising a computer information program.

The reports of the fellows served as valuable resource and reference tools which the state directors used for internal agency planning. In some cases, the reports were disseminated to all members of the state legislature and to other state government agencies.

The fellows devoted considerable time to devising various techniques to meet the needs assessment surveys, which are mandated by law. Since, in many cases, the agency personnel had little or no training in research design and implementation, the needs assessment surveys often posed a definite problem.

OUTCOMES: THE ACADEMIC GERONTOLOGISTS

The Gerontological fellows in general found the summer internship to be an extremely valuable and enriching experience, providing new insights for their teaching and research. In a subcommittee report of the Gerontological Society on the summer intern project, there was a wide distribution of answers on the benefits to the academic gerontologists. At least a third of the respondents mentioned that their academic activities were changed as a result of their internship in the following ways: The existing gerontology curriculum was modified; personal research projects were redesigned; there was a change of career goals to a more applied orientation; research related to the summer experience was published; practical experiences for students were redesigned; and resident instruction activities were modified.

Others mentioned that the entry to the State Office on Aging had been important to them and their students; one had participated in the widespread interest in gerontology at the medical school level, and another found it valuable to be involved in monitoring AOA procedures in regard to discretionary grant projects.

One of the most valuable lessons the fellows learned was that their technical expertise—the theoretical skills, the survey techniques, the statistical competence—may pale in relation to the practical exigencies of the actual service delivery system. They found that contextual issues derived from political, bureaucratic, economic, and social considerations were highly important in determining the nature and outcome of the particular project. The researcher in the "real world" must bring to the situation his technical and professional expertise, but he must also know how to adapt and use it in a setting where he may control only a few of the parameters.

OUTCOMES: CAREER OPPORTUNITIES IN GERONTOLOGY

Various observers (Maddox and Wiley, 1976) have pointed out that gerontology has two sources: scientific and social problems. The work described here illustrates the dual nature of the discipline, and, in discussing the career opportunities in gerontology, it is useful to keep the distinction in mind.

The field of gerontology has grown enormously in the last decade. Formal courses are now offered in almost all four-year colleges and universities and in two-year community colleges. There are 170 university centers devoted to gerontological studies and programs. Thus, the number of persons who learn about gerontology as an academic discipline is enormous, and many are attracted to the field as a career. Seminars, workshops, and conferences are also an important and integral part of the academic scene. Outside the academic world, there has also been an increase in courses and programs sponsored by community service and action groups, by private groups of senior citizens, and by religious and civic organizations. These multifaceted activities provide opportunities for new careers.

To understand the job opportunities, one must be aware of the social trends of the coming decades. Although there has been a growth of gerontology in academic settings, the general growth of higher education has reached a plateau. Indeed, some colleges and universities are concerned about enrollments and various attempts—some almost desperate—have been initiated to cope with the possibility of fewer students. The decrease in student enrollment is related to the fact that the baby boom cohort has already entered higher education or has graduated. Furthermore, general demographic trends indicate that the college age population will not be increasing in the next decade.

The gradual decline in enrollment has also been accompanied by a decline of support for higher education. These trends suggest that academic positions will be in shorter supply than has been true in the past two decades. Although the study of aging has some growth potential among academic specialities in comparison to traditional fields in the social sciences and the humanities, it can absorb only a small percentage of trained gerontologists.

These trends lead us to predict that the greatest area of job opportunities in gerontology is likely to be in the public sector in service delivery, administration, and programming. At present, many persons working in the positions in these areas do not have an academic background in gerontology. Many have been recruited from other areas—service and administration in health, mental health, youth services, religion, etc. These gerontologists have found careers in the field primarily because it grew so rapidly, and they were available and interested.

However, the future job situation is likely to change if gerontology follows the pattern of longer established fields. Emphasis on specific training will probably take on greater importance, and there will gradually develop a trend toward certification and the acquisition of the required academic credentials. Indeed, the trend is already under way, and some persons now in the field are acquiring skills and credentials by means of short courses, summer institutes, workshops, etc.

One must ask: Does the current gerontology education prepare the student adequately for working in complex bureaucratic agencies? In most cases, it would have to be acknowledged that the present curriculum is usually deficient in this respect. Many social scientists—teachers and researchers—are trained to study individuals, their attitudes and behavior, and they are not technically proficient in the study of organizations. What is needed in the field of aging and in other human service programs is a more sophisticated knowledge of complex organizations and how they function.

Persons who wish to work in human service organizations are often motivated by a desire to "work with people." However, they frequently find that many of the staff do not deal directly with the client or individual members of the target population, and they may become disillusioned and frustrated.

This gerontology intern program has been particularly valuable in making academics aware of the settings in which their future graduates might work. A number of the fellows have recognized the need for new and revised curricula to meet the changing needs of the field and of the students. Thus, the academics have been sensitized to the bureaucratic complexities, and they can interpret these realities to their students and present a more accurate picture of service delivery to the elderly.

This model intern program has implications beyond the field of gerontology, for the problems of complex organizations are perennial in fields dealing with the young, the mentally ill, the handicapped, and others. The program might be used as a prototype for acquainting persons with the bureaucratic complexities of service delivery in other areas.

OUTCOMES: CASE STUDIES

Case I. Fauri

One of the basic mandates of the OAA is that information on the needs and living conditions of older Americans must be systematically collected. It states that special attention shall be given to the needs of low-income and minority older persons. Fauri drew up a very detailed and professional plan of the activities that would be required to carry out a needs assessment interview survey in Tennessee, although the general format could be adapted to the requirements of other states. However, the agency was not able to conduct such a survey because of lack of funds.

This case illustrates how legislative mandates may not be carried out because they were not clearly and fully communicated from the national level down through the regional to the state level of government where the research was supposed to be conducted. The state agency did not have sufficient or expert staff to monitor or to carry out the survey.

Fauri's work resulted in a detailed plan for a needs survey, and the preparation of such a plan was considered by state administrators to be an expression of *intent* to do a needs assessment survey. Thus, the work of the consultant might be judged unsuccessful in one sense; however, from another standpoint, the work could be used as a first step in the attempt to initiate the undertaking. Thus, the short-term organizational goals may have been met by this temporizing approach even though the requirement for developing assessment data as part of long-range planning was not met.

The case clearly illustrates the complexity of implementing what appears to be a clear-cut federal mandate, which, because of inadequate communication, lack of follow-through, and unavailability of personnel and resources, was not carried out.

Case II. Moen

The variety of consulting experiences is illustrated by comparing the work of David Fauri and Elizabeth Moen. Both were interested in needs assessment, and the directors of the state offices in each case, Tennessee and Oregon, wanted assistance in complying with the federal mandate that needs assessment surveys be used as the basis for planning. However, the two professionals carried out the study of needs assessment in very different ways.

Moen did an intensive qualitative field study of needs assessments in a rural area of Oregon, and, with the collaboration of her husband, a professional photographer, was able to establish excellent rapport with a small number of low-income persons and determine their social and economic situations. The outcome was a detailed case study of a small number of the elderly to whom special attention should be given. The research was published by the Oregon State Program on Aging, and more than three thousand copies were distributed. In a different form, Moen's report was published in one of the leading professional sociological journals, *Social Problems*.

Moen produced a product—a report—which was of use to the state agency. It focused on the fact that low-income older persons in Oregon are unwilling to seek out and demand services. We can only speculate as to the generalizability of Moen's findings, but it seems likely from what we know generally of rural Americans in other parts of the country that older rural Americans are affected by situational and generational factors which influence them to avoid seeking aid from government agencies unless the service is defined as a form of *earned* assistance.

Moen's work also suggests a problem faced by planners and administrators in the human service fields, namely, that of raising the expectation of clients by the needs assessment survey and then not being able to offer the desired services. Some administrators use the kind of information Moen gathered in an advocacy and adversarial way to enhance their programs and to obtain more funds for delivery of services. However, there may be a time gap of several years between the advocacy of new services and the actual implementation when the required money or staff is available. The administrators must walk a fine line between promising too much before they can deliver what is needed and being able to persuade the decision-makers (local, state, or federal) that additional monies are necessary. Reallocation of existing resources is not the solution to this dilemma. When funds are limited, reallocation means that some other services must be eliminated—an act that brings protest from other target populations and other staff persons.

Case III. Allen

All ten tribes surveyed by Michael Allen in his study of American Indians in the Southwest stated that they preferred that the funding, monitoring, and evaluating of aging programs should be done directly by the Washington office of the AOA, rather than through the State Office on Aging. Allen indicated this in his final report in 1974 to the Governor's Advisory Council on Aging. It is not known precisely what affect the report had in the bureaucratic power struggle, but the 1978 amendment to the OAA provides for funding and monitoring between the Indians and the AOA.

Allen's case also points out that witnesses who speak in behalf of minorities may not always represent their needs accurately. The discrepancies between perception of needs by the agency staff and the reservation residents is striking. For example, 43 percent of the reservation residents cited a need for transportation to procure food and water, while only 16 percent of the agency staff perceived this as a need. In contrast, 50 percent of the agency staff saw a need for nursing or convalescent homes on the reservation, while only 23 percent of the residents considered this a need.

Allen's study also demonstrates the difficulties and personal frustration for a consultant who operates between two antagonistic groups. Some of their suspicion of each other carried over to him.

Case IV. Peters

In a sense, the case study by George Peters on the aging network provides an analytical framework for understanding many of the other cases in the book as they relate to the governmental bureaucratic structure. Peters shows how a conventional goal attainment model employed by administrators, sociologists, and others is not adequate for understanding how the administrative aging network operates in the "real world." His careful research, based on participant observation and the use of a structured interview guide, illustrates how the perspectives of staff at the state and local levels are similar and how they are varied. Beyond the perceptions of goals, problems, and resources, Peters offers a view on the interactions between the staff in each of the two levels of government.

This case imparts a new appreciation of what is meant by the social context of service delivery and also the day-to-day constraints under which it operates. Kansas is similar to many other states—one might assert most states—because it has a history of minimal support and involvement by the state government in aging problems and programs. Indeed, those persons who are critical of how the federal government sets guidelines and provides matching funds must acknowledge that without the stimulus of federal monies and requirements, many states would probably be doing even less than they do now for their older citizens. If this is federal "influence" with all of its ambiguities, frustrations, paperwork, and the like, it must be underscored that without federal stimulus and monitoring, much less would be accomplished.

Peters' general conclusion is that the problem of Kansas' network for services is a structural problem and not a "people problem." While he acknowledges that attention must be given to psychological considerations, he strongly recommends structural changes. This is an understandable emphasis by a sociologist interested in complex organization. However, some readers might place less emphasis on structural change and more on the personnel component, for fundamentally the structure becomes reality only through the personnel. Obviously, the organizational structure exists as a table of organization, a line of authority, and a set of regulations and rules, but it is the specific individuals, both as individual bureaucrats and in a collective sense, who constitute the organization. Peters notes that one weakness in the Kansas situation is the lack of training or even general orientation for staff responsibilities. Persons do not know clearly what their duties are. The employee hired for the network receives "on-the-job training." Peters views this as a structural problem, but it is also a personnel problem. In the "real world" it is a combination of these two factors, plus the amount of available resources that account for this situation. Kansas, like other states, does not have the pressure derived from a political consensus to appropriate more resources for human services programs. Thus, many structural and staff problems are often reduced to this underlying resource problem.

Case V. White

One of the challenging and most difficult situations a private or public organization must face is a crisis—an unusual situation that poses a serious threat to the clientele or to the service which is offered. Public utilities, such as telephone and power companies, have some experience in dealing with technical failures. However, the large blackouts which have occurred in recent years indicate that even seemingly well-organized bureaucracies can be caught off-guard and experience great difficulties.

Charles White's case study is an instructive example of how an administrative agency concerned with serving the elderly in New York tried to anticipate what would happen if an energy shortage should occur. White's assignment was to develop a telephone survey methodology that would ascertain one particular type of need. This work is one specific form of needs assessment and is atypical in the sense that the regulations and guidelines formulated by the AOA are designed to deal with recurring, long-range kinds of problems, rather than crisis situations.

Like the other cases described here, the technical aspects of developing a telephone survey must be understood in relation to the larger social service bureaucracy of which aging programs are only a small part. Finally, the issue of how research and research techniques are viewed by the personnel in the state social service bureaucracy is of strategic importance.

Plans for an energy crisis must be placed in the larger social context of the industrialized, urban, bureaucratic society in which we all live and with which we must cope. Many older persons live alone, and a substantial proportion have limited incomes and mobility. Thus, a shortage of energy can create considerable hardship for a small but significant proportion of the older persons. One can assume that in many emergencies, family members will look after relatives. In addition, there are specified organizations and their personnel—police, fire departments, public utilities, hospitals—who are trained and dedicated to deal with a variety of critical situations in contemporary communities. But in any community, there is bound to be a certain percent of the population who is isolated or overlooked and, at a time when energy is in short supply, might suffer considerable deprivation, illness, and even death.

Fortunately, the anticipated energy crisis did not take place. It may occur in the future. One hopes that somewhere in the large bureaucracy of New York State, Charles White's telephone survey methodology will be remembered if the critical situation should occur.

Beyond the chance occurrence of an emergency, the methodology could be utilized in less critical situations and by other states and other agencies. It is an efficient and inexpensive way to gather information quickly.

Case VI. Solem

Solem's case is presented in a form somewhat different from the others for Robert Solem uses a six phase time framework to organize his work. Like

Sigler (Case IX), he consulted with a regional office of the AOA which monitors the offices of four states in the Northwest. The regional director with whom he worked saw the role of the regional office as more than a "watchdog" and believed that it should identify and initiate new activities which would improve the delivery networks.

Solem's work could be considered to be within the framework of state and regional planning, and it emphasized the need for accurate and timely information on the elderly populations. He proposed to devise an instrument that dealt with the area agency population and which would obtain the facts about housing, transportation, access to medical services, etc. without the use of a comprehensive and expensive survey method.

The idea behind his new approach to information gathering was to utilize secondary data sources (not the older person himself). These data were originally collected from primary sources by other organizations which plan, monitor, or evaluate various programs and activities. The primary advantage of this technique is that it is much less expensive than others.

An instrument was carefully developed and pretested; on the basis of limited field experience it was modified and prepared for use by the area agencies along with a procedures manual. However, the majority of area agencies were either unable or unwilling to engage in systematic information gathering beyond compiling the basic facts required for the area plan and for minimal compliance with monitoring service vendors.

The Solem case is another illustration of the importance of a structural problem in the network of government agencies concerned with the older population. Facts are required for planning and monitoring, and in this instance the areas and states would have to cooperate in completing the instrument, so that the regional office could develop a unified profile of the region which would accurately reflect the "real world." However, it was decided that the information obtained was not worth the staff time to implement and manage the reporting system, and to engage in the kind of persuasion and "arm twisting" which bureaucrats must employ to produce at least minimal useful information.

The "Peter Principle" of emphasizing structural considerations was certainly an important factor in the situation. Therefore, this case could be considered another example of how uncoordinated levels of government are detrimental to genuine planning in the delivery of human services. Perhaps uncoordinated is a euphemistic way of saying that in some spheres authority is relaxed and that persuasion is the strongest mechanism that can be employed to induce local and state offices to comply with reasonable and useful requests. The local offices are primarily concerned with day-to-day services, such as preparing and delivering meals, and other tasks which have a higher priority than gathering planning data. Critics of government programs often do not realize that local autonomy implies some activities are voluntary and that regional offices may employ weak sanctions, if any at all. Local offices may choose not to participate in all programs sponsored by the regional office.

Case VII. Carpenter

James Carpenter describes the complexity of a large metropolitan area where in just one county the AAA may have to deal with the needs of 450,000 older persons of diverse ethnic, economic, and social backgrounds. The kind of detailed qualitative study carried out by Moen in rural Oregon is not of great help in trying to develop a broad plan for a metropolitan area.

Carpenter shows that available statistical information can be reanalyzed and disaggregated for the needs of a particular area. He used census data, a previously conducted survey from a statewide project, plus gerontological research carried out in other parts of the country to generate information on generic needs in Wayne County, Michigan.

He also discovered that the ideal type of needs assessment is not possible in the "real world" of the local community agency. The staff may acknowledge the value and the importance of a careful and methodologically sound assessment. However, they also realize that a careful survey would be a diversion of scarce resources and that the results may be irrelevant to meeting survival goals of the organization.

It is also difficult to approximate the ideal kind of assessment because needs may be defined and prioritized at the national level, and these may be incongruent with the way needs are defined at the community level. Yet, in order to insure funding, the agency must make an attempt to satisfy needs defined by higher levels of jurisdiction. In summarizing, Carpenter writes: "Need surveys tend to become sort of bookkeeping activities rather than rendering a meaningful contribution to improved knowledge essential to comprehensive service delivery at the community level."

This case illustrates the difficulty of translating national goals and priorities into concrete services and programs for the older persons at the local level.

Case VIII. McConnel

Gerontology is a multidisciplinary field, but to date sociologists, psychologists, and social psychologists have dominated the behavioral and social science aspects. Income is the top priority issue for many elderly persons, yet only a small number of economists have been active in gerontology. This situation is changing, and the work of Charles McConnel is indicative of a trend in which economists are giving increasing attention to the study of aging and the aged.

McConnel focused on the issues related to work and the employment services for older workers. He found that these programs do not give as much attention to the older person as is mandated by legal regulations and guidelines. His research moves beyond technical economic analysis— which is complex and fine-grained—to broader system considerations involving power and decision-making.

McConnel points out an interesting example of what sociologists call "normative evasion"—social rules may not be adhered to because they are too difficult or too stringent to expect full conformity. Nonconformity with rules and regulations, as Robin Williams (1970) has pointed out, is widespread and is patterned. Indeed, Williams suggests that patterned evasion may be one of the dominant themes of American culture.

Rules, regulations, and guidelines are not followed for a complicated network of reasons. However, patterned evasion of rules is perplexing for economists because their analyses are based on the assumption that resources will be used "rationally." Such rationality involves adherence to the rules and regulations governing economic behavior. In the case of a labor market analysis of the vulnerability of older workers, other factors, such as the pressure of younger workers, may alter adherence to the rules.

Case IX. Sigler

Students of complex bureaucratic organizations (such as Peters, Case IV) point out the importance of training as a component of a well-organized agency. Jack Sigler illustrates the value of clearly differentiating the various kinds of training. Generally, education on aging can be separated into two major categories: education *of* older persons for their own enlightenment and benefit and education *about* aging and aging services. Sigler specified further by type of program, by whether it involves substantial programming, by its location, and by the kind of resources required.

His hatrack model can undoubtedly be applied to other geographical settings, and to the other kinds of training situations (mental health, criminal justice, etc.) The logic and clarity of his analysis results in a practical and adaptable tool. He shows how his model may be used in a dynamic and political way within the aging network. As a chart, it can be employed in negotiating in the planning, coordinating, and funding processes.

Sigler points out that his hatrack approach should be helpful in coordinating programs and funding by showing where gaps exist and what areas or programs are already being planned or are in operation. He is aware that persuasion and cooperation often involve what he calls a poker game, a complex game combining elements of skill and chance in which the players (administrators of agencies) attempt to obtain support for their program or agency. There are formal and informal rules to this game, and, like many other systems, the formal rules have to be bent on occasion in order to make the system workable. Complex bureaucracies are very much like the New York subway system which on occasion has been slowly brought to a halt by adhering to every rule in the book. From his observations of a regional office and its component agencies, he concludes that rule bending is effected usually in order to bring services to the older persons more efficiently.

CONCLUSION: BRIDGING THE GAP BETWEEN ACADEMICS AND THE REAL WORLD

Many academic gerontologists utilize a paradigm which is individualistic in its focus. The emphasis is on how the aging person copes with and adapts to his situation, and his attitudes towards it. When there is maladaptation, service agencies offer assistance to alleviate the difficulty of the older person.

In the studies reported here, which are samples of the fifty cases completed in the first three years of the Gerontological Fellowship program, the predominant paradigm is an organizational model, and the "outsider," the Gerontology Fellow, had to think in structural terms about how organizations function. We regard this shift in perspective as particularly valuable in broadening and enriching the professional stance of academic gerontologists.

The general objectives of the OAA are lofty indeed and constitute a praiseworthy set of goals that no one would challenge. They focus on the older person with an *individualistic* value system (U.S. Dept. of HEW,

1976, pp. 2–3), specifying that, among other things, he is entitled to "The full enjoyment of an adequate income. . .the best possible physical and mental health which science can make available and without regard to economic status. . . pursuit of meaningful activity within the widest range of civic, cultural and recreational opportunities . . . and immediate benefit from proven research knowledge which can sustain and improve health and happiness," etc. However, specification of how to reach these excellent goals are not precise, and the huge bureaucratic structure, to say nothing of the immense resources, required to actualize such rights and privileges to 22,000,000 older Americans is not fully acknowledged in the law.

Some of the academic gerontologists were struck with the contrast between the high goals set forth in the law and the actual operations at the service delivery level. These gerontologists and the administrative agencies share the belief that all older Americans are entitled to the privileges and satisfactions specified in the OAA—a dignified style of life; freedom to choose; health, recreation, housing, and transportation services; and so forth. However, the agency staff also has a secondary agenda—the preservation of their organization, which they see as absolutely necessary to reach the goals of service delivery.

It was the demands of this secondary agenda that sometimes frustrated the fellows. Many began their internships with the idea that by providing a sound knowledge base, they would have an important role in improving service delivery. They viewed knowledge and research as the proper bases for policy. In actuality, the situation is more like that described by Laurence E. Lynn, Jr. (1977, p. 71), an expert in social policy at the John F. Kennedy School of Government, Harvard University. He said, "In moving through various stages, policy making does not usually wait for relevant knowledge to become available. . . . Indeed the process often works the other way around: the systematic accumulation of knowledge on an appropriate scale may not begin until policies and programs are implemented."

In the constant battle for resources, power, and influence, bureaucracies may use information to show "proof" of the efficacy of their actions or the correctness of their past decisions. Thus, some activities are carried on to protect the organization, not primarily to serve the aged directly. It must be acknowledged, however, that the efforts of an agency to maintain itself are not simply self-serving behaviors, as some critics have charged. Under our system of funding, federal money is funneled through the state and area agencies. After proper procedures and applications have been completed, grants for programs are received. If an agency does not remain strong and viable, the elderly will get few or no services at all. Therefore, the prudent director must spend considerable time and effort "selling" his program to state and local legislators, and to the general public, if he is to obtain the necessary matching funds. Part of his activities are of necessity public relations, "fence mending," and self-promotion.

These considerations led many academics to new insights into the imperatives of bureaucratic organizations and their operating practices. They also gained some understanding of the components of policy-making. The remarks of Nathan Caplan (1977, p. 359) are pertinent here: "The rather narrow and instrumental-like, or parochial use of knowledge in policy-making reported by the respondents studied appears to start with the policy-maker himself and then to evolve through a combination of organizational controls and information procurement procedures which progressively delimit the opportunity for new ideas and research findings to reach those who make decisions at the top level of governmental power."

Some readers may believe "policy" is formed only at the top of the governmental hierarchy, at the national level. However, policy is a multilevel phenomenon. Although the fellows were working in the regional, state, and area offices, policy was being formulated at all of these levels. What is called "implementation" is actually a restatement of broad policy to make it relevant to the priorities of the state and local agencies.

In this context, Charles Taylor's cogent remarks on the "insider" and the "outsider," presented in chapter 2, are relevant. The academic gerontologist, as "outsider," has a detached view and is safe from job recriminations. He is not subject to the same constraints, chain of command, and sanctions as is a person who is part of the permanent staff. Being an outsider is the precise quality that could make him a valuable resource in policy-making. It is hoped that he could be a vehicle for introducing new ideas and fresh perspectives to the policy-maker that may be of value in the decision-making process.

It is essential in an open society that this type of relationship be fostered so that the administration of programs and services does not become locked into rigid and sclerotic procedures. If the Gerontology Fellowship program is continued, it is our hope that this could be one of the most important contributions of the academic—serving in an "outsider" role and participating in the decision-making process. Such opportunities are important steps in bridging the gap between academic gerontologists and practitioners and, at the same time, help to achieve the goals sought by all concerned—a better life for older Americans.

REFERENCES

Caplan, N. 1977. Social research and national policy: What gets used, by whom, for what purposes, and with what effects. In *Evaluation Studies Review Annual,* vol. 2, ed. Marcia Guttentag. Beverly Hills, Calif.: Sage Publications.

Department of Health, Education, and Welfare. 1976. Older Americans Act of 1965, as Amended. DHEW Publication No. (OHD) 76–20170. Washington: Government Printing Office.

Lynn, L. E., Jr. 1977. Policy relevant social research: What does it look like? In *Evaluation Studies Review Annual,* vol. 2, ed. Marcia Guttentag. Beverly Hills, Calif: Sage Publications.

Maddox, G., and Wiley, J. 1976. Scope, concepts and methods in the study of aging. In *Handbook of Aging and the Social Sciences,* ed. R. H. Binstock and E. Shanas. New York: Van Nostrand.

Williams, R. M., Jr. 1970. *American Society: A Sociological Interpretation.* New York: Knopf.

Appendix. Research Fellows of the Gerontological Society of America, 1974–80

THE list in this appendix contains the following information when it was available: name (degree), placement, year of fellowship, topic, and present address. An effort was made to obtain the most recent and complete information at the time of publication. The editor regrets any omissions or any changes not included.

Adams, David L. (Ph.D.), Iowa State, Region VII, 1974.
"Observations on Title III and Title VII Sites and Program Delivery of Custodial Housing."
Iowa Commission on the Aging.

Allen, Michael A., (M.A.), Arizona State, Region IX, 1974.
"A Profile of Needs and Recommendations for Implementing Aging Programs on Ten Arizona Reservations: A Summer Study, 1974."
Sociology Department, George Fox College, Newberg, Oregon.

Bader, Jeanne E. (M.A.), San Francisco Area Agency, Region IX, 1975.
"Considerations Regarding the Development of Interdepartmental Relationships, in This Case, Aging with City Planning."
Center for Gerontology, University of Oregon, Eugene, Oregon.

Banziger, George (Ph.D.), Ohio Board of Regents, 1979.
"An Applied Setting of Geriatric Medical Education in Ohio."
Psychology Department, Marietta College, Marietta, Ohio.

Barber, Clifton E. (Ph.D.), Wyoming Office on Aging, Department of Health and Social Services, 1980.
"Functional Status, Perceived Conditions of Personal Well-Being, and Service Utilization among the Rural Elderly in Two Wyoming Communities."
Department of Human Development and Family Studies, Colorado State University, Ft. Collins.

Bayliss, Brad (Ph.D.), Missouri State, Region VII, 1976.
"Review of Information and Referral Services in the AAA's, with Recommendations."
Cooperative Aging Program, Missouri Valley College, Marshall, Missouri.

Bearon, Lucille (Ph.D.), Gerontological Society, 1979.
"The 1981 White House Conference on Aging."
Center for Aging and Human Development, Duke University, Durham, North Carolina.

Beatty, David J. (D.S.W.), Washington State, Region X, 1974.

"Program Development for High School Educators. Data Collection and Analysis, Technical Assistance."
School of Social Work, University of Washington, Seattle.
Benner, Larry (Ph.D.), Rohm and Haas Company, 1979.
"The Impact of the Planning Program on Planning Activities, Psychological Preparation for Retirement, and Assessments of Current Life Situations."
Sociology Department, Beaver College, Glenside, Pennsylvania.
Bettinghaus, Carol O. (Ph.D.), Michigan Office, Region V, 1977.
"Demographic Planning: Data for Planning and Service Area Boundaries."
East Lansing, Michigan.
Bikson, Tora K. (Ph.D.), Western Gerontological Society, 1979.
"Getting it Together: Gerontological Research and the Real World."
The Rand Corporation, Santa Monica, California.
Bognar, John B. (Ph.D.), Ohio State, Region V, 1976.
"Information and Referral for the Elderly," with recommendations (improving outreach training program).
Department of Social Work, Wright State University, Dayton, Ohio.
Bricknell, Ann T. (Ph.D.), Federal Region III Office, 1975.
"An Approach to Coordination of Education and Careers in Gerontology."
Psychology Department, Slippery Rock State College, Slippery Rock, Pennsylvania.
Broberg, Merle (Ph.D.), Pennsylvania State, Region III, 1975.
"Hourly Cost of Homemaker Service in Pennsylvania, 1975."
School of Social Work and Social Research, Bryn Mawr College, Philadelphia, Pennsylvania.
Brown, Patricia A. (Ph.D.), Illinois State, Region V , 1974.
No report submitted.
Jane Addams School of Social Work, University of Illinois, Chicago.
Butcher, Loretta (M.A.), American Association of Community and Junior Colleges, 1979.
"Free and Reduced Tuition Policies for Older Adult Students at Community, Junior, and Technical Colleges."
Ann Arbor, Michigan.
Capitman, John (Ph.D.), California Department of Health Services, 1980.
"Adult Day Health Care: Setting, Type, Client Characteristics, and Judgments of Appropriate Level of Care."
Department of Psychology, Duke University, Durham, North Carolina.
Carpenter, James O. (Ph.D.), Detroit/Wayne County Area Agency, Region V, 1975.
"Development of a Monitoring Device for the Technical Review of New Proposals. Analysis and Evaluation of the Consultantship and Work in Terms of that Evaluation. Address to the Need for Synthesis of Theory and Practice and Suggestion of Topics of Interplay between Them."
Lazarus-Goldman Center, University of Pennsylvania, Philadelphia.
Carpenter, James O. (Ph.D.), Detroit/Wayne County Area Agency, Region V, 1976.
"Consultation and Monitoring of Knowledge Base for Improving Agency's Service Delivery System. Contributing to Needs Assessment of Target Se-

nior Population. Assisting in Development of Possible Approach to Examining Service Profile of AAA toward Improving Agency Decision-Making."
Lazarus-Goldman Center, University of Pennsylvania, Philadelphia.
Carson, Linda Gross (Ph.D.), California State, Region IX, 1975.
"The Stress Index for the Aged: An Instrument for AAA Use for Planning and Advocacy in Mental Health Agencies."
Christiansen, David (Ph.D.), North Bay Area Agency on Aging, Region IX, 1977.
"A Needs Assessment Survey."
Center for Planning and Developmental Research, University of California, Berkeley.
Cline, Barry G. (M.A.), Lakawanna Area Agency on Aging, 1977.
"Automated Client Tracking: Management by Information."
Mechanicsburg, Pennsylvania.
Collier, Charlotte M. (Ph.D.), New Jersey Department of Community Affairs, 1979.
"Congregate Services Needs Assessment for Older People in Subsidized Housing in New Jersey."
Chilton Research Services, Philadelphia, Pennsylvania.
Cowgill, Donald O. (Ph.D.), Missouri State, Region VII, 1974.
"Informal Program Evaluation. Recommendations Regarding Research Priorities and Suggestions of Hypotheses."
Sociology Department, University of Missouri, Columbia.
Cox, Harold G. (Ph.D.), Indiana State, Region V, 1975.
"Statewide Training Needs and Program Design. Gerontology Program Availability."
Holmstead Hall, Indiana State University, Terre Haute.
Cranz, Galen (Ph.D.), New Jersey State, Region II, 1975.
"Toward a Sociology of Taste: Aesthetic Preferences of Elderly in a High-Rise Apartment."
Department of Architecture, University of California, Berkeley.
Crawford, Jean K. (Ph.D.), Asociacion Nacional Pro Personas Mayores, 1980.
"An Analysis of Knowledge, Use, Adequacy, and Needs among Older Hispanics."
Sociology Department, California State University, Fullerton.
Davis, Linda J. (Ph.D.), Federal Region III Office, 1976.
"Development of an Evaluation Research Design to Study Programs of the Handicapped, Disabled, and Aged Target Populations."
Division of Health-Related Professions, University of Southern California, Los Angeles.
Day, Robert A. (Ph.D.), New York City Department for the Aging, 1980.
"Design and Undertake a Survey to Gather Data and Evaluate Certain Aspects of a Wider Research and Development Project Recently Funded by AoA and HCFA." The project concerns the delivery of medical and health services to homebound elderly and will examine the coordinating role of this agency.
Department of Sociology, University of Louisville, Louisville, Kentucky.
Durgin, Owen (Ph.D.), New Hampshire, Region I, 1978.
"Current Status and Recommendations for Extension of Transportation of the Elderly."

Institute of Natural and Environmental Resources, University of New Hampshire, Durham.

Ehrlich, Phyllis (M.S.S.A.), Illinois Department of Public Health, 1980.
"Elderly Health Advocacy Group Handbook of Organizing Principles."
Rehabilitation Institute, Southern Illinois University, Edwardsville.

Eve, Susan B. (Ph.D.), Texas Area 5 Health Systems Agency Inc., 1979.
"Health Needs of Older Adults in Texas Health Service Area 5."
Center for Studies in Aging, North Texas State University, Denton.

Fabian, Dorothy (Ed.D.), Maine Bureau of Elderly Affairs, 1979.
"Comparison of Content and Organization of Source-Oriented and Problem-Oriented Nursing Home Records."
Princeton, New Jersey.

Falkman, Peter W. (Ph.D.), Minnesota Office on the Aging, 1977.
"Transportation Policy."
Sociology Department, Hamline University, St. Paul, Minnesota.

Fauri, David P. (Ph.D.), Tennessee State, Region IV, 1975.
"Report on Proposed Organizational Structure Revisions for the Tennessee Commission on Aging."
"Plan for a Model Project: Status and Needs Assessment Survey of Older Americans in the State of Tennessee."
Division of Social and Community Services, Southern Illinois University, Carbondale.

Fengler, Alfred P. (Ph.D.), Vermont State, Region I, 1976.
"Data Utilization in the Vermont Office on Aging: Assessment and Recommendations." A plan for reorganization and development of a data library.
Department of Sociology, University of Vermont, Burlington.

Fox, Sandra S. (Ph.D.), Delaware State, Region III, 1976.
"Identification of Post-Secondary Educational Programs and Activities in Gerontology."
"Educational and Training Interests and Needs of the Elderly and Those Working with the Elderly."
"Stimulation and Encouragement of Interest in the Field of Gerontology."
National Catholic School of Social Service, Catholic University, Washington, D.C.

Frank, Murray W. (Ph.D.), New Jersey State, Region II, 1974.
No report submitted.
American Federation of State, County, and Municipal Employees, New York.

Gagnier, Dorothy R. (M.A., M.E.), Minnesota Board on Aging, 1979.
"Alternatives to Nursing Home Care in Minnesota."
Minnesota Board on Aging, St. Paul.

Gelfand, Donald E. (Ph.D.), American Health Care Association, 1978.
"Nursing Home Aide Screening Instrument."
School of Social Work, University of Maryland, Baltimore.

Gottlieb, Amy Z. (Ph.D.), Illinois State, Region V, 1975.
"Manpower Program Policy Recommendations to the Division on Aging, State of Illinois," following "Research into Manpower Programs Designed to Benefit Unemployed Older Persons in the United States, England, and Germany."
Institute of Labor and Industrial Relations, University of Illinois, Urbana.

Greene, Richard D. (M.A.), Wisconsin State, Region V, 1975.
"Review of the Division on Aging's Evaluation Instruments and the Procedures of Area-Wide Agencies, with Recommendations."
Faye McBeath Institute on Aging, University of Wisconsin, Madison.
Gresson, Aaron D. (Ph.D.), Massachusetts Mental Health Center, 1980.
"Building a Clinical Research Model of Day Care Service Utilization and Efficacy for Nursing Home Residents."
Department of African and Afro-American Studies, Brandeis University, Waltham, Massachusetts.
Hanhardt, Arthur M. (Ph.D.), Portland Oregon: Columbia Regional Association of Governments, Region X, 1975.
"Coordination of Planning among Regional Agencies (Service Definitions, Planning Schedule, Issue Identification)."
Department of Political Science, University of Oregon, Eugene.
Harootyan, Robert (M.A.), California State Office, Region IX, 1978.
"Demographic Data Base/Needs Assessment Project."
Western Gerontological Society, San Francisco, California.
Heilman, Robert (M.A.), American Association of Homes for the Aged, 1978.
"Long-Term Care Public Policy Analysis."
Herman, Jimi (M.A.), North Carolina, Region IV, 1978.
"Alternatives to Institutionalization."
Wilmington, Delaware.
Hicks, Donald (Ph.D.), Houston/Galveston Area Agency on Aging, Region VI, 1977.
"Needs Assessment Alternatives and Rationales among Rural and Non-Care Metropolitan Elderly."
Department of Sociology, University of Texas, Richardson.
Holtzman, Joseph M. (Ph.D.), Illinois State, Region V , 1976.
"Adult Day Care in Illinois: A Preliminary Review."
School of Medicine, Southern Illinois University, Edwardsville.
House, Gail (Ph.D.), Utah State, Region VII, 1978.
"The Alternatives Program for the Elderly."
Hudis, Ann (Ed.D.), New York City Area Agency, Region II, 1976.
"Proposed Project: Review, Delivery of Home-Care Services and Program Evaluation of These Services."
Irvington-on-Hudson, New York, New York.
Jeffrey, Dwight W. (Ph.D.), Dallas Area Agency, Region VI, 1975.
"Program Evaluation/Technical Assistance."
Center for Studies in Aging, North Texas State University, Denton.
Jones, Ann A. (Ph.D.), National Association of Home Health Agencies, 1979.
"Home Health Care: A Profile of Providers."
Johns Hopkins School of Hygiene, Johns Hopkins University, Baltimore, Maryland.
Jones, Joseph H., Jr. (Ph.D.), Arkansas State and Louisiana State, Region VI, 1974.
"Nutrition Program Evaluation," a preliminary report. No final report submitted.
Department of Sociology, Louisiana State University, Baton Rouge.
Kaszniak, Alfred W. (Ph.D.), Handmaker Jewish Geriatric Center, 1980.

"The Development of an Instrument for the Assessment of the Psychological, Social, and Economic Impact of Adult Day Care Upon the Families of Elderly Participants."

Department of Psychiatry, University of Arizona College of Medicine, Tucson.

Kincaid, Jean (Ph.D.), Cleveland Mayor's Office, 1977.

"Evaluation of Title VII Nutrition."

Tulsa, Oklahoma.

Kubey, Robert W. (M.A.), National Broadcast Communication, 1979.

"The Experience of an Academic Working in the Television Industry." (A one-hour video tape, "Maytime," was also produced as part of this fellowship.)

Committee on Human Development, University of Chicago, Chicago, Illinois.

Landis, Larry M. (Ph.D.), Iowa State and Des Moines Area Agency, Region VII, 1976.

"Refining AAA Capabilities in Data Collection, Analysis, and Tabulation."

Department of Sociology, Drake University, Des Moines, Iowa.

Lane, William C. (Ph.D.), Health Systems Agency of Southeastern Pennsylvania, 1980.

"Nursing Homes and Medicaid Certification: Study of the Fifty Percent Medicaid Requirement for Southeastern Pennsylvania Region Nursing Homes."

Department of Sociology/Anthropology, SUNY-College at Cortland, New York.

Levin, Barry L. (Ph.D.), Missouri Office of Aging, Region VII, 1979.

School of Social Work, School of Public and Community Services, University of Missouri, Columbia.

Lind, Donna S. (Ph.D.), American Association of Homes for the Aging, 1980.

"Self-Assessment of Quality of Life in Homes for the Aging."

Department of Health Services Administration, George Washington University, Washington, D.C.

Little, Virginia C. (Ph.D.), Connecticut State, Region I, 1975.

"Home Care Systems."

School of Social Work, University of Connecticut, West Hartford.

Lurie, Elinore (Ph.D.), Federal Region IX Office, 1975.

"Older Americans/Target Populations for Service in DHEW Region IX." (Data available for program planning for older Americans.)

"Policy Implications of Data Use for Programs Planning in DHEW Region IX."

"Notes on Future Administration on Aging/Gerontological Society Consultants in Aging Agencies."

College of Nursing, University of California, San Francisco.

Lynch, Rufus S. (D.S.W.), Federal Region III, 1978.

"Utilization and Dissemination of AoA Funded Research."

Center for Studying Social Welfare and Community Development, Philadelphia, Pennsylvania.

McAdoo, John (Ph.D.), National Caucus on the Black Aged, 1977.

"The Effects of Fear of Crime on the Social and Psychological Well-Being of Black Aged in Washington, D.C."

Columbia, Maryland.

McAuley, William J. (Ph.D.), Wisconsin State, Region V, 1976.
"Human Resources and Needs Assessment: Recommendations for a Practical Approach."
Virginia Center on Aging, Virginia Commonwealth University, Richmond.
McConnel, Charles E. (Ph.D.), Los Angeles County Area Agency, Region IX, 1976.
"Mature Labor Market Risk Factors and National Manpower System Outcomes."
Gerontology Program, University of Texas at Dallas, Dallas.
Mahoney, Kevin J. (Ph.D.), Connecticut State, Region I, 1978.
"Recommendations on the Role of Adult Day Care in the Continuum of Extended Care Services."
Coventry, Connecticut.
Mandell, Betty E. (Ph.D.), South Carolina State, Region IV, 1975.
"Development of Methodology for Needs Assessment for Use with Supervisors in South Carolina."
Social Problems Research Institute, University of South Carolina, Columbia.
Maxwell, Robert J. (Ph.D.), and Maxwell, Eleanor K. (M.A.), Alaska State, Region X, 1976.
"Cooperative Independence: Support of the Elderly in Tlingit and Non-Native Alaskan Communities."
Department of Anthropology, California State College, Bakersfield, California.
Miller, Phyllis R. (Ph.D.), Maryland State, Region III, 1976.
"Mental Health and Mental Illness of Elderly in Maryland," a study mandated by the Maryland Legislature to determine whether the mentally ill elderly were appropriately placed in hospital centers, with recommendations.
School of Social Work, University of Maryland, Baltimore.
Moen, Elizabeth (Ph.D.), Oregon State, Region X, 1976.
"Exploratory Study for the Development of a Survey Assessment of Needs of the Rural Elderly."
Department of Sociology, University of Colorado, Boulder.
Olson, Laura K. (Ph.D.), Madison Area Agency on Aging, 1978.
"Poles of AAA: An Assessment of District I."
Government Department, Lehigh University, Bethlehem, Pennsylvania.
O'Neal, Daniel J. III (M.A.), National Association of State Units on Aging, 1980.
"A Report on Initiatives from the National, State and Area Agency Levels Regarding Expansion of Services within the Continuum of Long-Term Care, Particularly in Home Services, in Order to Help State Units in their Efforts in Service System Development."
Gerontology Nursing Graduate Program, University of Pennsylvania, Philadelphia.
Osako, Masako M. (Ph.D.), United Nations Center for Social Development, 1979.
"Coping with Subtle Diplomatic Constraints: Internship with the U.S. Center for Social Development."
Department of Sociology, University of Illinois at Chicago, Chicago.
Peters, George R. (Ph.D.), Kansas State, Region VII, 1976.
"Interagency Relations and the Aging Network: A Study of the State Unit on Aging and AAA's in Kansas."
Center for Aging Studies, Kansas State University, Manhattan.

Peterson, John (Ph.D.), Massachusetts State Office, Region I, 1977.
   "Demographic Characteristics."
   Harvard Center for Community Health and Medical Care, Harvard University,
      Cambridge, Massachusetts.
Pippin, Roland (Ph.D.), New Orleans Area Agency on Aging, Region VI, 1978.
   "View in Need and Priorities."
   Department of Sociology, University of Louisiana, Lafayette.
Ralston, Penny A. (M.Ed.), Iowa Commission on the Aging, 1979.
   "The Identification and Description of Senior Center Programs in Iowa."
   Ames, Iowa.
Richards, Debra (M.A.), Mississippi State Board of Health, 1980.
   "Study the Feasibility of Using Churches as Contact Settings to Provide
      Screening for Hypertension and Other Age-Related Diseases among Rural,
      Predominately Black Elderly."
   Jackson Public Schools, Jackson, Mississippi.
Riedel, Robert G. (Ph.D.), Ebinezer Center for Aging, 1980.
   "A Report Analyzing the 'Philadelphia Model' of In-Home Service Delivery to
      the Elderly and Its Applicability to the City of Minneapolis."
   Department of Psychology, Southwest State University, Marshall, Minnesota.
Roberts, Betty H. (Ph.D.), New Hampshire, Region III, 1978.
   "Post-Secondary Gerontological Offerings and Provider of Training Needs in
      New Hampshire."
   Social Service Department, University of New Hampshire, Durham.
Robertson-Tchabo, Elizabeth A. (Ph.D.), Virginia State, Region III, 1976.
   "Evaluating the Alternatives to Institutionalization," a proposed project. No
      final report submitted.
   Reston, Virginia.
Rocheleau, Bruce (Ph.D.), American Hospital Association, 1980.
   "Hospitals and Innovative Programs for Elderly Persons."
   Center for Governmental Studies, Northern Illinois University, Dekalb.
Rosenkranz, Catherine R. (Ph.D.), Federal Region I Office, 1976.
   "Increasing the Effectiveness of Staff Development Activities for Personnel in
      State and Area Agencies and Service Providers in Aging Programs in Region
      I."
   Cuyahoga Community College-Metro Campus, Cleveland, Ohio.
Rubenstein, James M. (Ph.D.), Cincinnati Area Senior Services, Inc., 1980.
   "Displacement in a Cincinnati Neighborhood."
   Department of Geography, Miami University, Oxford, Ohio.
Sack, Ann (Ph.D.), Federal Region V Office, 1976.
   "Report of a Survey of Career Training and Model Project Grants in Region V:
      Relationships with Components of the Network on Aging."
   Social Rehabilitation Department, Drexel Home, Inc., Chicago, Illinois.
Sadowski, Bernard (Ph.D.), Federal Region X Office, 1978.
   "The Expansion of Quality Satisfaction Instruments to Include Additional
      Social Centers."
   Nichols & Association, Seattle, Washington.
Santos, John F. (Ph.D.), New Mexico State, Region VI, 1975.
   "Preliminary Planning for Geriatric Training in the State of New Mexico."

Department of Psychology, University of Notre Dame, Notre Dame, Indiana.

Sherman, Edith M. (Ph.D.), Denver Area Agency, Region VII, 1974.
"A Subjective and Impressionistic Evaluation of a Vast Social Service System." Structure and function of Colorado State Division of Services for the Aging; Assessment of state programs; Summary and recommendations.
Graduate School of Social Work, University of Denver, Denver, Colorado.

Sigler, Jack E. (M.A.), Federal Region VII Office, 1975.
"Assessment of Training Needs, Plans and Availability in HEW Region VII." Appendix: "A Functional Model of Education and Training in Aging: A Hat Rack for Planning and Coordination."
Swope Ridge Health Care Center, Kansas City, Missouri.

Smith, Carol R. (Ph.D.), Delaware, Region III, 1978.
"Architectural Accessibility for Title VII Nutrition Programs."
College of Human Resources, University of Delaware, Newark.

Smyer, Michael (Ph.D.), Pennsylvania Department of Aging, 1980.
"Long-Term Care in Pennsylvania: Projections for 1990–2000."
College of Human Development, Pennsylvania State University, University Park.

Solem, Robert A. (Ph.D.), Federal Region X Office, 1975.
"The Development of a Working Instrument for Baseline Data." With the use of secondary information.
Office of Research, Department of Social and Health Services, Olympia, Washington.

Steinhauer, Marcia B. (Ph.D.), Illinois State Office, Region V, 1978.
"Geriatric Foster Care: Needs and Feasibility of Service."
Institute of Community Development, University of Louisville, Louisville, Kentucky.

Stunkel, Edith L. (M.S.W), Federal Region VIII, 1977.
"Alternatives to Mandatory Retirement for Regular State Employees."
Department of Social Work, Kansas State University, Manhattan.

Turner, Robert G. (Ph.D.), Florida State, Region IV, 1974.
"Florida Area Agencies on Aging: An Evaluation . . . of the Concept as it Relates to Goals and Goal Achievement, and the Current Problems and Potential. . . ."
College of Business, Florida State University, Tallahassee.

Wan, Thomas T. H. (Ph.D.), Baltimore Area Agency, Region III, 1975.
"An Organizational Analysis of the Determinants of Unmet Service Needs for the Elderly."
Department of Sociology, University of Maryland, Baltimore.

Warren, Linda R. (Ph.D.), Alabama Office, Region IV, 1977.
"Needs Assessment of Jefferson County Aged."
Department of Psychology, University of Alabama, Birmingham.

White, Charles B. (Ph.D.), New York State, Region II, 1975.
"Use of the Telephone Survey in Assessing the Needs and Attitudes of the Aged: Methodological Review and Analysis."
"General Report to the Summer Consultantship Program of the Gerontological Society."
Department of Psychology, Trinity University, San Antonio, Texas.

Whitelaw, Nancy A. (M.S.), Minnesota Office, Region V, 1978.
"A Background Report on In-Home Services for the Aged."
Department of Sociology, University of Minnesota, Minneapolis.
Wilson, Wallace (Ph.D.), Federal Region V Office, 1978.
"Advances in Needs Assessment of the Elderly in Illinois and Wisconsin."
Medical Center, University of Illinois, Chicago.
Windley, Paul G. (D.Arch.), North Central Kansas/Flint Hills Area Agency, Region VII, 1976.
"Environmental Intervention: Case Studies in Independent Living among the Rural Elderly."
Department of Architecture, Kansas State University, Manhattan.
Winogrond, Iris R. (Ph.D.), New York State Office for the Aging, 1979.
"Research Project on Manpower Development for Services to the Aging of New York State." A summary report.
Milwaukee, Wisconsin.
Woehle, Ralph E. (Ph.D.), Virginia Office, Region III, 1977.
"An Interpretation of Social and Economic Indicators."
Department of Sociology, University of Virginia, Charlottesville.
Zaki, Gamal E. (D.Ed.), Rhode Island State, Region I, 1974.
"Day Care Centers for the Elderly in Rhode Island."
Department of Sociology, Rhode Island College, Providence.